# The 20th Century Book

# The 20th Century Book

Its illustration and design

Second Edition

John Lewis

The Herbert Press

**To Griselda**
whose patience has been infinite during the production of this and many
other books

Copyright © John Noel Claude Lewis 1967, 1984
First edition published in 1967
This new and revised edition first published in Great Britain by
The Herbert Press Limited, 46 Northchurch Road, London N1 4EJ

Designed by John Lewis FSIAD

Printed and bound in Great Britain by W. S. Cowell Ltd, Ipswich, Suffolk

Lewis, John, 1912–
    The 20th century book. — New and rev. ed
    1. Book design
    I. Title    II. Lewis, John 1912–
    Twentieth century book
    686    Z116.A3

ISBN 0-906969-41-7

# CONTENTS

## ACKNOWLEDGEMENTS

A book like this depends on the work of others. My first acknowledgements are to the artists and designers whose work appears here and to the publishers who have given their permission for reproduction and in many cases helped with information. My next are to those who have written about this subject and particularly for the following books:

Dr. G. K. Schauer's *Deutsche Buchkunst 1890–1960,* Mr Albert Kapr's *Buchgestaltung,* Mr Philip Hofer's and Miss Eleanor Garvey's *The Artist and the Book 1860–1960,* Mr David Bland's *A History of Book Illustration,* Mr Percy Muir's *English Children's Books* and the various editions of *The Art of the Book,* published by Studio Ltd.

My thanks are also due to the Trustees of the British Museum for permission to photograph the book illustrated on page 13; to the Victoria and Albert Museum for permission to photograph the books shown on pages 11, 39, 40–1, 82–3, 85, 88–9, 112–13, 114–15, 116–17, 120–1, 122–3, 194–5; to the Bibliothèque Nationale for the photographs on pages 60, 72–3.

My gratitude to all my friends who have helped me either with the loan of books or in other ways including Mr Edward Ardizzone, Mr Tom Balston, Mr R. A. Bevan, Mr Louis Bondy, Mr Max Caflisch, Mr Geoffrey Cumberlege, Mr Robin Don, Mr Charles Ede, Miss Eleanor Garvey, Mr Bob Gill, Mr Felix Gluck, Mr John Hadfield, Mr John Harthan, Mr David Herbert, Mr George Him, Mr Philip Hofer, Mr Blair Hughes-Stanton, M. André Jammes, Mr Jean Koefoed, M. Edy Legrand, Mr James Mosley, Mr John Nash, Mr Walter Neurath, Mr John O'Connor, Mr Francis Odle, Mr David Pearce, Mr James Pfeufer, Mr Hugh Radcliffe-Wilson, Mrs Herta Ryder, Mrs Margaret Rideout, Mr Anthony Rota, Mr Hans Schmoller, Mr Martin Simmons, Mr Geoffrey Smith, Mr Reynolds Stone, Mme J. Veyrin-Forrer.

Also to Messrs John R. Freeman Ltd, Mr John Lunnis, and to Mr Robert Alcock and Miss Shirley Notton of the Butter Market Studio, Ipswich for the care they have taken in photographing several hundred books, and to Mr Ben Clark and all those at the Press in the Butter Market who helped in the production of this book.

And finally to Mr Ruari McLean for helpful advice and for reading the proofs and to Mr John Dreyfus for much valuable criticism and advice at various stages in the production of this book.

## PREFACE

This book is not an attempt to catalogue the hundred (or any other arbitrary figure) best books of either this year or of the last sixty or seventy years. The pages and covers from the books shown here are a designer's personal choice. Most of them I like, a few of them I don't, but all of them I feel, were in some way significant. Amongst the books that I like and which are not here are those books whose *raison d'être* relies on superb colour printing and also those whose beauty depends on fine composition and presswork and beautiful paper. In the first case, the futility of trying to re-reproduce by a different process work that has already been done well is fairly obvious, so coffee table books have had to be left out. In the second case, the finely printed private press or even commercially published book with impeccable qualities of precise craftsmanship, is quite beyond the limits of photography and process reproduction. So, the excellent work of such presses as Giovanni Mardersteig's Officina Bodoni is likewise excluded.

In reproduction, the arrangement of type and illustrations on paper, or an individual illustration can be shown. The presswork, unless it is appallingly bad, cannot be seen; and one illustration does not make a book. So this book has become a 'sample tasting', but I hope that by comparison and juxta-position the tasting may be given some point. The comparative method may produce some pretty odd bedfellows, but widely different attitudes to design were prevailing in different countries at the same time and utterly similar influences were affecting the design of books, that were often separated in time by years or even decades.

There have been a lot of handsome books printed since the beginning of the century. It would not be difficult to fill a book of this size with, say, the best of Scandinavian, or Russian or South American books and none of these appears here. My limitations had to be self-imposed. Amongst my reasons for compiling this book is an attempt to communicate something of my enthusiasm for, and interest in, the design and illustration of books. My livelihood is concerned with the production, editing, designing and publishing of books. My most absorbing and life-long hobby has been the collecting of books — and in particular of illustrated books and of books whose design shows some evidence of 'a directing intelligence'.

As for the book's title, it is fair comment· to suggest that the twentieth century began in 1901, but the forces governing the design of the twentieth century book do not fit the calendar so conveniently. The art nouveau movement and the historicism of the first of the English private presses all began before the end of the Victorian era, but they provide the foundations of the design of the modern book.

Auguste Heckscher, in opening a recent A.I.G.A. exhibition of 'Fifty Best Books' in New York said: 'Books used to be made, today they are designed.' After looking at a recent exhibition of 'The Fifty Best Books of the Year' in London, I was forcibly reminded of these words. Though many of the books in this exhibition were well laid out (and, reproduced in miniature in the catalogue, looked well), in fact they were often ill-made, some were ill-printed and often on unsuitable paper, and mostly they were bound in badly blocked, sloppily fitting cases. When a book is *well* made, and is printed on good stock with good presswork, where the binding case fits snugly and is cleanly blocked on nice material, the most unadventurous typographic arrangement will look well. Design is no substitute for craftsmanship. For a book to be a work of art, however, it needs to be both well designed and well made. The feel of a well-made book, its weight in the hand, its texture, even its smell — these qualities that mean so much to anyone who cares for books — the reader of this book will have to take on trust for I cannot show them here.

1893. *Le Voyage d'Urien* by André Gide,
illustrated with lithographs by Maurice Denis,
published by the Librairie de l'Art Indépendant,
Paris. Lithographs printed by Edw. Ancourt, text
printed by Paul Schmidt. Limited to 300 copies.
8″ × 7½″. Lithograph.

# 1. ART NOUVEAU OR PRIVATE PRESS HISTORICISM?

Since the end of the last century there has been a dichotomy of ideas about the design of books. In the 1890's the two opposing influences were the historicism of the private press movement and the aesthetics of art nouveau. These threads have continued with surprising persistence; though on occasions book designers have moved from camp to camp, sometimes without being aware of their inconsistency. Modern designers are increasingly aware of this dichotomy. It is the modern graphic artist who has made the first real attempt to resolve it — as I hope later pages of this book will show.

One of the first artists in the modern movement to concern himself actively with the relationship of illustration to the design of the book as a whole was Maurice Denis. As a painter he was heavily influenced by Gauguin; but he was more important as a writer on modern art than as a practitioner. His first attempt at illustration was for Paul Verlaine's *Sagesse*. These illustrations, daring in their simplicity of conception, were carried out in 1889, but not published until 1911. André Gide saw them in their unpublished state and asked Denis if he would illustrate his *Le Voyage d'Urien*; the result was a small and little-known book, described by Philip Hofer as a masterpiece of art nouveau. Denis expressed the art nouveau attitude to books when he said, 'A book ought to be a work of decoration and not a neutral vehicle for transmitting a text'; and 'For each emotion, each thought, there exists a plastic equivalent and a corresponding beauty'.

Art nouveau was essentially new art and in no way historical. Its origins, by now only too often explained, were largely oriental, the influences springing from the Japanese prints of Utamaro, Hiroshige, Hokusai and others that were at this time appearing on the bookstalls and in the art shops of Paris, Munich and London.

One of the first Western artists to take a serious interest in this oriental art was James McNeill Whistler, who incorporated in his paintings and in the typography of his books the qualities he found in Japanese prints. He was soon followed by French painters such as Gauguin, Bonnard and Lautrec, and by the poster artists Alphonse Mucha, Jules Chéret and the American Will Bradley. In art nouveau posters, the designs are flat, essentially two-dimensional and without perspective; and the white paper is as important as the flat colours. Although Bradley made full use of art nouveau principles in his posters, in his book work he produced designs that owed more to William Morris's mediaevalism. Alphonse Mucha on the other hand — working, like Bradley, on both posters and book design — used a style that was consistently art nouveau.

Mucha, a Slav from South Moravia, came to Paris when he was twenty-eight to study at the Académie Julian. His work soon developed the characteristics to be seen in his illustrations to *Ilsée, Princesse de Tripoli*. His cover design of lilies is printed in a typical art nouveau 'greenery-yallery' colour scheme; and the lithographed illustrations, which have a feverish, hectic feeling, are mostly in the same greens and yellows. His very solid females, strongly outlined like the leading of a stained glass window, move through a web of febrile tendrils. Mucha, in spite of his origins, was as much France's contribution to art nouveau as Beardsley was England's.

Charles Ricketts, the founder of the Vale Press in Chelsea, was one of the first typographic designers influenced by art nouveau who still based the typography of his books on historic principles.

Before Charles Ricketts founded the Vale Press he practised as a commercial book designer and typographer. He must have been one of the first practising typographers. He designed books for John Lane, and in 1889 laid out several of Thomas Hardy's books, for a London publishing house called Osgood,

1882. *Selections from the Hesperides and Noble Numbers of Robert Herrick.* Illustrated by Edwin A. Abbey. Published by Harper & Brothers, New York. Printed by the Leadenhall Press, London. 11⅝″ × 8⅞″. Case-binding blocked in gold, black, red and green, on a cream-coloured cloth.

McIlvaine, including the first edition of *Tess of the D'Urbervilles.*[1] The most distinctive feature of this book, apart from its art nouveau cover, is the curious asymmetric title-page, with the copy placed high on the page, and a 2-line, drop initial T for 'Tess'. This asymmetry is carried into all the chapter openings. In contrast to the title-page is the equally unconventional contents page, where the copy begins nearly two-thirds of the way down the page. The book gives abundant evidence of an attempt to break away from current commercial convention. It is also clear that Ricketts had taken a look at Whistler's *The Gentle Art of Making Enemies,* but had not reached the assurance or the bravado of the 'Butterfly'.

The effect of art nouveau on the appearance of books and particularly on the covers was very considerable. In 1882 Harper and Brothers, in New York, had published *Selections from the Hesperides and Noble Numbers of Robert Herrick* with drawings by Edwin A. Abbey. The cover design of this book, possibly by Abbey, is one of the earliest examples of this influence, the choice of green and gold on a cream background being typical of many art nouveau colour schemes.

By 1900, art nouveau was already an international style. In Germany, as early as the 1890's, the movement had inspired experiments in the layout of books and in the design of new typefaces. The publication of the journals *Pan* and *Jugend* gave encouragement to such experiments. *Pan,* edited by Julius Meier-Graefe, an art historian, and Otto Julius Bierbaum, an amateur typographer, engaged the services of a number of young designers, who were showing an interest in the typographic arts. These included E. R. Weiss, Peter Behrens and Otto Eckmann. *Pan,* which ran for twenty-one issues, was international in its scope and included articles on Beardsley, Corinth, Toulouse-Lautrec and Van de Velde. *Jugend* was published in Munich and first appeared in 1896; its title (*Youth*) implied a criticism of anything old, and it soon achieved a wide popularity, lending its name to Jugendstil, the German art nouveau movement.

[1] Ricketts, writing in his *A Defence of the Revival of Printing* in 1899, said: 'Some of my earliest experiments in the shaping of books, crude and hesitating as they are, were done for Messrs Osgood, McIlvaine in 1890 and 1891 . . . they were unlike the ordinary books in the matter of title-page, proportion of margin, and in the designs upon their boards.'

1897. *Ilsée Princesse de Tripoli* by Robert de Flers. Illustrated with 132 lithographs by Alphonse Mucha. Lithographed by L'Imprimerie Champenois. Printed and published by L'Édition d'Art. 12⅝″ × 10″. Cover design printed in blue and yellow on grey-green paper; and illustrated pages.

## Painters as book designers

1890. *The Gentle Art of Making Enemies* by
J. McNeill Whistler. Published by William
Heinemann, London. Printed by the Ballantyne
Press, London and Edinburgh. 8″ × 6¼″. Text
spread and chapter half-title, showing two
variations of Whistler's 'Butterfly' signature.

*Whistler v. Ruskin*

*ART & ART CRITICS*

*Chelsea, Dec. 1878.*

---

#### Serious Sarcasm

PARDON me, my dear Whistler, for having taken
you *au sérieux* even for a moment.

I ought to have remembered that your penning,
like your painting, belongs to the region of " chaff."
I will not forget it again ; and meantime remain yours
always,

TOM TAYLOR.

LAVENDER SWEEP,
Jan. 9, 1879.

#### Final

WHY, my dear old Tom, I never *was* serious with
you, even when you were among us.   Indeed, I killed
you quite, as who should say, without seriousness, " A
rat !  A rat !" you know, rather cursorily.

Chaff, Tom, as in your present state you are beginning to perceive, was your fate here, and doubtless
will be throughout the eternity before you.   With
ages at your disposal, this truth will dimly dawn
upon you ; and as you look back upon this life, per-
chance many situations that you took *au sérieux*
(art-critic, who knows ? expounder of Velasquez, and
what not) will explain themselves sadly—chaff ! Go
back !

*The World,*
*Jan. 15, 1879.*

THE WHITE HOUSE,
Jan. 10, 1879.

1889. *Tess of the D'Urbervilles* by Thomas Hardy.
Designed by Charles Ricketts; bound in brown
cloth-covered boards, blocked in gold. Published
by J. R. Osgood McIlvaine and Co., London. In
three volumes. Printed by R. & R. Clark,
Edinburgh. 7½" × 5½". Case-binding and title-page.

1901. *De Cupidinis et Psyches Amoribus.* A
version by C. I. Holmes. Illustrated with wood
engravings by Charles Ricketts and printed by
Hacon & Ricketts at the Ballantyne Press.
Published by John Lane. 11½" × 7¾". Text
spread with wood engraving.

celeritate nauigabant. tunc sic iterum momentarius maritus suam
Psychen admonet dies ultima et casus extremus. sexus infestus
et sanguis inimicus iam sumpsit arma et castra commouit et aciem
direxit et classicum personauit. iam mucrone destricto iugulum
tuum nefariae tuae sorores petunt. heu quantis urguemur cladibus,
Psyche dulcissima! tui nostrique miserere religiosaque contin-
entia domum maritum teque et istum paruulum nostrum immin-
entis ruinae infortunio libera. nec illas scelestas feminas, quas tibi
post interneciuum odium et calcata sanguinis foedera sorores
appellare non licet, uel uideas uel audias, cum in morem Sirenum
scopulo prominentes funestis uocibus saxa personabunt.'

His verbis et amplexibus mollibus decantatus maritus, la-
crimasque eius suis crinibus detergens, facturum spopondit, et
praeuertit statim lumen nascentis diei.

Sic adfectione simulata paulatim sororis inuadunt animum,
xii

statimque eas lassit-
udine uiae sedilibus
refotas et balnearum
uaporosis fontibus
curatas pulcherri-
me triclinio miris-
que illis et beatis ed-
ulibus atque tuccetis
oblectat. iubet cith-
aram loqui, psallit-
ur; tibias agere, so-
natur; choros can-
ere, cantatur. quae
cuncta nullo praese-
nte dulcissime mo-
dulis animos audie-
ntium remulcebant.
nec tamen scelestar-
um feminarum neq-
uitia uel illa melli-
ta cantus dulcedine
mollita conquieuit, sed ad destinatam fraudium pedicam ser-
monem conferentes dissimulanter occipiunt sciscitari, qualis ei
maritus et unde natalium, secta cuia proueniret. tunc illa sim-
plicitate nimia pristini sermonis oblita nouum commentum in-
struit, atque maritum suum de prouincia proxima magnis pe-
cuniis negotiantem iam medium cursum aetatis agere, intersper-
sum rara canitie. nec in sermone isto tantillum morata rursum
opiparis muneribus eas onustas uentoso uehiculo reddidit.

Sed dum Zephyri tranquillo spiritu sublimatae domum
redeunt, sic secum altercantur 'quid, soror, dicimus de tam mon-
struoso fatuae illius mendacio? tunc adulescens modo florenti
lanugine barbam instruens, nunc aetate media candenti canitie lu-
cidus. quis ille quem temporis modici spatium repentina senecta
reformauit? nil aliud repperies, mi soror, quam uel mendacio ista
pessimam feminam confingere uel formam mariti sui nescire.
quorum utrum uerum est, opibus istis quam primum extermin-
anda est. quod si uiri faciem ignorat, deo profecto denupsit
et deum nobis praegnatione ista gerit. certe si diuini puelli—
quod absit—haec mater audierit, statim me laqueo nexili suspen-
dam. ergo interim ad parentes nostros redeamus et exordio
sermonis huius quam concolores fallacias adtexamus.'
xiii          c

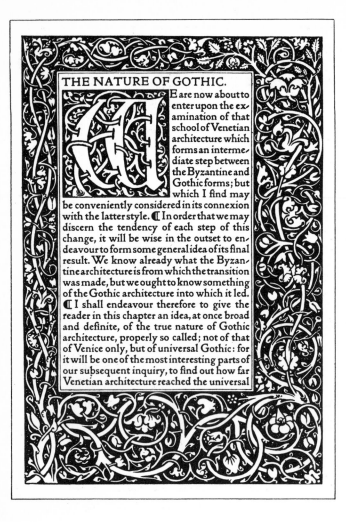

## The influence of Morris

1893–4. *Le Morte d'Arthur* by Sir Thomas Malory. Illustrated by Aubrey Beardsley. Published by J. M. Dent and Co., London. Printed by Turnbull and Spears, Edinburgh. First published in parts and then issued in two volumes. (Second edition issued in a single volume and limited to 1,000 copies for U.K. and 500 for U.S.A.). 10" × 7⅝". Chapter opening with border designed by Beardsley.

*Opposite left:*
1892. *The Nature of Gothic* by John Ruskin. Decorated, printed and published by William Morris at the Kelmscott Press, Hammersmith. Bound in vellum with green silk petersham ties. 8" × 5½". First text page with border design by Morris.

*Opposite right:*
c. 1910. *The Campbell Book* with decorations by Will Bradley. Reproduced from *The Art of the Book* 1914: Studio. Text page, area of illustrations 7¾" × 5½".

**Book ij. Chapter j.**

OF A DAMOSEL WHICH CAME GIRT WITH A SWORD FOR TO FIND A MAN OF SUCH VIRTUE TO DRAW IT OUT OF THE SCABBARD. FTER the death of Uther Pendragon reigned Arthur his son, the which had great war in his days for to get all England into his hand. For there were many kings within the realm of England, and in Wales, Scotland, and Cornwall. So it befell on a time when King Arthur was at London, there came a knight and told the king tidings how that the King Rience of North Wales had reared a great number of people, and were entered into the land, and burnt and slew the king's true liege people. If this be true, said Arthur, it were great shame unto mine estate but that he were mightily withstood. It is truth, said the knight, for I saw the host myself. Well, said the king, let make a cry, that all the

The German typefounders were soon turning to art nouveau letter forms, and in 1900 Karl Klingspor commissioned Otto Eckmann (an admirer of Beardsley) to design a typeface 'appropriate for the printing of books in the new style'. This Germanic type, called Eckmann-Schmuck, was very like the style of lettering that was appearing on the poster hoardings of Paris and Berlin.

In contrast to art nouveau the historically based work of the English private presses may seem a little humdrum, but the influence they exerted on commercial book production was powerful and lasting. In this revival of fine book printing, the most influential of all the private presses was William Morris's Kelmscott Press in Hammersmith, London. Morris was a mediaevalist and, though his first typeface was based on the fine roman used by Nicholas Jenson in Venice in 1468, all his leanings were towards dark-textured, black-letter books. Morris's pre-occupation with mediaevalism might seem a curious point of departure for modern book design, yet he was really at the beginning of the diverging lines of development in twentieth-century design. Morris contributed much to the decorative arts; for printing, he established the belief in standards of quality in workmanship, and in the use of good materials. Morris aimed at perfection. He stated that he was determined to obtain the very best types, ink and papers as well as the best of illustrations and decorations. His illustrations were always cut on the wood to be printed by the same methods as the type. As far as I know, he never considered using lithography as a method of illustration. Morris's insistence on quality in workmanship, design and materials provided the qualities which were the basis of the revival of fine printing in England and America, in much of the continent of Europe, and particularly in Germany. Morris's interest in early printing was also responsible for producing the last thing he would have wished for — a reactionary revivalism.

*Opposite:*
1906. *Alles um Liebe*. Edited by Ernst Hartung. Designed by Käte Vesper-Waentig. Published by Wilhelm Langewiesche-Brandt, Düsseldorf and Leipzig. 7½" × 4¾". Title-page spread.

AVBREY
BEARDSLEY

1906. *The Dream and the Business* by John Oliver Hobbes. Published by T. Fisher Unwin. Design by Aubrey Beardsley, printed in three colours and mounted on the cover. 6⅝" × 2⅞". This design was also used as a poster for T. Fisher Unwin's 'Pseudonym and Antonym Library'.

In 1893, two years after Morris had started his press, Aubrey Beardsley began work on his drawings for *Le Morte d'Arthur*, for a most enterprising London publisher called J. M. Dent. In spite of the subject, and the Burne-Jones influence, Beardsley's work was the antithesis of everything Morris believed in. The air of decadence in Beardsley's work is an essential part of the aesthetics of art nouveau, itself essentially a cult of the precious. This precious quality can be seen at its best in many fine art nouveau book bindings, but if art nouveau had nothing but this to offer, its influence would not have lasted. Beardsley's sinuous line, his massing of areas of black and white, his choice of subjects, rarefied as hothouse orchids and with a lurking sense of eroticism is the epitome of art nouveau. The most interesting of his qualities as a designer is this use of white space, an ethereal quality which is a component of art nouveau. His cover design for *The Dream and the Business* by John Oliver Hobbes shows this well.

In 1894, Beardsley undertook the art editorship of *The Yellow Book*, to be published by Elkin Mathews and John Lane in England, and by Copeland and Day in Boston. With Henry Harland as editor, and under Lane's supervision, its preliminary announcements had an effect comparable to the notoriety attained by the magazines *Playboy* or *Penthouse* in the 1960's. The first volumes lived up to expectation. The sour yellow covers, with (on the first four books) Beardsley's drawings, the Beardsley title-pages and the wide margins, added up to something quite new and rather shocking. The sheer physical weight, because of the solid board covers and coated stock, the more than adequate printing of Ballantyne's, the writings of Henry James, Max Beerbohm and Baron Corvo *and* Beardsley's exotic drawings, were all factors contributory to the remarkable impact of these quarterly books. These books in some way capture the imagination and are, at least to our eyes, very much of their time.

*The Yellow Book* ran for thirteen numbers, but Beardsley only stayed with it for the first four. As an indirect result of the Oscar Wilde scandal he was sacked; and with his departure, the fire went out of the series. If Beardsley perhaps found John Lane's rather windy supervision too confining, his next publisher, Leonard Smithers, was quite a different kettle of fish. The new production was to be called *The Savoy* and have Beardsley as art editor and Arthur Symons as literary editor. It had a larger format (quarto) and sold for 2*s* 6*d*, half the price of *The Yellow Book*. The Beardsley covers, for the first two numbers, were printed in black on pink paper-covered boards; abandoning the massed blacks of *The Yellow Book* covers, he used intricate cross hatching to give an engraved effect.

The contributors to the first volume of *The Savoy* included George Bernard Shaw, Havelock Ellis, and Beardsley himself, with the first pages of his novel *Under the Hill*. In Volume 2, Max Beerbohm drew Beardsley and Beardsley drew himself, Sickert showed a drawing of the Rialto and Charles H. Shannon drew a naked girl diving. The standard of illustration in *The Savoy* is much higher than that of *The Yellow Book*; Beardsley had matured in these two years; and his *Under the Hill* drawings are amongst his finest work. *The Savoy* ran for eight volumes; yet, curiously, it is the memory of *The Yellow Book* that lingers on, whilst *The Savoy* is all but forgotten. Yellow always possesses the power to shock, far more than does the dusty cosmetic pink of the first of *The Savoy* covers.

Yellow was always an essential feature of the pulp magazine covers, as for example in the '20's; for the work of Edgar Wallace and Sidney Horler, 'Horler for Excitement!' Gollancz made good use of it in the '30's with the Stanley Morison-designed book jackets. If *The Yellow Book* had been called *The*

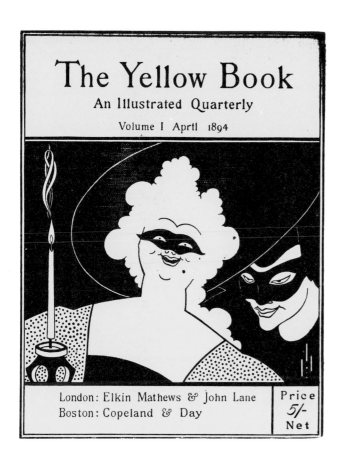

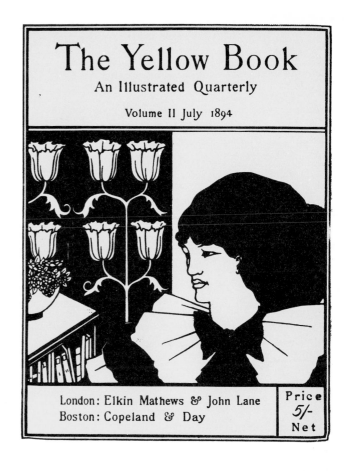

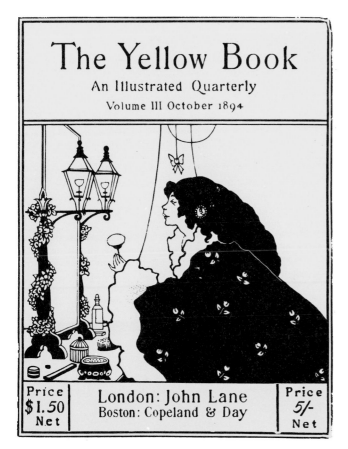

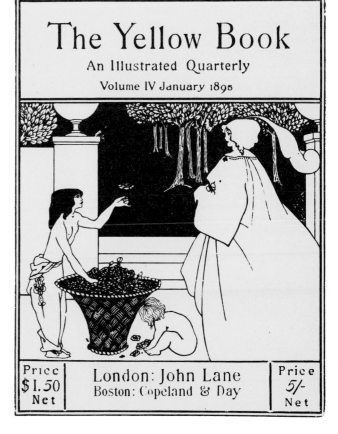

1894–5. *The Yellow Book* Volumes 1–4. Edited by Henry Harland. Published by Elkin Mathews and John Lane, London. (Vols 3 and 4 John Lane, Bodley Head). In Boston by Copeland and Day. Printed by the Ballantyne Press, London and Edinburgh. 8″ × 6⅛″. These cover designs for the first four volumes of *The Yellow Book* were by Aubrey Beardsley.

1909. *Histoire de Soliman Ben Daoud et de la Reine du Matin* by Gérard de Nerval. Published by the Eragny Press, Hammersmith. Designed, engraved and printed by Lucien and Esther Pissarro. 8½" × 5½". Commissioned by the Society of 'Cent Bibliophiles'. Combined title-page and chapter opening. Gold leaf was used for the printing of the initial letters.

*Grey Book*, it is doubtful if we would have remembered it. In 1900 Emery Walker, who had been Morris's adviser at Kelmscott (May Morris is reported as saying: 'Without Mr Walker the Kelmscott Press could not have existed – at any rate in the form it took')[2] – went into partnership with T. J. Cobden-Sanderson and started the Doves Press, near the Doves Inn at Hammersmith. The Doves policy was that their books should be free from ornament and owe their design quality to the 'architectural beauty of their pages'. The immaculate productions that resulted from this philosophy are not particularly endearing. The only concessions to decoration were initials drawn for them by Graily Hewitt and Edward Johnston.

Johnston, a pioneer in the teaching of calligraphy in two London art schools, first at the Central School of Arts and Crafts and later at the Royal College of Art, maintained that in the practice of calligraphy the letter cutter and the type designer could learn the fundamentals of their craft. The falling away of this method of teaching is a sad thing. Maybe too many scribes have had their horizons limited to writing Rolls of Honour and the like, yet artists such as Berthold Wolpe, Imre Reiner and Hermann Zapf have successfully carried this craft into the world of type founding and modern graphics. Unhappily there are not many Wolpes, Reiners and Zapfs in each generation.

Of the English private presses at the turn of the century the most interesting was the Eragny. This was run by Lucien Pissarro, a son of the French painter, Camille Pissarro, and a close friend of Ricketts. Lucien married an English girl, Esther Bensusan, and settled in Hammersmith. Together they produced some of the most delightful and, until recently, the least sought after of the private press books. They are beautifully printed and usually decorated with Lucien's coloured woodcuts, which are a curious mixture of his father's down-to-earth impressionism, blended with something derived from Charles Keene's drawings and the whole overlaid with art nouveau decoration. Possibly it is these qualities and particularly the art nouveau influences that have until now detracted from their popularity.

English commercially published books in 1900 showed various influences in their appearance. The most dominant of these was still art nouveau, which showed particularly in decorated covers. John Lane's productions led the field in the elegance of their covers and in their typography. Percy Muir, a partner in another famous book house, wrote: '. . . the actual design and layout (of Lane's Books) were largely the work of two men – Charles Ricketts, who was a genius at that sort of thing . . . and Walter Blaikie, of the firm of T. & A. Constable of Edinburgh, whose unmistakable layout is to be seen in so many of the early productions of the firm'.[3] In illustration the stylistic unrealities of Aubrey Beardsley were mingling with post Pre-Raphaelite illustrators and the robust drawings of William Nicholson, Gordon Browne and Phil May. The airy wide-margined typography of Whistler had had its effect, but so had the eighteenth-century revivalist typography of Pickering and Whittingham and the consciously 'olde worlde' chapbook style of Field and Tuer at the Leadenhall Press. Behind all this confusion lay the heroic work of William Morris at the Kelmscott Press. The commercial publishers of Europe and America had, as yet, paid little heed to Morris's observations about type, presswork and paper. Imitations of Kelmscott proliferated, but, lacking Morris's qualities of design and presswork, were often sorry objects.

[2] *Emery Walker:* C. V. Nordlunde. Copenhagen 1959.

[3] *Minding my own business:* Percy Muir, Chatto and Windus 1956.

2*

PSYCHE BORNE OFF BY ZEPHYRUS, DRAWN BY EDWARD BURNE-JONES & ENGRAVED BY WILLIAM MORRIS

1898. *A Note by William Morris on his aims in founding the Kelmscott Press.* The last book published by the Kelmscott Press. Frontispiece by Edward Burne-Jones. 8″ × 5¾″.

*Opposite:*
1896. *The Savoy,* an illustrated quarterly edited by Arthur Symons, with Aubrey Beardsley as art editor. Published by Leonard Smithers. Printed by the Chiswick Press, Charles Whittingham and Co. 10″ × 7⅝″. This publication ran for eight issues. Cover design by Aubrey Beardsley.

## The influence of Burne-Jones on Beardsley

The Kelmscott influence was felt in one or two unexpected places, and showed even in Beardsley's work. In his *Le Morte d'Arthur* the decorative borders and initial letters were a direct development of Morris's borders and letters. In all Beardsley's figure drawings, from *Le Morte d'Arthur* to his work for *The Savoy,* there are traces of Edward Burne-Jones's sad elongated, rather sexless creatures. The cross-fertilization of anti-pathetic movements in art is a recurring factor in the design and illustration of twentieth century books. When viewed sixty or seventy years later, their dissimilarities are often submerged by their period flavour.

1907. *Riquet à la Houppe* by Perrault with four-colour wood engravings by Lucien Pissarro. Published and printed by the Eragny Press. 5¼″ × 4¼″. Cover quarter bound in vellum and grey Ingres paper with a printed label. Chapter opening and text spread.

**The influence of the English private presses**

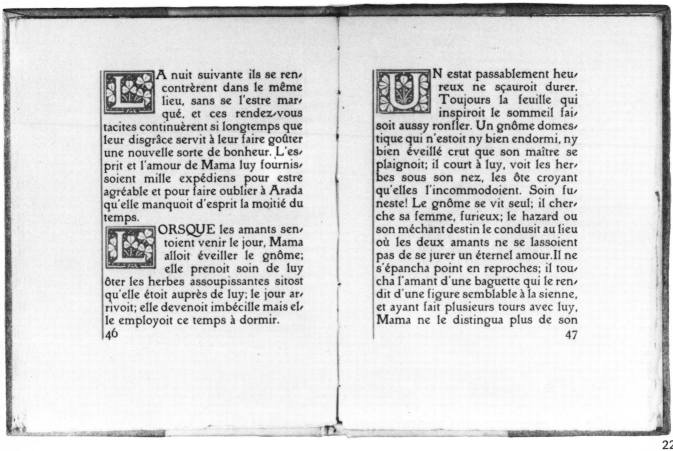

The Autocrat of the
Breakfast-Table by
Oliver Wendell Holmes
author of 'The Poet at
the Breakfast-Table'

London *Walter Scott Limited*
Paternoster Square

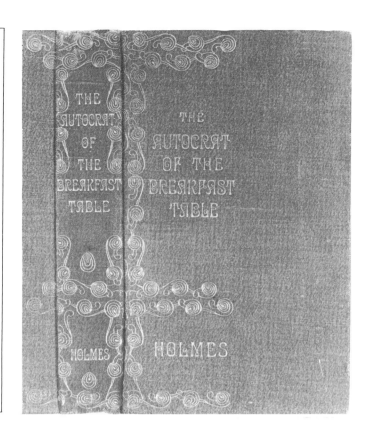

*c.* 1897. *The Autocrat of the Breakfast Table* by Oliver Wendell Holmes. Published by Walter Scott Ltd, London. Printed by the Walter Scott Press, Newcastle upon Tyne. 6⅞″ × 4⅜″. Title-page and red cloth-covered case-binding blocked in gold.

*c.* 1914. *Routine et Progrès en Agriculture* by R. Dumont. Binding designed by G. Auriol. Published by Maison Larousse. Reproduced from *The Art of the Book* 1914: Studio.

1883–4. *Olde ffrendes wyth newe Faces,* with hand-coloured woodcut illustrations by Joseph Crawhall. Published by Field and Tuer, London and Scribner and Welford, New York. Printed by the Leadenhall Press, London. 11½″ × 8¾″. Title-page.

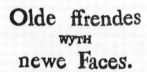

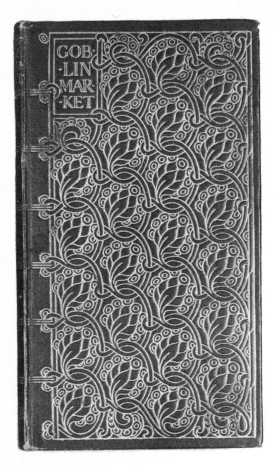

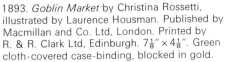

1893. *Goblin Market* by Christina Rossetti, illustrated by Laurence Housman. Published by Macmillan and Co. Ltd, London. Printed by R. & R. Clark Ltd, Edinburgh. 7⅛″ × 4⅛″. Green cloth-covered case-binding, blocked in gold.

*To the right:*
1896. *Green Arras* by Laurence Housman, illustrated by the author. Published by John Lane at the Bodley Head, London. Printed by R. Folkard and Son, London. 7½″ × 5″. Green cloth-covered case-binding, blocked in gold.

The revival of good typography both on the continent and in the U.S.A. was due largely to the work of the English private presses. The typographic interests of these press printers were almost exclusively limited to the reviving of the old style typeface of the fifteenth-century Venetian printers. This pre-occupation makes them more than a little dull. Good presswork, good paper, good types and good composition are essential ingredients for the making of a good book; but they do not necessarily make a visually exciting one. For example, the charm of the Eragny books is due to other factors than these, including art nouveau influences and Pissarro's Gallic taste. And however well printed it may be, there is not much charm about a Doves Press page. The covers of books in the 'nineties were often their most attractive features. Those for *Goblin Market* and *Green Arras* are both of a smooth sage-green cloth, with arabesque patterns based on leaves, blocked in gold; on each case the title on the front is tucked away in the top left-hand corner. These slim volumes are most elegant little books, both designed and illustrated by Laurence Housman.

Housman's work appeared in various periodicals and he illustrated a number of books, including several that he had written himself. His illustrations for Christina Rossetti's poem are shown in a later chapter of this book. His title page for his own *Green Arras* is certainly remarkable, not only for the intricate border, no doubt inspired by William Morris, but also for the extreme economy of space occupied by the actual copy.

The first illustrated edition of *The Picture of Dorian Gray* was planned to be published in 1908, the date that actually appears on the title-page; but the illustrator, Paul Thiriat, fell ill and the book did not appear until 1910. Thiriat's illustrations are more like magazine drawings than book illustrations. They have been most skilfully engraved on the wood by E. Dété. This is an attractive book, with very wide margins, but rather uneven presswork. It has a handsome case, half bound in white buckram and grey Ingres paper, blocked in gold. The asymmetric title page, printed in black and red, is evidence of someone's thought and attention.

1896. *Green Arras* by Laurence Housman, illustrated by the author. Published by John Lane at the Bodley Head, London. Printed by R. Folkard and Son, London. 7½" × 5". Title-page spread.

1910. *The Picture of Dorian Gray* by Oscar Wilde. Illustrated by Paul Thiriat (engraved by E. Dété). Published by Charles Carrington, Paris. 10" × 7½". Title-page spread printed in black and red.

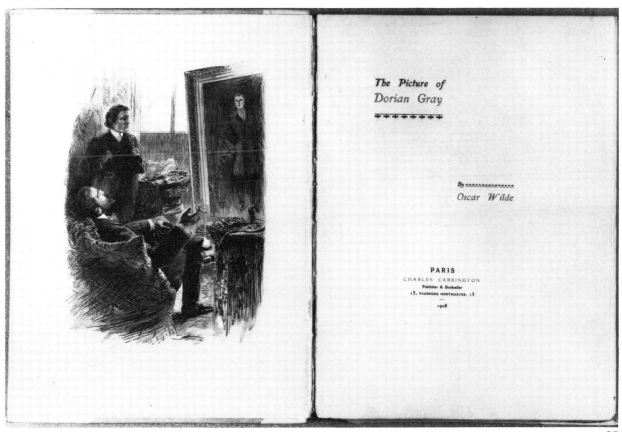

1900. *Vom Lieben Gott und Anderes* by Rainer
Maria Rilke. Illustrated and designed by E. R.
Weiss. Published for Insel-Verlag by Schuster
and Loeffler, Berlin and Leipzig. Printed by
W. Drugulin, Leipzig. Set in Luthersche Fraktur.
8⅜″ × 5⅞″. Title-page. Cased in paper-covered
boards with labels on front and spine printed in
black. End-paper design printed in red.

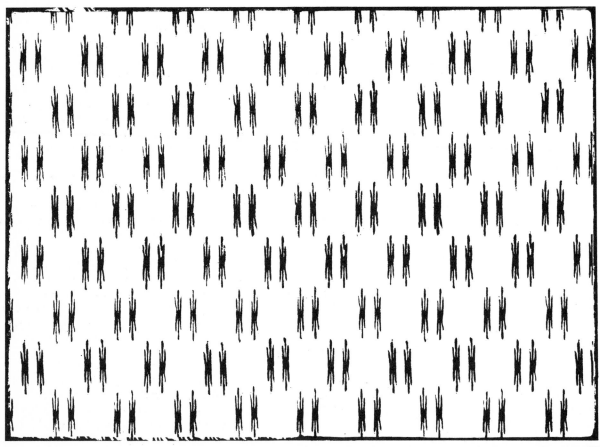

1908. *Ecce Homo* by Friedrich Nietzsche.
Designed by Henry van de Velde. Published by
Insel-Verlag, Leipzig. Printed by Friedrich
Richter. $9\frac{5}{8}'' \times 7\frac{1}{2}''$. Title-page.

### Book design in Germany in 1900

Morris had not lived in vain, yet it was not in England but in Germany where
his work had most impact. The revival of good printing in Germany spread
directly from his influence. Amongst the first publishers there to consider
book design as something that mattered were Insel-Verlag of Leipzig, and
J. Fischer and Bruno Cassirer, both of Berlin. Another pioneer of fine book
work in Germany was C. E. Poeschel, the proprietor of the important printing
works Poeschel and Trepte of Leipzig, and for a short while in part control
of Insel-Verlag.

In 1905, Poeschel and Harry Graf Kessler (who later was to have his own
private press) invited Emery Walker to design a series of German classics for
Insel-Verlag. This was the *Grossherzog Wilhelm Ernst* edition. These octavo
books, designed on the proportion of the golden section, with calligraphic
title-pages by Edward Johnston and Eric Gill and attractively cased in limp
calf, had a marked effect upon German book production.

The foremost typographers and book designers in Germany at this time were
Otto Eckmann, Peter Behrens and Rudolf Koch who all designed for the
Klingspor foundry, F. W. Kleukens who designed a series of roman types for
the Stempel foundry, Walter Tiemann who was an instructor at the Royal
Academy of Graphic Arts at Leipzig, and E. R. Weiss who designed for the
Bauer typefoundry. Of these Weiss was the most versatile, and Koch the
most dedicated.

Koch carried Edward Johnston's doctrine to its logical conclusion and most
successfully linked the art of the scribe with the arts of typefounding and
printing. In 1911, Willy Wiegand founded the Bremer Press, and produced
private editions, which followed the style of the Doves Press. The books were
without illustration, but were decorated with fine initial letters drawn by
Anna Simons, a former pupil of Edward Johnston.

27

1902. *Ex Libris* by Bernhard Wenig. Published by
Fischer and Franke, Berlin. Privately printed and
limited to 500 copies. 9⅝" × 7". Bound in grey
paper-covered boards, blocked in blue. Title-page.

1898. *Johannes*, a tragedy by Hermann
Sudermann. Published by J. G. Cottasche,
Stuttgart and Berlin. Printed by Union Deutsche
Verlagsanstalt, Stuttgart. 7⅝" × 4⅞". Paper cover
designed by Otto Eckmann, printed in black
and red.

**Die zehnte Muse**

Dichtungen vom Brettl
~ und fürs Brettl ~

Aus vergangenen Jahrhunderten
und aus unsern Tagen gesammelt

von

Maximilian Bern

Sechsundzwanzigstes Tausend.

Recht des Jüngern.
Wer auf des Alten Schultern steht,
Der kann ihm Dank bezeigen;
Doch kann er nicht aus Dankbarkeit
Zu ihm heruntersteigen.
E. F. Ludw. Robert
(1779 1832).

Berlin 1908
Verlag von Otto Elsner

1908. *Die zehnte Muse* edited by Maximilian
Bern. Published by Otto Elsner, Berlin. 8″ × 4½″.
Red cloth-covered case-binding blocked in
white and title-page, set in Eckmann-Schmuck.
*Below*: 1913 edition cover with paper wrapper
printed in red and green.

Jubiläums-Auflage

**86.–100. Tausend!**

Maximilian Bern

**Die zehnte Muse**

Enthält fünfhundert

galante, heitere und ernste

**Dichtungen**

Romanzen aus realem Leben — Erotische Lyrik
Bunte Lieder — Satiren — Vagabundenlieder
Moderne Fabeln — Sinngedichte — Soziales
Ernste Vorträge — Heitere Vorträge

*Berns Brettlanthologie aus vergangenen Jahr-
hunderten und aus unsern Tagen: „Die zehnte
Muse" ist in ihrer Art klassisch und hat bleiben-
den literarhistorischen Wert.* (Neue Freie Press.)

*Dieses Buch kann gar nicht genug gelobt werden.
Die Auswahl ist direkt bewundernswert.* (Die Zeit.)

Preis zwei Mark.

In 1913, Harry Graf Kessler started the Cranach press at Weimar. He had a
special typeface cut by Edward Prince (who had worked for the Kelmscott
Press), under the supervision of Emery Walker: the roman was based on that
used by Jenson in 1470; the italic was designed by Edward Johnston. A
number of English artists worked for Kessler including Eric Gill and Edward
Gordon Craig. Craig produced a set of woodcuts for a truly magnificent edition
of *Hamlet*, based on the designs for his production of the play at the Moscow
Arts Theatre in 1912. He worked on them for seventeen years; so this, one of
the most outstanding of the Cranach books, did not appear until 1929 (in
German) and in 1930 in an English edition.

The classicism of the Cranach *Hamlet* is in marked contrast to Koch's block-
book *Elia*, when, working in a mediaeval tradition, he cut both illustrations and
letters on the wood.

Many years later, Francis Meynell published an edition of *Genesis* from his
Nonesuch Press; its pages had much the same block-book appearance, for
Meynell made use of Koch's Neuland typeface, which combined effectively
with woodcuts by Paul Nash. Maximilian Bern's *Die zehnte Muse*, published
by Otto Elsner in 1908, is set in Eckmann-Schmuck, the typeface Otto Eckmann designed for Klingspor. It was Jugendstil's answer to black letter, and
is comparable to Morris's rejection of the roman typeface. The layout of the
title page for *Die zehnte Muse* is judiciously asymmetric. The paper cover,
from a later edition, is interesting but a poor piece of work in comparison with
the first edition cover.

GOETHES
DRAMATISCHE
DICHTUNGEN
BAND I

LEIPZIG
MDCCCCIX
IM INSELVERLAG

1905–17. *Goethes Dramatische Dichtungen*
Volume I. Grossherzog Wilhelm Ernst Edition.
Pocket edition of the German classics. Layout by
Harry Graf Kessler and Emery Walker, with
titling by Eric Gill. Published by Insel-Verlag.
Printed by Brierkopf and Hartel, Leipzig.
$6\frac{7}{8}$" × 4". Bound in flexible calf and gold
blocked. Case-binding, title-page and text spread.

---

208      FAUST

MEPH. (*zur Hexe*). Und kann ich dir was zu Gefallen tun,
So darfst du mirs nur auf Walpurgis sagen.
DIE HEXE. Hier ist ein Lied! wenn Ihrs zuweilen singt,
So werdet Ihr besondre Wirkung spüren.
MEPHISTOPHELES (*zu Faust*).
Komm nur geschwind und laß dich führen;
Du mußt notwendig transpirieren,
Damit die Kraft durch Inn- und Äußres dringt.
Den edlen Müßiggang lehr ich hernach dich schätzen,
Und bald empfindest du mit innigem Ergetzen,
Wie sich Cupido regt und hin und wider springt.
FAUST. Laß mich nur schnell noch in den Spiegel schauen!
Das Frauenbild war gar zu schön!
MEPH. Nein! Nein! Du sollst das Muster aller Frauen
Nun bald leibhaftig vor dir sehn.
(*Leise.*) Du siehst, mit diesem Trank im Leibe,
Bald Helenen in jedem Weibe.

STRASSE.

*Faust. Margarete vorübergehend.*

FAUST. Mein schönes Fräulein, darf ich wagen,
Meinen Arm und Geleit Ihr anzutragen?
MARGARETE. Bin weder Fräulein, weder schön,
Kann ungeleitet nach Hause gehn.
(*Sie macht sich los und ab.*)
FAUST. Beim Himmel, dieses Kind ist schön!
So etwas hab ich nie gesehn.
Sie ist so sitt- und tugendreich,
Und etwas schnippisch doch zugleich.
Der Lippe Rot, der Wange Licht,
Die Tage der Welt vergeß ichs nicht!
Wie sie die Augen niederschlägt,
Hat tief sich in mein Herz geprägt;
Wie sie kurz angebunden war,
Das ist nun zum Entzücken gar!

*Mephistopheles tritt auf.*

FAUST. Hör, du mußt mir die Dirne schaffen!

ERSTER TEIL      209

MEPHISTOPHELES. Nun, welche?
FAUST.          Sie ging just vorbei.
MEPHISTOPHELES. Da die? Sie kam von ihrem Pfaffen,
Der sprach sie aller Sünden frei;
Ich schlich mich hart am Stuhl vorbei,
Es ist ein gar unschuldig Ding,
Das eben für nichts zur Beichte ging;
Über die hab ich keine Gewalt!
FAUST. Ist über vierzehn Jahr doch alt.
MEPHISTOPHELES. Du sprichst ja wie Hans Liederlich,
Der begehrt jede Blum für sich,
Und dünkelt ihm, es wär kein Ehr
Und Gunst, die nicht zu pflücken wär;
Geht aber doch nicht immer an.
FAUST. Mein Herr Magister Lobesan,
Laß Er mich mit dem Gesetz in Frieden!
Und das sag ich Ihm kurz und gut:
Wenn nicht das süße junge Blut
Heut nacht in meinen Armen ruht,
So sind wir um Mitternacht geschieden.
MEPHISTOPHELES.
Bedenkt, was gehn und stehen mag!
Ich brauche wenigstens vierzehn Tag,
Nur die Gelegenheit auszuspüren.
FAUST. Hätt ich nur sieben Stunden Ruh,
Brauchte den Teufel nicht dazu,
So ein Geschöpfchen zu verführen.
MEPHISTOPH. Ihr sprecht schon fast wie ein Franzos;
Doch bitt ich, laßts Euch nicht verdrießen:
Was hilfts, nur grade zu genießen?
Die Freud ist lange nicht so groß,
Als wenn Ihr erst herauf, herum,
Durch allerlei Brimborium,
Das Püppchen geknetet und zugericht't,
Wie's lehret manche welsche Geschicht.
FAUST. Hab Appetit auch ohne das.
MEPHISTOPH. Jetzt ohne Schimpf und ohne Spaß.
Ich sag Euch, mit dem schönen Kind
Gehts ein- für allemal nicht geschwind.
GOETHE VI 14.

VIERTER AKT
FÜNFTE SZENE

DIE TRAGISCHE GESCHICHTE VON

HAMLET PRINZEN VON DÆNEMARK

VIERTER AKT
SECHSTE SZENE

Befürchte nichts für unsere person.
Denn solche göttlichkeit schirmt einen könig:
Verrat, der nur erblickt, was er gewollt,
Steht ab von seinem willen. - Sage, Hamlet,
Was bist du so entrüstet? - Gertrud, laß ihn! -
Sprich, junger mann!
Ham. Wo ist mein vater?
König Tot.
Königin Doch nicht durch ihn.
König Laß ihn nur satt sich fragen. -
Ham. Wie kam er um? Ich lasse mich nicht äffen.
Zur hölle, treu! Zum ärgsten teufel, eide!
Gewissen, frömmigkeit, zum tiefsten schlund!
Ich trotze der verdammnis; so weit kam's:
Ich schlage beide welten in die schanze,
Mag kommen, was da kommt! Nur rache will ich
Vollauf für meinen vater.
König Wer wird euch hindern?
Ham. Mein wille, nicht der ganzen welt gebot.
Und meine mittel will ich so verwalten,
Daß wenig weit soll reichen.
König Höre, Hamlet,
Wenn du von deines teuren vaters tod
Das sichre wissen willst: ist's deiner rache schluß,
Als sieger in dem spiel, so freund als feind,
Unschuldige und schuldge zu vernichten?
Ham. Die schuldgen nur.
König Wollt ihr sie kennen lernen? -
Ham. Den freunden will ich weit die arme öffnen
Und, wie der lebensopfrer pelikan,
Mit meinem blut sie nähren.

England, the messengers presented themselves to the king, giving him Fengons letters; who having read the contents, sayd nothing as then, but stayed convenient time to effect Fengons desire, meane time using the Danes familiarly, doing them that honour to sit at his table (for that kings as then where not so curiously, nor solemnely served as in these our dayes), for in these dayes meane kings, and lords of small revenewe are as difficult and hard to bee seene, as in times past the monarches of Persia used to bee; or as it is reported of the great king of Aethyopia, who will not permit any man to see his face, which ordinarily bee covereth with a vaile. And as the messengers sate at the table with the king, subtile Hamlet was so far from being merry with them, that he would not taste one bit of meate, bread, nor cup of beare whatsoever, as then set upon the table, not without great wondering of the company, abashed to see a yong man and a stranger not to esteeme of the delicate meates and pleasant drinkes served at the banquet, rejecting them as things filthy, evill of tast, and worse prepared. The king, who for that time dissembled what he thought, caused his ghests to be conveyed into their chamber, willing one of his secret servantes to hide himselfe therein, and so to certifie him what speeches past among

140

Laer. Doch meine hand wird eisen, und nur ein
Gedanke nistet noch in meinem hirn.
König Wie denkt ihr's euch?
Laer. Ihn in der kirch' erwürgen.
König Auf andre art, wenn ihr entschlossen seid.
Laer. Der würger würgte meinen vater hin,
Er würgte meine schwester und wird mich
Erwürgen, doch ich komme ihm zuvor.
König Mit einem wohlgezielten, sichern stoß.
Wollt ihr dies tun, so haltet euch zuhaus.
Kommt Hamlet, soll er wissen ihr seid hier.
Wir laden beide euch zu diesem spiel,
Des ende tödlich sein muß für den prinzen,
Kein wenn und aber ist hier mehr am platz.
Laer. Mit meines basses gift salb ich die spitze
Des degens.
König Gebt zum apotheker, kauft
Ein richtges gift, ein tödliches: geritzt nur,
Geb er die gottverdammte seele auf.
Doch muß der plan noch einen rückhalt haben.
Ich hab's: wenn ihr vom fechten heiß und durstig
seid -
Ihr müßt deshalb die gänge kräftger machen -
Und er zu trinken fordert, soll ein kelch
Bereitstehn, der, wenn er davon nur nippt,
Entging er etwa eurem giftgen stich,
Noch unsern anschlag sichert.
Laer. Herr, ich zittre,
Dem rüden gleich, der einen eber wittert.

HARANGUE D'AMLETH
AUX DANOIS
S'il y a quelqu'un d'entre vous, Messieurs de Dannemarch, qui aye encore fraische memoire du tort faict au puissant Roy Horwendille, qu'il ne s'esmeuve en rien, voyant la face confuse et hideusement espouvantable de la presente calamité: S'il y a aucun qui aye la fidelité pour recommandee, et cherisse l'affection qu'on doit à ses parens, et trouve bonne la souvenance des ou trages faits à ceux, qui nous ont produits au monde, que celuy ne s'esbahisse, contemplant un tel massacre, et moins s'offense en advisant une si effroyable ruine, et d'hommes, et des plus superbes edifices de tout le pays, car la main qui a execute ceste justice, ne pouvoit en chevir à meilleur marché, et ne luy estoit loisible d'autrement se prevaloir, qu'en ruinant, et l'insensible, et le sensible, pour garder la memoire d'une si equitable vengeance. Je voy bien, Messieurs, (et suis joyeux de cognoistre une telle vostre si affectionnee devotion) que vous estes marris, ayans devant vos yeux Fengon ainsi mutile, et celuy sans teste, que d'autresfois vous avez recogneu pour chef, mais je vous prie penser que ce corps n'est le corps d'un Roy, ains d'un tyran execrable, et d'un parricide plus detestable.

145

1929. *Die Tragische Geschichte von Hamlet, Prinzen von Daenemark* by William Shakespeare illustrated with woodcuts by Edward Gordon Craig. Published and printed by the Cranach Press, Weimar. Produced under the direction of J. H. Mason and Max Goertz. 14" × 9½". Text pages.

1921. *Elia*, a block-book with letters and pictures cut on the wood by Rudolf Koch. 11" × 9⅜". Printed by Wilhelm Gerstung, Offenbach-am-Main, in an edition of 200 copies. Double spread.

1902. *The Art of Walter Crane* by P. G. Konody. Published by George Bell and Sons. Printed by the Chiswick Press. $13\frac{1}{2}'' \times 9\frac{1}{2}''$. The title-page design by Walter Crane was also blocked in gold on the cloth cover.

## The Arts and Crafts Exhibition Society and art nouveau

Walter Crane was both an illustrator and a book designer. He was also, under William Morris's influence, one of the prime movers in the Arts and Crafts Exhibition Society, a society founded to promote a revival in the decorative arts. Crane stated the aims of this Society with clarity and persuasion in the introductory essay to the catalogue of the 1888 exhibition. The ideas of the various members of the Society were assembled in *Arts and Crafts Essays,* which Morris edited and Rivington, Percival published in 1893. (In this same book was the admirable essay, *Printing*, by Morris and Emery Walker.) Crane was a vociferous opponent of art nouveau, yet his work reveals marked art nouveau characteristics. His earlier illustrations, drawn for the colour printer Edmund Evans, have some charm, but as he became more interested in book *decoration*, as opposed to illustration, so his work became more lifeless. He subordinated everything to the design of the printed page and, though to some extent he avoided the archaism of Morris and Burne-Jones, his work lacked the magnificent quality of inevitability so apparent in all Morris's work. Crane influenced a number of young artists, including Anning Bell, and taught for a number of years at the Royal College of Art. His professional career spanned over half-a-century, during which time he illustrated a great number of books.

1900. *Line and Form* written and designed by Walter Crane. Published by George Bell and Sons, London. Printed by Charles Whittingham and Co., London. 9⅛″ × 5¾″. The title-page design was also blocked in gold on the cover.

1913. *Le Nouveau Monde* by Villiers de l'Isle-Adam. Illustrated by woodcuts by P. E. Vibert. Published by Georges Crès et Cie, Paris. 9⅞″ × 6⅜″. Art Nouveau title-page designed by P. E. Vibert and printed in black, green and orange.

*c.* 1912. *Corner Stones* by Katharine Burrill. Binding designed by Reginald L. Knowles. Published by J. M. Dent and Sons Ltd, London. Reproduced from *The Art of the Book* 1914: Studio.

1888. *Troy Town* by Q. (Sir Arthur Quiller-Couch). Published and printed by Cassell and Co. Ltd, London. 7¼″ × 5″. Brown cloth cover blocked in gold and black.

**The beginning of the illustrated case-binding**

Sir Arthur Quiller-Couch's *The Astonishing History of Troy Town* was first published in Cassell's Five Shilling Series in 1888. The cover, by some anonymous artist, is printed in black on a smooth dun-coloured cloth. Only the words 'Troy Town' on the spine are blocked in gold. The letter forms are a firm break away from any traditional roman, and antecede art nouveau with their vaguely oriental characteristics. The history of the late nineteenth- and early twentieth-century illustrated cover is still to be written. The *Troy Town* cover is a relatively modest example of the genus.

In contrast Reznicek's cover for Eduard Fuch's *Die Frau in der Karikatur* is a colourful thing, combining blocking on a suede-finished cloth and a woman's figure printed in colour, cut out and inlaid. The laborious process of mounting four-colour prints on cloth cases, particularly for gift books and children's books, continued well into the 1920's. Though this has been regarded as a bastard process, some pretty covers resulted. The influence of the poster hoarding on such a cover as that for *Die Frau in der Karikatur* is obvious, but it was a golden age for posters and their influence on book covers was considerable.

34

1906.  *Die Frau in der Karikatur* by Eduard
Fuchs. Published by Albert Langen, Munich.
Printed by Hesse and Becker, Leipzig. Bound by
E. R. Enders, Leipzig. 10¾″ × 7⅛″. Case-binding.

1920. *Theodor Hosemann* by Lothar Brieger. Published by Delphin-Verlag, Munich. With a catalogue of the works of art by Karl Hobrecker. 9⅜″ × 6¼″. Bound in a rough mustard-coloured cloth, blocked in black. Sugar-bag blue end-papers. Case-binding, title-page and text spread.

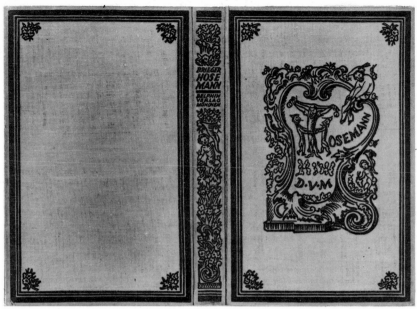

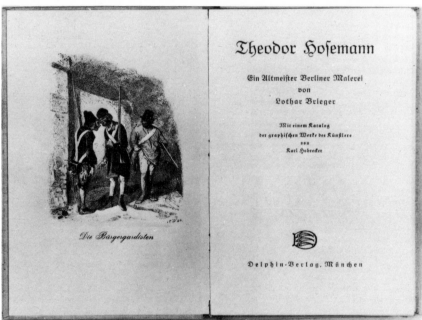

HISTOIRE

DE

L'IMPRIMERIE

EN FRANCE

AU XVᵉ ET AU XVIᵉ SIÈCLE

PAR A. CLAUDIN

LAURÉAT DE L'INSTITUT

TOME PREMIER

PARIS

IMPRIMERIE NATIONALE

MDCCCC

1900. *Histoire de l'Imprimerie en France* by A. Claudin. Published and printed by l'Imprimerie Nationale, Paris. 16¾″ × 13″. Title-page.

Lothar Brieger's monograph on the nineteenth-century German illustrator, Theodor Hosemann, has an interesting cover. The mustard-coloured case is blocked with a design that combines art nouveau, William Morris and rococo motifs. The case-binding is set off with sugar-bag blue end paper. The book, which looks as if it belonged to the end of the nineteenth century, was actually printed and bound in 1920.

**The typographic book in France**

In French book production more attention was paid to the illustrations than to the typefaces or the *mise-en-page*. But there were exceptions to this amongst publishers and printers; and of these, the Imprimerie Nationale very properly led the field. The French National Printing House at this time was under the enlightened direction of Arthur Christian. In 1900, Christian published Anatole Claudin's monumental *Histoire de l'Imprimerie en France*. This was printing in the grand manner, not seen in France since the times of Barbou and Didot. Typographically traditional, the book was set in large sizes of Garamond and Grandjean typefaces; the folio pages had ample margins and impeccable presswork.

An interest in France in the typographic, illustrated book, rather than the *édition de luxe*, where every other feature was subordinated to the illustration, was largely due to the publisher Édouard Pelletan. Pelletan was almost unique amongst his contemporaries. He demanded a high standard from his printers, was an exacting typographer and made good use of the typefaces of Jannon and Grandjean.

1902. *L'Album: les Maîtres de la Caricature,*
with a preface by Roger-Milès. Published by
Librairie Illustrée, J. Tallandier, Paris. Printed by
l'Imprimerie Générale Lahure, Paris. Bound by
Engel. 12¼″ × 9½″. Cover design by Lucien
Métivet, printed in full colour, on a cream-
coloured buckram.

1900. *Histoire du Chien de Brisquet* by Charles Nodier, with 25 illustrations by Théophile Alexandre Steinlen, engraved by Deloche, E. Froment, Ernest and Frédéric Florian. Published by Édouard Pelletan, Paris. 11⅜" × 9". Title-page printed ih black from a wood engraving and in blue and red, and vignette half-title printed in black and red.

CHARLES NODIER

Histoire
du
Chien de Brisquet

PRÉCÉDÉE
D'UNE LETTRE A JEANNE
PAR
M. ANATOLE FRANCE
de l'Académie française

*25 Compositions de Steinlen*

GRAVÉES PAR DELOCHE, E. FROMENT
ERNEST ET FRÉDÉRIC FLORIAN

KTHMA ΕΣ ΑΕΙ
E    P

PARIS
ÉDOUARD PELLETAN, ÉDITEUR
125, BOULEVARD SAINT-GERMAIN, 125

1900

4 *The New Book Illustration in France* (1924) Léon Pichon, Studio Ltd, London.

When Pelletan established himself as a publisher of 'artistic' books at 125 Blvd. Saint-Germain on 1st February 1896, there was plenty of exciting French book illustration but little good French book design. Léon Pichon, another French publisher of judgment writing nearly thirty years later, stated that at that time the English book, as conceived by William Morris, had a perfect unity; that the German books, derivative though they were (from Morris), matched the character of the race; but that French books were devoid of personality or harmony of style. Above all, Pichon went on, they lacked any 'directing intelligence'.[4] With that last remark, Pichon established the essential factor in book design. The 'directing intelligence' can be publisher, printer, typographer or illustrator, but without such direction, design is absent.

Pelletan, at a time when most French publishers thought only of the illustrations (for this kind of book, Pelletan's 'artistic' book), considered first the book as a whole, then the general typographic arrangement that would help to display the illustrations, and lastly, the illustrations themselves.

He helped to re-establish (at a time of insipidity in French books) a precise classification of the component parts of a book, subordinating everything to the elucidation of the author's text.

Pelletan's typography always took precedence over the illustrations, but this is not to say that he was unaware of the quality of the artists he employed. He used many illustrators, including Steinlen, Daniel Vierge and Willette, but his books, even when illustrated by an artist of the power of Steinlen, were never overpowered by the illustrator's personality. In such a book as Charles Nodier's *Histoire du Chien de Brisquet*, one's first impression on turning the pages is not of the skill of Steinlen's drawings of the woodcutter or his dog, but of the immaculate typography and the superb presswork.

nir chez Jean Paquier. — « As-tu vu nos
« enfants? » lui dit Brisquette.

« Nos enfants? dit Brisquet. Nos enfants?
« mon Dieu! sont-ils sortis? »

« Je les ai envoyés à ta rencontre jusqu'à
« la butte et à l'étang, mais tu as pris par un
« autre chemin. »

Brisquet ne posa pas sa bonne hache. Il

se mit à courir du côté de la butte.
« Si tu menois la Bichonne? »
lui cria Brisquette.

La Bichonne étoit déjà bien
loin.

Elle étoit si loin que Brisquet la perdit bientôt de vue.
Et il avoit beau crier :
« Biscotin, Biscotine! » on
ne lui répondoit pas.

Alors il se prit à pleu-
rer, parce qu'il s'ima-
gina que ses enfants
étoient perdus.

Après avoir couru
longtemps, longtemps,
il lui sembla recon-
noître la voix de
la Bichonne. Il
marcha

1900. *Histoire du Chien de Brisquet* by
Charles Nodier with 25 illustrations by Théophile
Alexandre Steinlen. Published by Édouard
Pelletan, Paris. 11¾" × 9". Text and illustration
spread. Cover engraved on the wood by Froment
and printed in full colour.

Steinlen's drawings for *Histoire du Chien de Brisquet* were beautifully
engraved by Deloche, E. Froment, and Ernest and Frédéric Florian. They
marry most happily with the handsome neo-classical typeface. The book is an
interesting typographic mixture: the title-page has strong art nouveau
influences, particularly in the title lines; the cover belongs to the new age of
the French poster. *Histoire du Chien de Brisquet* is a successful example of
a book conceived typographically, rather than solely as a vehicle for illustration. It is a beautiful book.

The 1900's might seem to be something of an anti-climax after the splendours
of the 'nineties. Yet there was plenty of confidence in the world of books. The
development of photographic methods of reproduction led to wide use of
illustration, not only inside books but also on their covers. This was the age
of the picture cover, sometimes crudely printed, often superbly blocked. In
most of these illustrated covers art nouveau motifs can be detected, which
were often repeated in the endpapers and title-pages.

But, however lively their covers, the presswork and typography of these books
were often deplorable; the papers used were wretched puffed-up antiques,
or not very good coated stock (though the bindings were often made up of
firm boards and excellent book cloths, well blocked). The wide margins that
Whistler had used so successfully in his books helped ro relieve the otherwise
rather undistinguished typography. It was only in the private press book and
in the work of a few commercial publishers that the typographic virtues one
looks for in fine books were to be found.

Histoire du Chien de Brisquet

illustrée par Steinlen

se vend chez Édouard Pelletan aux Éditions d'Art

1900. *Sie*, an album of drawings by Reznicek.
Published by Albert Langen, Munich. 14¾″ × 11″.
Bound in calendered unbleached linen, printed
in black and Indian red.

### The illustrated case-binding

The brashness of many of the commercially produced books of the 1900's
often has more vitality than the impeccable work of private press productions.
This is particularly true of their covers, which were frequently colourful and
decorative. They look perhaps a little modest alongside the jewel-like block-
ings of the '60's and '70's; or against such exotic materials as tortoiseshell or
*papier mâché* (which had to be cast in moulds), or cloths such as silk and
velvet. Blocking in gold or blind blocking came into use in the 1830's, and
the mounting on cloth covers of printed panels of paper some thirty years later.[5]
These two techniques provided the hard core of decorative and illustrative
bindings well into the twentieth century. The printing of coloured designs on
paper-covered boards shown so splendidly by the yellow-backed novels,
which were printed in three or four colours from designs cut on wood, fell
into disuse. (A development of this method – printing cover designs by
offset lithography on cloth – is used rather less often than it might be
nowadays.) The cover for *Sie* is by Reznicek and is printed in colour on linen-
covered boards. The silhouette treatment of the woman's black dress is
worthy of the Beggarstaffs.
The cloth cover for the first American edition (1893) of Robert Louis Stevenson's *Island Nights' Entertainments* is printed in black and a terracotta red.
It is an effective and appropriate design by some anonymous designer at
Scribner's. The book is illustrated by Gordon Browne and W. Hatherell.

[5] See *Victorian Book Design and Colour Printing*
by Ruari McLean. Faber and Faber, London 1963.

1893. *Island Nights' Entertainments* by Robert
Louis Stevenson. Published by Charles Scribner's
Sons, New York. Printed by Trow Directory,
Printing and Bookbinding Company, New York.
$7\frac{1}{4}'' \times 5''$. Case-binding printed in black and
Indian red on an oatmeal coloured cloth.

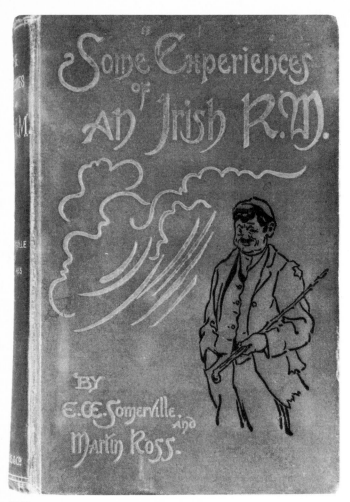

1900. *Some Experiences of an Irish R.M.* by
E. Œ. Somerville and Martin Ross. Illustrated by
E. Œ. Somerville. Published by Longmans,
Green and Co., London. 7¼″ × 4¾″. Case-binding
of dark green cloth blocked in red and black.

1907. *A Tarpaulin Muster* by John Masefield.
Cover designed by 'Mr Symington', reproduced
from *The Inchcape Rock*. Published by E. Grant
Richards. 7½″ × 4⅞″. Case-binding of unbleached
canvas blocked in navy blue and orange.

1913. *The Pavilion on the Links* by Robert Louis
Stevenson, illustrated by Gordon Browne.
Published by Chatto and Windus, London.
Printed by Ballantyne, Hanson and Co. Ltd,
Edinburgh. 8⅛″ × 5¼″. Case-binding blocked in
six colours on a grey cloth. (*Opposite left.*)

1905. *Ghost Stories of an Antiquary* by
Montague Rhodes James, illustrated by James
McBryde. Published by Edward Arnold, London.
Printed by Billing and Sons Ltd, Guildford.
8¼″ × 5⅝″. Case-binding of unbleached canvas
blocked in red and black. (*Opposite right.*)

The book covers shown here are very typical of those published at the turn
of the century. The title for *Some Experiences of an Irish R.M.* is blocked in
red and black, on a green cloth from a design by E. Œ. Somerville. The same
treatment is used for the Will Owen design for *A Master of Craft*. Owen, who
was a successful poster artist, illustrated both this book and *At Sunwich Port*,
though the cover design for the latter is by a designer with the initials G.M.W.
*The Pavilion on the Links* by Robert Louis Stevenson is illustrated with some
very lively drawings by Gordon Browne, who also designed the cover. This
is effectively blocked in white, two yellows, black and dark grey on the mid-
grey cloth. Gold for the letters on the spine brings the total of blocking
operations to six! M. R. James's *Ghost Stories of an Antiquary* makes a
pleasant contrast to these picture covers. It has a square-backed, rough, unbleached canvas cover, blocked in black and red. 'Square-backing' was a
continental rather than an English binding method; the English binders, more
than those of any other country, have remained faithful to rounding-and-
backing.

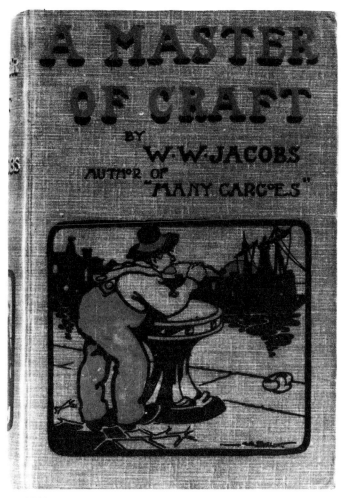

1900. *A Master of Craft* by W. W. Jacobs, illustrated by Will Owen. Published by George Newnes, London. 7¾″ × 5⅛″. Green cloth case-binding blocked in black and orange.

1902. *At Sunwich Port* by W. W. Jacobs, illustrated by Will Owen. Published by George Newnes, London. 7¾″ × 5⅛″. Cloth binding blocked in black, blue and pink.

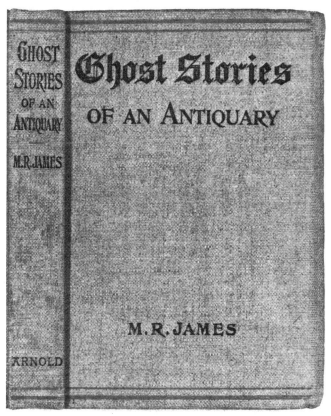

## PRINTING TYPES

THEIR HISTORY, FORMS, AND USE

*A STUDY IN SURVIVALS*

BY

DANIEL BERKELEY UPDIKE

WITH ILLUSTRATIONS

"*Nunca han tenido, ni tienen las artes otros
enemigos que los ignorantes*"

VOLUME I

*SECOND EDITION*

*GEOFFREY CUMBERLEGE*
OXFORD UNIVERSITY PRESS
LONDON

1922. *Printing Types* by Daniel Berkeley Updike. Published in Great Britain by Oxford University Press, London; and published and printed by Harvard University Press, Cambridge, Mass., in the United States of America. 9¼" × 6¼". This title-page is taken from the second edition, 1937

### Daniel Berkeley Updike and Bruce Rogers

The effects of Morris's work at Kelmscott were certainly felt in the U.S.A., most strongly in New England, and by no one more so than by Daniel Berkeley Updike. In 1893, Updike started the Merrymount Press. Until that time, from the age of twenty, he had been working for Houghton Mifflin at the Riverside Press. He said: 'None of us were very sensible or businesslike, and if we had been we would have been heard of no more.'[6]

His Merrymount Press achieved an outstanding reputation in both the U.S.A. and Europe for fine typography and presswork and the most painstaking care in every stage of book printing. Updike's career was crowned by the publication in 1922 of his *Printing Types,* of which he wrote 'The book has, by those who know, been called a monumental work, and came, as far as I was concerned, fatally near being so.'[7]

The other great American typographer in the twentieth-century renaissance of book design was Bruce Rogers. Whereas Updike was essentially a scholar-printer, Rogers was an artist who happened to express himself through the design of books. His typographic art, like that of all his contemporaries, was based on the work of the past. His knowledge of period was extensive, yet his books were not slavish copies; he took a period style and made the fullest use of it, producing something quite personal.

[6] Updike: *American Printer and his Merrymount Press.* Notes on the press by Daniel Berkeley Updike and essays by Stanley Morison, T. M. Cleland *et alia.* Published by the American Institute of Graphic Arts, New York, 1947.

[7] *Ib.*

## Directoire and other period influences

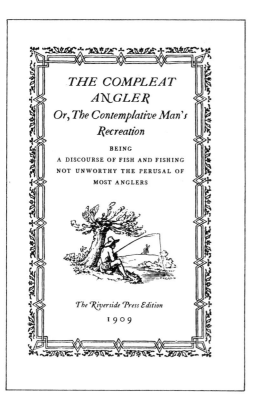

1909. *The Compleat Angler* by Izaac Walton, designed by Bruce Rogers. Published and printed by the Riverside Press, Cambridge, Mass., for Houghton Mifflin Co., Boston. $6\frac{1}{4}'' \times 4\frac{1}{8}''$. Title-page.

An edition of *The Compleat Angler,* which Bruce Rogers designed in 1909, was printed at the Riverside Press, Cambridge, Mass., and published by Houghton Mifflin Company, from Boston and New York. It is a charming book, square-backed and bound in a brown, crumpled Japanese paper with a simple printed label on the spine. In spite of the very short lines, the setting is remarkably close knit. The title-page has been reproduced many times, but it is so pretty and so typical of its designer that it is worth showing just once again.

By the beginning of the First World War, art nouveau had lost much of its appeal. There was a general return to Directoire (1795–9) and Louis XVI (1774–93) designs. Shepherds, shepherdesses and powdered wigged gallants vied with Pierrots and Columbines as subjects for book decorations. It was a somewhat sentimental period. Popular illustrators in this manner were Emil Preetorius in Germany, Daniel Vierge in France and Hugh Thomson in England. Books continued to look much as they had done for the last twenty years, except for the wider use of coated stock, that was needed for printing halftone illustrations, in monochrome and colour.

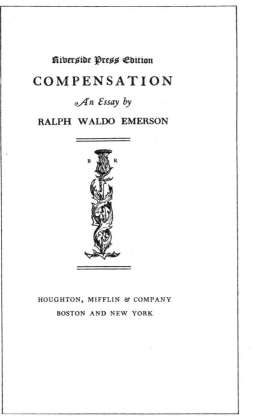

1903 *Compensation,* an essay by Ralph Waldo Emerson. A prospectus designed by Bruce Rogers. Published by Houghton Mifflin and Co., New York. Printed by the Riverside Press. $7\frac{1}{4}'' \times 4\frac{5}{8}''$.

1939. *The Work of Bruce Rogers* published by the Oxford University Press, New York. Half-title for 'Progressive Layouts for On Dry-Cow Fishing' as designed by Bruce Rogers. $9\frac{1}{4}'' \times 5\frac{3}{4}''$.

47

1913. *Tartarin von Tarascon* by Alphonse Daudet. Translated by A. Gerstmann, with illustrations by Emil Preetorius. Published by Der Gelbe Verlag Mundt and Blumtritt. Printed by M. Müller and Sohn, Munich. 7¾″ × 5¼″. Drawn-on orange coloured paper cover printed in black. Title-page and chapter opening.

Jetzt, mein lieber Leser, möchte ich ein Maler sein, ein großer Maler, damit ich hier bei Beginn des zweiten Teiles unserer Geschichte vor deinen Augen die verschiedenen Lagen skizzieren könnte, die der rote Fez des Herrn Tartarin aus Tarascon an den drei Tagen der Überfahrt von Frankreich nach Algier an Bord des „Zuaven" einnahm. Ich würde ihn zuerst gezeichnet haben bei der Abreise auf der Landungsbrücke. Ach, wie heldenhaft und stolz, wie eine Aureole, schmückt er das schöne tarasconische Haupt.

Dann würde ich ihn zeigen bei der Ausfahrt aus dem Hafen, als der „Zuave" auf den Wellen sich zu wiegen und zu schaukeln begann; man würde ihn zitternd und zagend sehen, als spüre er schon die ersten Vorboten des nahenden Unheils.

Zum dritten würde ich den Fez im Golf du Lion malen. Je breiter hier die Meeresfläche zwischen den Küsten wird,

87

*c.* 1912. *Briefe der Ninon de l'Enclos* translated
by Lothar Schmidt. Illustrated with etchings by
Karl Walser. Published by Bruno Cassirer. 7″ × 5″.
Title-page and frontispiece.

**Series design**

The cheap reprints of books dates at least back to the time of the Venetian
printer-publisher Aldus, who was producing pocket editions by the first years
of the sixteenth century. The great age of mass-produced series of books
started with the railway age and railway bookstalls. George Routledge's
Railway Library in the 1850's was followed by a number of cheap and (usually)
nasty series. The first serious attempt to combine quality with cheapness was
made by J. M. Dent, with his Temple Library (1888), followed by his Temple
Shakespeare (1894), for which series Walter Crane drew the title-page. The
greatest and most lasting success (in the hard-back field) came with Grant
Richards' World's Classics in 1901 which the Oxford University Press took
over in 1906. Dent's Everyman also began in 1906. Both these series flourish
to this day.

The World's Classics were in a small format (6 in. by 3¾ in.) with green or
maroon cloth-covered binding cases, blocked in gold on the spine with the
title and an entwined leaf pattern (by an anonymous designer). The early
volumes were well set and well printed by, amongst others, two Edinburgh
printing firms, R. & R. Clark and Turnbull and Spears, and the famous East
Anglian book house, William Clowes and Sons of Beccles.

The Everyman series was issued in both grey cloth and red leather-covered
cases. The format was slightly larger than that of the World's Classics.

For Everyman, J. M. Dent commissioned an English architect called R. L.
Knowles to design the covers, endpapers and title-pages. Knowles's designs
were made up of swirling, macaroni-like lines, essentially art nouveau in
character.

The books were of an ideal size for holding in the hand (or reading in bed)
and were extremely legible and well printed by such firms as William Clowes
and Sons of Beccles in Suffolk. (The concentration of good printing in East
Anglia and Scotland is worth noting.)

1902. *The Opium Eater* by Thomas de Quincey. Published by E. Grant Richards as No. 23 in The World's Classics Series. Spine blocked in gold on a green cloth.

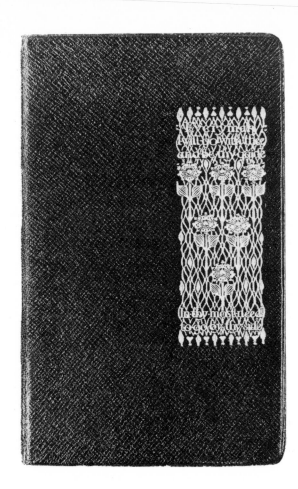

1907. *American Notes and Pictures from Italy* by Charles Dickens. Everyman Library, edited by Ernest Rhys. Published by J. M. Dent and Co. Ltd and in New York by E. P. Dutton. This edition had a gold blocked leather binding and rounded corners. Printed by the Temple Press, Letchworth. $6\frac{3}{4}$" × $4\frac{1}{8}$". (*To the right.*)

1928. *Memoirs of Mary Wollstonecraft* by William Godwin. Published by Constable and Co., London. Title-page spread. 7" × $4\frac{3}{8}$".

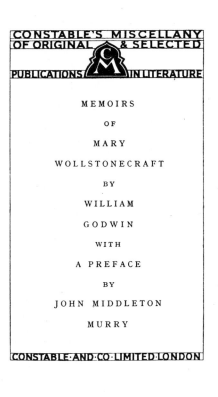

1907. Everyman Library title-page design by
Reginald L. Knowles. Published by J. M. Dent
and Co. Ltd, London.

*c.* 1905. Everyman Library endpaper design by
Reginald L. Knowles.

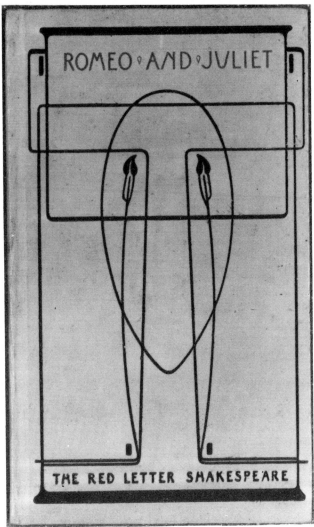

1910. *Paul et Virginie* by Bernardin de Saint-Pierre. Published by Nelson, Paris, London, Edinburgh and New York. Printed in Edinburgh by Nelson. 6⅛″ × 4″. White cloth case-binding, blocked in green and mauve.

1904. *Romeo and Juliet* by William Shakespeare. The Red Letter Shakespeare. Published by Blackie & Sons Ltd. 6⅛″ × 3½″. White cloth case-binding blocked in dark green and vermilion, designed by Talwin Morris.

In the years before the first war, a number of English publishers entered this cheap reprint field. Most of these series were fairly short lived. The Scottish firm of Nelson brought out one with very pretty white cloth covers, blocked in green and mauve. A white cloth cover was also used by the Gresham Publishing Company for 'The Red Letter Shakespeare', so called because the names of the characters were printed in red.

Blackie and Sons of Glasgow were the publishers of 'The Red Letter Shakespeare'. These little books were designed by Talwin Morris (1865–1911), who came from the south to work for Blackies, as art director. His simple geometric designs were ideal for blocking in gold or colour and were architecturally strong enough to be very effective. His output was enormous. As John Russell Taylor has recently said, Talwin Morris was one of the great purveyors of art nouveau to the fast expanding book buying public.[8]

[8] *The Art Nouveau Book in Britain:* John Russell Taylor, Methuen, London 1966. If it had not been for Mr Taylor's book, which I saw just as I was completing my proof corrections, I should never have known of Talwin Morris's work and I should also have credited 'The Red Letter Shakespeare' to the Gresham Publishing Company. The volume in my possession had had the original title-pages removed and a replacement leaf had been tipped in with the Gresham Publishing Company's name on it. I can only think it must have come from remainder stock.

Various publishers continued to produce reprints in a 'series' format. Amongst these, Constable's 'Miscellany of Original and selected Publications in Literature', was a well-produced series, with smooth light-blue cloth covers blocked in gold and dark blue. One of the most successful and attractive series on either side of the Atlantic is 'The Modern Library'. These little books, published by Random House, the New York publishers, have classically simple covers of smooth grey cloth, with a rectangle of colour on the front and spine, on which the title is blocked in gold. Series designs continued to proliferate, until the overwhelming competition of paperbacks put an effective brake on that kind of publishing.

In England, by the beginning of the 1920's, the beneficial influence of the private press movement was at last having an effect on commercial printing and publishing. One of the last great romantics, Claud Lovat Fraser, nearing the end of his tragically short life, was contributing colour and gaiety both to books and to ephemeral printing for the Curwen Press. The great revival of classic typefaces was under way at Monotype, but in England and America there was little evidence of experimental typography. In Germany the effect of the Jugendstil typographers was not quite exhausted and a new impetus came from the Russian Constructivists and the Swiss Dadaists, resulting in a sudden blaze of typographic innovation.

### The typography of George Bernard Shaw's plays

George Bernard Shaw's plays were published in a uniform style. Shaw took a very close interest in every detail of printing and publishing. His *Plays, Pleasant and Unpleasant* was published by Grant Richards, 'that habitual bankrupt', and printed by the Edinburgh firm of R. & R. Clark; but Shaw soon deserted the unstable Grant Richards and himself arranged with Constable to publish his plays on commission. To do this, he had to deal directly with the printer and pay the print bills himself; his connections with W. R. Maxwell at R. & R. Clark is almost unique in the context of author-printer relationships. Shaw had firm ideas about book design and based his page layout and general format on William Morris's *Roots of the Mountains*. He likewise used the same solidly set Long Primer Caslon Old Face. As for a typeface he had little choice; James Shand described the typographic limitations of the times in an article in *Alphabet and Image*, December 1948:

'In 1897 we must remember that there were only two text-types available in most book-houses: Old Style or Modern. More often than not, before mechanical typesetting, there was not even any choice. Publisher and author often had to accept the type of which there happened to be, at any given moment, the greatest amount of "dis".'

It was not until the middle 1920's, when the Limited Collected Edition of his works was proposed, that Shaw was willing to accept machine setting, and then only on the evidence of a specimen page that Maxwell put before him. Maxwell also succeeded in weaning him from his beloved Caslon; the new editions of the Standard Edition were reset in Fournier, in spite of Shaw's saying 'I'll stick to Caslon until I die'!

There have been collected editions of the works of a number of authors, including Macmillan's Pocket Edition of Rudyard Kipling's works. These handsome, slim books were bound in limp maroon calf and blocked in gold.

Three Plays for Puri-
tans: The Devil's Dis-
ciple, Cæsar and Cleo-
patra, & Captain Brass-
bound's Conversion. By
Bernard Shaw.

London: Grant Richards,
48 Leicester Square, W.C.

Androcles and the Lion,
Overruled, Pygmalion.
By Bernard Shaw.

Constable and Company
Ltd. London: 1916.

1901. *Three Plays for Puritans* by Bernard Shaw.
Published by E. Grant Richards, London.
$6\frac{7}{8}'' \times 4\frac{3}{4}''$. Set in Caslon Old Face. Title-page.

Text spread for *Pygmalion*, set in Caslon Old Face.

1916. *Androcles and the Lion, Overruled and
Pygmalion* by Bernard Shaw. Published by
Constable and Co. Ltd, London. Printed by
R. & R. Clark, Edinburgh. $6\frac{7}{8}'' \times 4\frac{3}{4}''$. Set in
Caslon Old Face. Title-page.

---

120    Pygmalion    Act II

*when he is neither bullying nor exclaiming to the heavens
against some featherweight cross, he coaxes women as a child
coaxes its nurse when it wants to get anything out of her.*

HIGGINS [*brusquely, recognizing her with unconcealed dis-
appointment, and at once, babylike, making an intolerable
grievance of it*] Why, this is the girl I jotted down last
night. Shes no use: Ive got all the records I want of the
Lisson Grove lingo; and I'm not going to waste another
cylinder on it. [*To the girl*] Be off with you: I dont want
you.

THE FLOWER GIRL. Dont you be so saucy. You aint heard
what I come for yet. [*To Mrs Pearce, who is waiting at the
door for further instructions*] Did you tell him I come in a
taxi?

MRS PEARCE. Nonsense, girl! what do you think a gentleman like Mr Higgins cares what you came in?

THE FLOWER GIRL. Oh, we are proud! He aint above
giving lessons, not him: I heard him say so. Well, I aint
come here to ask for any compliment; and if my money's
not good enough I can go elsewhere.

HIGGINS. Good enough for what?

THE FLOWER GIRL. Good enough for ye-oo. Now you
know, dont you? I'm come to have lessons, I am. And
to pay for em too: make no mistake.

HIGGINS [*stupent*] Well!!! [*Recovering his breath with a
gasp*] What do you expect me to say to you?

THE FLOWER GIRL. Well, if you was a gentleman, you
might ask me to sit down, I think. Dont I tell you I'm
bringing you business?

HIGGINS. Pickering: shall we ask this baggage to sit
down, or shall we throw her out of the window?

THE FLOWER GIRL [*running away in terror to the piano,
where she turns at bay*] Ah-ah-oh-ow-ow-oo! [*Wounded
and whimpering*] I wont be called a baggage when Ive
offered to pay like any lady.

*Motionless, the two men stare at her from the other side of the
room, amazed.*

Act II    Pygmalion    121

PICKERING [*gently*] What is it you want, my girl?

THE FLOWER GIRL. I want to be a lady in a flower shop
stead of selling at the corner of Tottenham Court Road.
But they wont take me unless I can talk more genteel.
He said he could teach me. Well, here I am ready to pay
him—not asking any favor—and he treats me as if I was
dirt.

MRS PEARCE. How can you be such a foolish ignorant girl
as to think you could afford to pay Mr Higgins?

THE FLOWER GIRL. Why shouldnt I? I know what lessons
cost as well as you do; and I'm ready to pay.

HIGGINS. How much?

THE FLOWER GIRL [*coming back to him, triumphant*] Now
youre talking! I thought youd come off it when you saw
a chance of getting back a bit of what you chucked at me
last night. [*Confidentially*] Youd had a drop in, hadnt you?

HIGGINS [*peremptorily*] Sit down.

THE FLOWER GIRL. Oh, if youre going to make a compliment of it—

HIGGINS [*thundering at her*] Sit down.

MRS PEARCE [*severely*] Sit down, girl. Do as youre told.
[*She places the stray chair near the hearthrug between Higgins and
Pickering, and stands behind it waiting for the girl to sit down*].

THE FLOWER GIRL. Ah-ah-ah-ow-ow-oo! [*She stands, half
rebellious, half bewildered*].

PICKERING [*very courteous*] Wont you sit down?

LIZA [*coyly*] Dont mind if I do. [*She sits down. Pickering
returns to the hearthrug*].

HIGGINS. Whats your name?

THE FLOWER GIRL. Liza Doolittle.

HIGGINS [*declaiming gravely*]

> Eliza, Elizabeth, Betsy and Bess,
> They went to the woods to get a bird's nes':

PICKERING. They found a nest with four eggs in it:

HIGGINS. They took one apiece, and left three in it.

*They laugh heartily at their own wit.*

54

The Smoker
*The Splendid Wayfaring*

1923. *The Book of Lovat* by Haldane McFall.
Projected colour illustration by Lovat Fraser for
*The Splendid Wayfaring*.

Published by J. M. Dent and Sons Ltd, London.
Printed by the Morland Press. $10\frac{3}{4}'' \times 8''$.

1927. *Das Entfesselte Theater* by Alexander
Tairoff. Published by Gustav Kiepenheuer, Berlin.
Printed by Gebr. Feyl, Berlin. 9½″ × 6¾″. Binding
designed by El Lissitsky.

The origins of modern book design and the New Typography can be traced back to the work of William Morris, his preoccupation with materials and workmanship and his rejection of the culture of the Italian Renaissance. They also developed from art nouveau with its anti-historical bias. Other influences that contributed to the New Typography were Marinetti and his Futurist Manifesto in 1909, the Dadaists, the Stijlists, the Cubists and the Constructivists. These influences were synthesised at the Bauhaus; and, mainly under the direction of Moholy-Nagy and El Lissitsky, the New Typography grew up with the same philosophical approach as was being applied to building by Walter Gropius.

In 1923, Bauhausverlag was established and, to coincide with the first Bauhaus exhibition, issued its first book. This was *Staatliches Bauhaus in Weimar 1919–1923,* edited by Gropius and Moholy-Nagy. The aim of the school press was to produce a series of books in which problems of art and design could be aired and elucidated.

Moholy-Nagy made the following observations about typography: clarity is of overriding importance, communications should not be constrained by old styles of presentation or preconceived aesthetic ideas, letters and words should not be squeezed into arbitrary shapes, such as a square.

The Bauhaus teachers El Lissitsky, Moholy-Nagy and Joost Schmidt were trying to create a new typographic language, combining freedom of layout and a fresh approach to the materials of printing. This interest in materials sounds a little like the credo of the Arts and Crafts movement, but instead of looking nostalgically to an Utopian idea of the Middle Ages, as the members of the Arts and Crafts movement did, they attempted to come to terms with the twentieth-century machine age.

Half a dozen years after the establishment of Bauhausverlag, Mr Stanley Morison, the most influential and the most rational of English writers on typographical matters, laid down his *First Principles of Typography*. This has, to a large extent, guided the more enlightened English and American printers and publishers since that time. The essence of his closely reasoned, utterly reasonable treatise is that 'typography is the efficient means to an essentially utilitarian and only accidentally aesthetic end'. This was coupled with the statement that the typography of books requires an obedience to convention which is almost absolute – a statement that presupposes a *status quo* for attitudes to design which today seem a little less assured than they did in 1930.

Morison wrote elsewhere, and some thirty years later: 'A designer needs to avoid an uncritical deference to what in some places is publicized as the only correct practice of this age. . . It is just as easy to be superstitious or sentimental about the present as it is about the past. The primary cause of superstition is ignorance of the historical causes of things. . . It is necessary to be aware of the difference between the mere perception of change and an appreciation of the reality underlying it'.[1]

In his *First Principles* Morison limited himself intentionally to composing room practice, to what Charles Peignot recently called *typolecture*, as opposed to *typovision* (or display). He makes no reference to design as such, except for a brief mention of modified margins for pocket books and some firm injunctions against the use of lower case in large sizes for title-pages.

For a postscript to a French edition (1965) of his *First Principles,* Morison makes a plea for tradition, which is, he concludes: 'another word for unanimity about fundamentals which has been brought into being by the trials, errors and corrections of many centuries'. Yet there is little unanimity about the fundamentals of design. However splendid the classical rules of proportion

[1] *The Typographic Book 1450–1935.* Stanley Morison and Kenneth Day, Benn, 1963.

# STAATLICHES BAUHAUS

# WEIMAR

# BAUHAUS

# 1919
# 1923

## WEIMAR - MÜNCHEN

## BAUHAUSVERLAG

1923. *Staatliches Bauhaus in Weimar 1919–1923.* Designed by L. Moholy-Nagy. Published by Bauhausbücher, Weimar. Title-page.

may be for architecture or book design, there are other rules, other proportions no less true and no less splendid.

And even the classical proportions may be reassessed.

The Golden Section, used by the Greeks and the artists of the Renaissance, has provided the basis of the International DIN paper sizes. The use of these sizes has not had much appeal to book publishers. A more useful related series of expanding relationships is the Fibonacci series. This Renaissance series used by Le Corbusier for his Modulor is based on the succeeding number being obtained by adding together the two preceding numbers i.e. 1, 2, 3, 5, 8. In addition to these there are an almost unlimited variety of ways in which a square or a rectangle can be subdivided, so that the divisions are related in a visually satisfying manner. This use of mathematical divisions of the page area, coupled with a repetition of these proportions throughout a book provide the essential quality in modern book design, the quality that Herbert Bayer, former Bauhaus teacher, called 'visual articulation'. That they

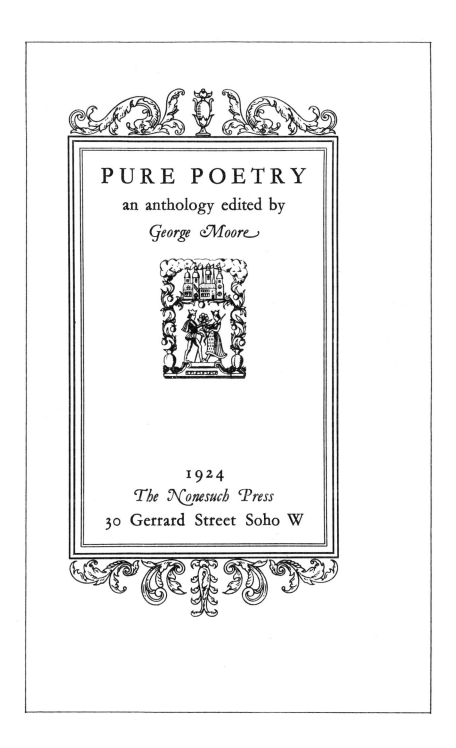

PURE POETRY
an anthology edited by
*George Moore*

1924
The Nonesuch Press
30 Gerrard Street Soho W

1924. *Pure Poetry* an anthology edited by
George Moore, designed by Francis Meynell.
Published by the Nonesuch Press. Bound in
grey boards, with a gold blocked vellum spine.
9¼" × 5½". Title-page.

apply more to the illustrated book than to the typographic book is obvious.
An infiltration of these features may well improve the look of the latter.
The belief in the importance of 'the historical causes of things' has governed
the attitudes of those involved in the twentieth-century English and New
England renaissance of printing. It has produced standards of book production
that are exceptional, though rarely as excellent as those followed in Germany
or Switzerland by typographers accepting the same historic principles. The
'English Book', as typified by the productions of the Nonesuch Press, or by
the Americans Bruce Rogers and D. B. Updike, is an agreeable thing, with a
feeling of rightness behind it. Sir Francis Meynell founded the Nonesuch
Press to re-issue old titles, because he could not find books he loved in an
acceptable format. (And what better reason, for such a publishing venture,
could one have than that?)
The insularity of England and the nature of English publishers have preserved
English books from the worst excesses of the new movement in typography

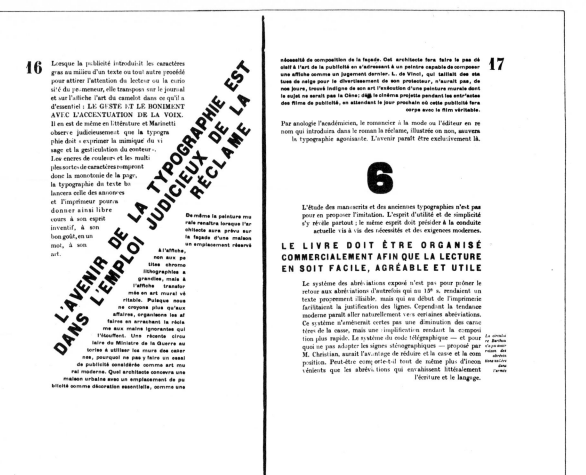

1922. *Causeries Typographiques* (No. 6).
Published by M. Audin and Co., 3 Rue Davout,
Lyon. 10¼″ × 6″. Text spread.

1921. *La Poésie* by Jean Epstein. Project for
title-page from *Causeries Typographiques No. 6*
published by M. Audin and Co., Lyon. 10¼″ × 6″.

and deprived them equally of the best features. However at last there are signs of change. It looks as if the New Typography has come to stay, at least for a while. But if it stays in as crystallized a style as sometimes seems possible, it will become even more sterile than the style it seeks to replace. Gropius once said: 'The development of a Bauhaus style would mean a return to academic stagnation and inertia.' Ways of life and methods of communication are changing fast; the design of books must keep pace in type and presentation. It seems to me that much of the sense of Morison's *First Principles* and particularly his statement '. . . any disposition of printing material which, whatever the intention, has the effect of coming between author and reader is wrong . . .', can with advantage be applied to new methods of typography; but with the over-riding proviso that design is a flexible weapon and that even the alphabet itself is liable to be questioned. What seemed a secure tradition in 1930 has changed, perhaps irrevocably, through the influence of the new movement in design.

The French acceptance of *Die Neue Typographie* was typical. They took solid German doctrine and stood it on its head. The spirited examples here are by a lively and erudite printer called Audin who worked at Lyons and periodically issued *Causeries Typographiques*.

In the English and American typographic revivals, borders cast on type bodies played a large part; they ranged from Fournier baroque to Bodoni neo-classical, like Francis Meynell's formal design for both the title and text pages of *Irish Wine*.

By the end of the 1920's, the influence of the Nonesuch Press in England, and of the Riverside and Merrymount Presses in America, was spreading to other commercial printing and publishing houses. *Toulemonde* by Christopher Morley is a sophisticated book, with a pretty title-page, whose title line is set in June, a version of one of Fournier le Jeune's decorative typefaces. This came from Doubleday, Doran, a commercial house which produced many good-looking books.

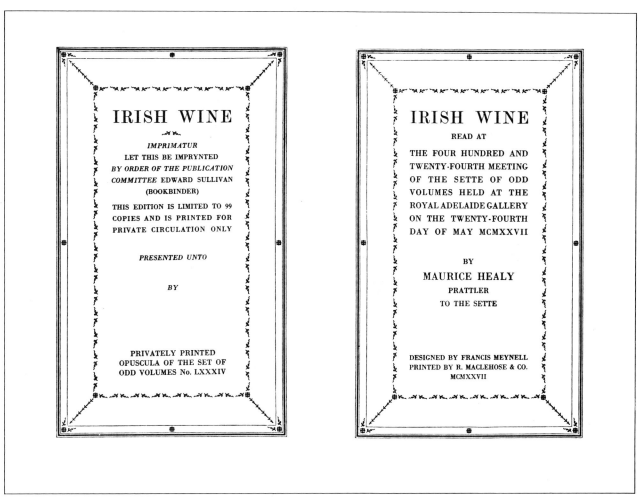

IRISH WINE

*IMPRIMATUR*
LET THIS BE IMPRYNTED
*BY ORDER OF THE PUBLICATION*
*COMMITTEE* EDWARD SULLIVAN
(BOOKBINDER)

THIS EDITION IS LIMITED TO 99
COPIES AND IS PRINTED FOR
PRIVATE CIRCULATION ONLY

*PRESENTED UNTO*

*BY*

PRIVATELY PRINTED
OPUSCULA OF THE SET OF
ODD VOLUMES No. LXXXIV

IRISH WINE

READ AT

THE FOUR HUNDRED AND
TWENTY-FOURTH MEETING
OF THE SETTE OF ODD
VOLUMES HELD AT THE
ROYAL ADELAIDE GALLERY
ON THE TWENTY-FOURTH
DAY OF MAY MCMXXVII

BY
MAURICE HEALY
PRATTLER
TO THE SETTE

DESIGNED BY FRANCIS MEYNELL
PRINTED BY R. MACLEHOSE & CO.
MCMXXVII

1927. *Irish Wine* by Maurice Healy, designed by
Francis Meynell. Printed by MacLehose and Co.,
Glasgow. Edition limited to 99 copies for private
circulation. 8″ × 5¼″. Title-page spread.

*TOULEMONDE*
BY
CHRISTOPHER
MORLEY

DOUBLEDAY, DORAN & COMPANY, INC.
GARDEN CITY · 1928 · NEW YORK

**The English and American typographic revivals**

1928. *Toulemonde* by Christopher Morley.
Published by Doubleday, Doran and Co. Inc.,
New York. 8¾″ × 5¾″. Title-page.

1931. *Mise en Page* by A. Tolmer. English
edition published by Studio Ltd, London. Printed
by A. Tolmer, Paris. $10\frac{3}{8}'' \times 8\frac{1}{4}''$. Cover design:
quarter-bound paper-covered boards printed in
silver, black and yellow. Title-page printed in
black and blue.

**The new typography
in France and Germany**

1930. *August Weltumsegler* by Knut Hamsun.
Published by Albert Langen, Munich. Project for
book design by Ludwig Schierle, Hamburg.
Printed by H. Broschek and Co., Hamburg.
$7\frac{5}{8}'' \times 4\frac{3}{4}''$. Inset from *Imprimatur II*.

## Grundsätzliches

## zur neuen

## Typographie

Von Philipp Albinus, Frankfurt am Main

Verlag des Bildungsverbandes der

Deutschen Buchdrucker, GmbH, Berlin

**1929**

---

### Über die Ausdrucksmittel der neuen Typographie

Was hat das alles mit Typographie zu tun? So wird man unwill-
kürlich fragen, wenn man die Typographie als ein selbständiges
Gebiet des Formschaffens ansieht. Aber das ist sie nie gewesen
und kann sie auch niemals sein. Immer war sie gebunden an das
Formempfinden ihrer Zeit, und immer wird sie ein Widerschein
sein vom Wollen und Vollbringen auf dem Gebiete des for-
malen Ausdrucks, der Kunst.
Also auch in der Typographie wird man an den grundsätzlichen
Änderungen auf dem Gebiet des allgemeinen Formschaffens
nicht achtlos vorübergehen können. Das heißt nun keineswegs,
daß man etwa die neue Form der Stütze, unten schmal, oben
breit, einfach ins Typographische übertragen soll. Nein, auch hier
heißt es, aus dem Material heraus im Sinne der neuen Lebens-
auffassung und des Zeittempos, des gesamten Lebensrhythmus,
zu gestalten und zu formen.
Das Bewegungsmoment ist auch für uns ausschlaggebend. Der
Empfänger einer Drucksache, die im Stil der geruhsamen Zeit aus-
geführt ist, wird unangenehm berührt, wenn er sich plötzlich um-
stellen muß, sich aus dem Moment der Bewegung, in dem er sich
befindet, in das der Ruhe versetzen soll, um die empfangene
Drucksache ganz auf sich wirken lassen zu können.
Und so ist das charakteristischste Merkmal in der neuen Typographie die Betonung eines Bewegungsrhythmus — die asym-
metrische Anordnung der Zeilen und Satzgruppen — gegenüber der Stellung auf Mitte, der Arbeit mit einem Ruhepunkt,
der symmetrischen Satzanordnung früherer Zeiten.
Es tut dabei nichts zur Sache, daß auch früher gelegentlich einmal
eine Verschränkung der Zeilen vorgenommen wurde. Denn es
ist doch ein Unterschied, ob man etwas bewußt, als Ergebnis

2*

---

1929. *Grundsätzliches zur neuen Typographie* by Philipp Albinus. Published by Verlag des Bildungsverbandes der Deutschen Buchdrucker, Berlin. Size unknown. Title and text pages. Reproduced from *Books for our time* 1951 by Marshall Lee, published by the Oxford University Press, New York.

*Mise en page*, written and compiled by a Parisian printer-publisher called A. Tolmer, is an extrovert hotch-potch of type and illustration, published in 1931. It was a book that had a lasting influence on the layout work of the advertising agencies of Paris, London and New York. It is packed with photo-montage and lively illustration. The pictures are much more interesting than the text. M. Tolmer's observations on book design are not particularly illuminating, though his opening remarks on this subject might serve for a fair comment, nearly forty years after they were written: 'The layout of books at the present day, except for a very few *éditions de luxe* produced in the modern spirit, is characterized by a respect for convention which amounts to timidity.'

From Tolmer's *Mise en page* to *Grundsätzliches zur neuen Typographie* by Philipp Albinus is a salutary jump. This book is a good example of 'visual articulation in typography'; that is, a repeating pattern of page design, established in the first place by a grid structure.

A number of German typographers began to lay down rules for the new typography. These designers included Paul Renner, the designer of the sans serif typeface Futura and author of *Die Kunst der Typographie*, and Jan Tschichold, the author of *Die neue Typographie* (1928) and *Typographische Gestaltung* (1935). Tschichold's writings had a very wide influence, and he more than any other writer was able to establish the fundamental principles of the New Typography, the key factors in which were freedom from tradition, geometrical simplicity and the acceptance of the utilitarian purpose of typography. Tschichold's work was much more refined than the earlier Bauhaus work, with which school he was never actually associated.

The project for a cover for Knut Hamsun's *August Weltumsegler* was a prize winner in a competition organized by Die Gesellschaft der Bucherfreunde in Hamburg. It was published in 1931 in the second volume of the German typographic annual, *Imprimatur*. The designer makes the most immaculate use of small, but heavy, grotesque capitals. In a very different vein, and in the same volume, was a lengthy survey of English private presses.

VERLAG DIE SCHMIEDE BERLIN

1926. *Kraft* by Henri Barbusse. Binding designed by Georg Salter. Published by Verlag die Schmiede, Berlin. Printed by Jakob Hegner, Hellerau. 7⅜″ × 4⅜″. Bound in unbleached linen blocked in blue and red. Binding case and title-page.

1931. *Russland Ja und Nein* by Hans Siemsen. Published by Ernst Rowohlt, Berlin. 8⅛″ × 5⅛″. Bound in rough greyish cloth blocked in red, black and grey.

### German binding designs

Georg Salter's lively case design for *Kraft*, where blue and red letters are blocked on an oatmeal-coloured cloth, contrasts with the impeccable formality of the book's title-page. (Salter, having made a name for himself as a typographic designer in Germany, has since carved out another career for himself in the United States.) The treatment of the binding case for *Russland Ja und Nein* has banished symmetry from front and spine. The two little American books opposite, one published in 1928 the other in 1934, might belong to a different world. They both come from the hands of distinguished practitioners. *On the Duty of Civil Disobedience* was designed and produced by Carl Purington Rollins from his private press at New Haven. For many years Rollins was the printer to the Yale University Press. The volume of *Emerson-Clough Letters* was designed and printed by William A. Kittredge from the Lakeside Press in Chicago. Kittredge brought distinction to much of the work that passed through the somewhat capacious maw of R. R. Donnelley and Sons. Both Rollins and Kittredge were masters of their craft.

1928. *On the Duty of Civil Disobedience* by
Henry David Thoreau, with decorations by
Rockwell Kent. Text set by Carl Purington
Rollins and published by Carl and Margaret
Rollins at the Sign of the Chorobates, New
Haven, Connecticut. 8½″ × 5½″. Edition limited to
300 copies. Title-page and cover.

**The American private presses**

1934. *Emerson-Clough letters* edited by Howard
F. Lowry and Ralph Leslie Rusk. Published by the
Rowfant Club, Cleveland. Printed by William A.
Kittredge at the Lakeside Press, Chicago. Edition
limited to 165 copies. 9¼″ × 6″. Cover of brown
marbled paper with a white label printed in
black. Title-page and cover.

ON THE DUTY OF
**Civil Disobedience**
HENRY DAVID THOREAU

New Haven Conne&ticut
**AT THE SIGN OF THE CHOROBATES**
Carl & Margaret Rollins

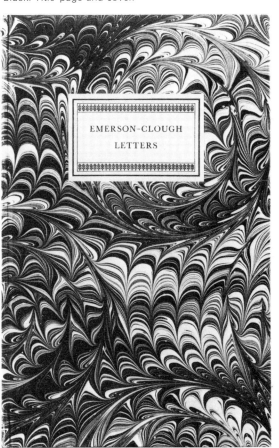

Emerson-Clough
Letters

EDITED BY

HOWARD F. LOWRY

AND

RALPH LESLIE RUSK

Cleveland
*THE ROWFANT CLUB*
1934

zjevů vnějšího světa. činí-li to, musí se tak díti tvůrčím úmyslem analogickým *fotomontáži* němého filmu. to je část úkolů zvukového filmu.

slyšitelná složka zvukového filmu by znamenala sotva obohacení proti filmu němému, rozuměli-li bychom tím zvukové podmalování, zvukovou ilustraci opticky vyřešených montážních částí. co bylo již dosaženo prostředkem — optickým —, je zařazením akustického pochodu jen zeslabeno. kvalitativní vzestup, nová pronikavá výrazová forma vznikne teprve tehdy, až budou zařazovány obě složky ve svém plném rozvinutí, střídavě účinkujíc. zde začíná skutečná ekonomie i reportážnost zvukového filmu.

**okamžitý problém zvukového filmu**

dříve než můžeme očekávati od zvukového filmu skutečných výkonů, musí býti naše akustická potence chápání značně uvolněna a rozšířena. ›hudebníci‹ nedospěli dosud ani k produktivnímu využití gramofonové desky, natož rozhlasu a éterových nástrojů. musí se v těchto oblastech neobyčejně důkladně přeorientovati.

kromě dokumentárního zápisu musí zvuková složka filmu obohatiti náš sluch dosud neznámými akustickými účiny. od akustické složky očekáváme totéž, čeho jsme v němém filmu očekávali po stránce optické a čeho jsme aspoň částečně obdrželi.

přes reprodukční přání obecenstva, zmateného s počátku materiálem, musí býti zvukový film veden k optofonetické synthese. jestliže zvukový film nastoupí cestu k takové synthese, pak to znamená konec konců: abstraktní *fonofilm*, odtud mohou býti všechny odrůdy filmu oplodněny. vedle kategorie ›dokumentárního zvukového filmu‹ a extrémní kategorie ›abstraktního zvukového filmu‹ vzniknou zde organicky ›montážní zvukové filmy‹. nejen montáž optických a akustických částí o sobě, nýbrž obou vzájemní.

znějící film měl by nejprve proto předběžně absolvovat období jen zvukových experimentů. to znamená: nejprve isolace od složky optické: prakticky: zvukovou část zvukoobrazového filmového pásma odděliti a jednotlivé kusy z toho zkusma navzájem kombinovati. (je jasné, že hudební konvence nejsou zde zrovna tak na místě, jako populární žánrové malířství nemůže míti ničeho společného s optickou stránkou filmu.) další etapa, která by však mohla probíhat souběžně s první, musela by přihlížeti k těmto směrnicím:

**45** l. moholy-nagy, 1933: fotografika . fotografik . photographic . photographique

94

**46–47** l. moholy-nagy, 1929: fotografie (positiv a negativ) . fotografie (positiv und negativ) . photography (positive and negative) . photographie (positive et négative)

1. zhodnocení reálných akustických fenoménů, pokud jsou nám k disposici přírodními šramoty, lidským ústrojím nebo nástrojem.
2. užití zvukových útvarů, opticky zaznamenatelných, ale na reálné existenci nezávislých, které se daří podle plánu předem stanoveného na zvukový filmový proužek nakresliti a pak převésti v reálné tóny. (u tri-ergon systému na příklad světlo-temnými proužky, jejichž abeceda musí býti dříve naučena. poněvadž všechno, co je na zvukový filmový proužek nakresleno, přesazuje projekční aparatura do zvuku nebo šramotu, podaly i mé experimenty s kreslenými profily, sledy písmen, otisky prstů, geometrickými značkami na zvukovém filmovém proužku překvapující zvukové výsledky.) k tomu přistupuje
3. mísení obou.

k 1:
a) mluvený film nemusí bezpodmínečně obsahovat souvislou akustickou událost.
akustická složka může působit dvojnásob intensivněji, vystupuje-li nečekaně, jsouc rozdělena v kratší nebo delší časové prostory.
b) jako má optický film možnost, aby různě fixoval objekt snímky shora a zdola, se strany a zpředu, frontálně a ve zkratce, musí něco podobného díti se i se zvukem. různým směrům pohledů musí tedy odpovídati různé směry slyšení (zejména myslíme zde na odstupňované kombinace hudby, řeči a šramotu). k tomu přistupuje akustický close up, snímek časorozptylný (rozšířeni), snímek časosběrný (stažení), skreslování, přeclonění, vůbec prostředky ›zvukové montáže‹: simultánnosti optické musí odpovídati akustická; to znamená: musíme míti odvahu během akustického průběhu dokonce prokládati *smyslový* proud řeči jinými zvukovými útvary nebo ho pojednou přerušiti a zařaditi jiné akustické dimense, skreslovati, roztahovati, stahovati, a teprve potom pokračovati v původní linii a podobné. urychlením nebo zpomalením normálních zvukových sledů vznikají nejpodivnější překlady, mnoho oktáv nahoru nebo dolů. tyto výsledky jsou opět překombinovatelny. (zde nejsou komise kladeny hranice.)
k 2:
a) správná výše tvůrčího využití bude však u mluveného filmu dosažena teprve tehdy, budeme-li ovládat akustickou abecedu ve formě fotografovatelných projekcí (na příklad u světelných zvukových systémů).
to znamená, že — bez reálných akustických událostí vnějšího světa — budeme plánovitě zaznamenávati na filmovém pásu akustické fenomeny, podle potřeby synchronisovanými s optickými; to znamená: komponista zvukového filmu

95

1936. *L. Moholy-Nagy.* Published by Fr. Kalivoda, Brno. 11¾″ × 8¼″. Text spread.

---

52    An Essay on Typography

mous blobs might be amusing to meet if they were the unaided efforts of some sportive letter designer. But having become common forms they are about as dull as 'Robots' would be if they all had red noses. As machinery & standardised production can only decently turn out the plainest of plain things, we shall have to steel our minds to a very ascetical and mortified future. This will be quite satisfactory to 'highbrows' like ourselves, but it is certain that the masses of the people will not stand it; & designers, who for inscrutable reasons 'must live', will continue to fall over one another in their efforts to design fancy forms which, like a certain kind of figure 9, are all tail and no body (see figure 19, 24).
¶ However, in spite of industrialism, letter designing is still an occupation worthy of the enthusiasm of rational beings, and, though a Q which were all queue & no Q would be 'past a joke', it is difficult to say exactly where a tail should end (see figure 21). The only thing to do is to make ourselves into such thoroughly and completely rational beings that our instinctive or intuitive reactions and responses and sympathies are more or less bound to be rational also. And just as we revolt from smells which are bad for our bodies without reasoning about it, so

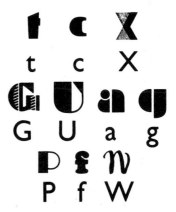

Figure 18

shall we revolt against the mentally defective.
¶ A final word may be said about the influence of tools in letter designing. The main stream of lettering to-day is undoubtedly the printed sheet or book. But whatever may be said about the derivation of our letters from the chisel-made or pen-made letters of the past, there is no doubt whatever that neither the chisel nor the pen has now any influ-

1936. *An Essay on Typography* by Eric Gill. Published by Sheed and Ward, London. Printed by Hague and Gill, High Wycombe. 6¾″ × 4¼″. Text spread and (*opposite*) title-page.

66

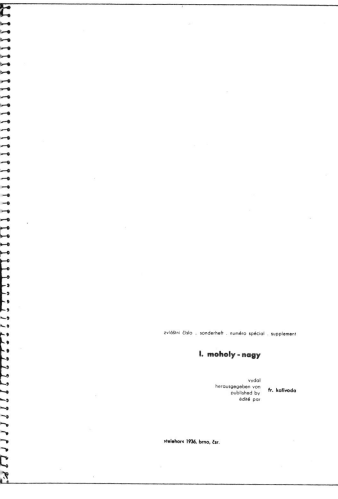

1936. *L. Moholy-Nagy.* Published by Fr. Kalivoda, Brno. 11¾″ × 8¼″. Spiral wire binding. Cover printed in black, and title-page.

AN ESSAY ON TYPOGRAPHY

BY ERIC GILL

Contents:

second edition

LONDON / SHEED & WARD / 1936

## A comparison: L. Moholy-Nagy and Eric Gill

László Moholy-Nagy was one of the most influential figures of the modern movement in design. With his influence on typography and photography, his written observations on these subjects, his work as a teacher at the Bauhaus and later at the Chicago Institute of Design, he has played as big a part in shaping the appearance of modern books as any of his typographic contemporaries; yet he was also an architect, a painter and a stage designer.
Moholy, as well as being a brilliant creative thinker, must have acted like a catalyst on the students and designers with whom he came in contact. It is difficult to gauge how much actual book designing he did, but he was certainly largely responsible for the first Bauhaus Press books.

Eric Gill, though older than Moholy-Nagy, played almost as great a part in English twentieth-century typography as the Hungarian did in German typography. Their lines of thought, however, were completely different.
Gill owed much to the teaching of Edward Johnston and was an Arts and Crafts product *par excellence.* Morris's doctrine, 'Every man ought to have joy in his labour', became Gill's credo. For many years he earned a rather precarious livelihood as a letter cutter and sign writer. His belief in tradition was implicit. He wrote: 'Lettering is a precise art and strictly subject to tradition. This is the secret, for letters are things, not pictures of things'. Gill's *An Essay on Typography,* first published in 1931, is an interesting book. It is set in his Joanna typeface, unjustified and freely sprinkled with ampersands and paragraph marks which replace indents. Gill shows here an example of his sans serif, but nothing would have induced him to set a book in a seriless typeface.

67

**Typographie, Photographie und Zeichnung**

Für die neue Typographie sind nicht nur die Schriften und Zeichen des Setz-
kastens Mittel der Gestaltung. Das Bild ist oft besser als das Wort; es bietet oft
mehr und kann manches leichter als Worte vermitteln. Die natürliche Dar-
stellungsweise unserer Zeit ist die Photographie, deren Gebrauch so vielfältig
geworden ist, daß wir ohne sie wohl nicht mehr auskämen. Die Qualität der
Photographie ist für den Wert der ganzen Arbeit mitbestimmend; für sich allein
unterliegt sie Gesetzen, die denen der neuen Gestaltung sinnverwandt sind.

Nicht nur die normale Photographie kann einen Teil neuer Typographie bilden; auch das Photogramm (die kameralose Photographie, deren Technik Moholy-Nagy und Man Ray für uns neu entdeckt und gestaltet haben), das Negativ-
photo, die Doppelaufnahme und weitere Kombinationen, legitimste Möglichkeiten des Lichtbildes (vergleiche das einzigartige Selbstbildnis Lissitzkys), die
Photomontage, die eine Idee verkörpern kann, sollen in den Dienst der typo-
graphischen Mitteilung gestellt werden. Sie können die Aussage verdeutlichen,
anziehend machen und optisch bereichern.

Die Photomontage muß jedoch auf Klarheit des Aufbaus bedacht sein und
unübersichtliche Anhäufungen vermeiden. Die normale Photographie kann als
rechteckige Fläche oder als Silhouette gebraucht werden; beide zusammen geben
neben reinen Größenkontrasten oft erwünschte Kontraste und Abwechslung.
Am Rande abfallende Photoklischees sind hin und wieder sehr wirksam; doch
wird ihr Gebrauch durch die technische Zweckmäßigkeit und ästhetische Er-
wägungen begrenzt. Mehr als eine bis höchstens zwei solcher bis zum Papier-
rande reichenden Photographien sollte man auf der gleichen Seite nicht zeigen.

Photoklischees können auch in einer bunten Farbe gedruckt werden; Über-
schneidungen verschiedenfarbig gedruckter Photos sind gelegentlich sehr wirksam.

Der Gebrauch der Photographie als der wichtigsten Bildform der Gegenwart
schließt den der freien und der Konstruktionszeichnung nicht aus. Beide können
sich ebensogut der Typographie einfügen und an der kontrastierenden Gestaltung teilnehmen. Alle drei können auch nebeneinander erscheinen und neue,
reiche Formen bilden.

Auch die amerikanische Retusche an Maschinendarstellungen und ihre Um-
kehrung als Negativ sind Möglichkeiten, die uns offenstehen und bei passenden
Gelegenheiten benutzt werden können.

Der Bildsatz dagegen, der aus meist eigens gegossenen geometrischen Satz-
elementen Bilder und Darstellungen erzeugt und lange Zeit von gewisser Seite

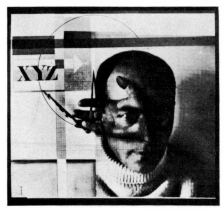

El Lissitzky: *Selbstbildnis* (Photogramm, Doppelbelichtung, Doppelkopie). 1924.

propagiert wurde, kann nur in der Hand zeichnerisch Begabter zu einem brauch-
baren Mittel der Gestaltung werden. So «gesetzte» Schriften sind fast immer
schlechter als selbst die gewöhnlichsten Typen. Jedenfalls ist es ziemlich schwer
und für Ungeübte technisch sehr umständlich, auf diesem Wege Brauchbares
herzustellen. Nicht alles ist so vollendet, wie der Bildsatz von Walter Cyliax-
Krauß, der auf diesem Gebiete das Beste hervorgebracht hat.

Innerhalb einer ganzen Arbeit sind Photo, Zeichnung und Bildsatz nur Teile,
die sich dem Ganzen fügen müssen. Ihre überzeugende Einordnung bestimmt
den Wert ihres Gebrauchs.

---

1935. *Typographische Gestaltung* designed and
written by Jan Tschichold. Published by Benno
Schwabe and Co., Basel. 8¼″ × 5¾″. Title-page
and text spread.

1936. *First Principles of Typography* by Stanley
Morison. Published and printed by the University
Press, Cambridge. 6⅝″ × 4¼″. Title-page.

*Jan Tschichold:*

**Typographische Gestaltung**

Benno Schwabe & Co . Basel 1935

FIRST PRINCIPLES

OF

TYPOGRAPHY

BY

STANLEY MORISON

━━━━

CAMBRIDGE

AT THE UNIVERSITY PRESS

1936

1936. *First Principles of Typography* by Stanley Morison. Published and printed by the University Press, Cambridge. $6\frac{5}{8}'' \times 4\frac{1}{4}''$. Text spread.

## The New Typography and the English and American revivals

Moholy-Nagy, Tschichold and Herbert Bayer on the one side, and Eric Gill, Francis Meynell at the Nonesuch Press and Oliver Simon of the Curwen Press on the other, represent the widely differing continental and English attitudes to book design. The continental New Typography, as we have seen, has close affinities with early twentieth-century movements in art and architecture, such as Cubism and Constructivism. The English style is based somewhat eclectically on the work of the best of the European printers since the time of the fifteenth-century Venetians. It has also been heavily influenced by a renewed interest in calligraphy and by Mr Morison's solid good sense. In comparing the work of the rationalist Morison and the intuitive Tschichold and in particular the title-pages shown on the opposite page, Morison's design is logical with a firm reliance on capital letters; Tschichold's is of an almost Whistlerian waywardness. Tschichold's typography was much less heavy-handed than the early Bauhaus books. In its precision and delicacy it helped to guide the post-war Swiss typographers. Five years after the publication of *Typographische Gestaltung*, Tschichold renounced the doctrine he has helped to establish and returned to an immaculate classicism. This was mainly due, as I have said elsewhere, to a personal reaction against 'militaristic, Nazi-minded New Typography'.[2] Morison stuck to his guns and authorised an unmodified reissue in French of his *First Principles* thirty-five years after its first publication. In a sparkling postscript, he vigorously explained why had had not changed his position.

[2] *Typography: Basic Principles. Influences and Trends since the 19th century:* John Lewis, Studio Vista/Reinhold (2nd Edn 1966).

**1919**

# BAUHAUS

*edited by*

HERBERT BAYER
WALTER GROPIUS
ISE GROPIUS

**1928**

THE MUSEUM OF MODERN ART · NEW YORK · 1938

1938. *Bauhaus 1919–1928* edited by Herbert Bayer, Walter Gropius and Ise Gropius. Typography and cover design by Herbert Bayer. Published by the Museum of Modern Art, New York. Printed in the United States of America. 10″ × 7½″. Title-page and cover of light yellow cloth, blocked in black and red.

### Design and typographic doctrine

After the Second World War, while England stuck firmly to her traditions, a new generation of American designers began to use with fluency and some freedom the New Typography vernacular, aided and abetted by such Bauhaus teachers and displaced Europeans as Moholy-Nagy, Herbert Bayer and Georg Salter. In Europe, the Swiss book designers, such as Max Bill, developed the new typography into an incredibly precise style. And Jan Tschichold (in 1940) made a complete *volte-face,* back from the New Typography to a rigid English classicism. In this vein, in the late 1940's, he did a magnificent re-styling job for Penguin Books.

70

1946. *The New Vision and Abstract of an Artist*
by Lázló Moholy-Nagy. Cover and typography
by Paul Rand. Published by Wittenborn and Co.,
New York. Printed by E. L. Hildreth and Co.,
Brattleboro, Vermont. 10″ × 7½″. Title-page.

The documents of modern art: Director  ● Robert Motherwell

**The New Vision** 1928 third revised edition **1946**
and
**Abstract of an Artist**

László Moholy-Nagy

Wittenborn and Company,      New York, 1946

OLIVER SIMON

INTRODUCTION TO
TYPOGRAPHY

The old artists of the classical school were
never egotists. Egotism has been and
remains responsible for many defects of
modern typography.      *Talbot B. Reed*

LONDON
FABER AND FABER
1945

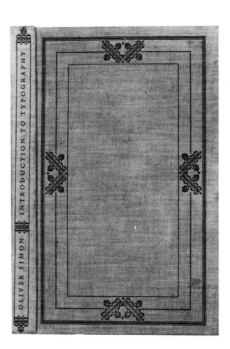

1945. *Introduction to Typography* written and
designed by Oliver Simon. Published by Faber
and Faber, London. Printed by the Curwen Press,
Plaistow. 8⅜″ × 5¼″. Cover of buff-coloured
cloth printed in blue and red, and title-page.

**Commentaire du catalogue de l'œuvre de Sophie Tæuber-Arp** par Hugo Weber

Je connaissais, un peu, l'œuvre de Sophie Tæuber depuis l'exposition bâloise de 1937 qui avait voulu nous présenter les «constructivistes». Je ne la compris pas bien, d'abord, et éprouvai peu d'intérêt. Je me méprenais complètement sur sa signification. C'est peu de semaines avant sa mort que je fis, à Bâle, la connaissance personnelle de Sophie Tæuber. Jean Arp et elle avaient réussi à fuir l'occupation allemande; ils venaient de passer en Suisse. La sincérité de ses enthousiasmes spirituels me fit alors une impression intense; mais je ne pensais guère à son travail, qui était pourtant la source de cette paix rayonnante. Encore moins aurais-je pu imaginer qu'il m'arriverait de me recueillir sur ses ouvrages durant plusieurs semaines dans le calme de son atelier de Meudon. Jean Arp me chargea en effet de dresser le catalogue de son œuvre.

A mon propre étonnement, je me mis un jour à mesurer des tableaux, à les marquer et à rechercher des dates. Mais surtout, je m'engageai dans une vaste contemplation des œuvres de Sophie Tæuber, en constituai le groupement, y distinguai des séries et tentai toutes les possibilités de comparaison qui me semblaient éclairer leurs rapports réciproques. La situation vraiment tragique de notre temps, qui condamne une œuvre aussi riche à s'amasser dans les tiroirs et les recoins d'un atelier, me permit du moins d'en prendre une facile vue d'ensemble. Un classement strictement chronologique présentait des difficultés, car Sophie Tæuber ne signa et data régulièrement ses travaux que dans les deux dernières années de sa vie. C'était un trait de l'esprit Dada de n'attacher aucune importance au temps ni à l'individualité artistique. Quelques points de repère me permirent néanmoins d'établir avec une approximation suffisante mon système de datation; j'eus recours au témoignage de certaines évidences visuelles, dans la mesure où des notes sur photographies, catalogues et publications ou la mémoire de Jean Arp me refusaient d'autres renseignements.

Mon travail ne devint vraiment convaincant que du jour où se dessina un groupement fondé sur les principaux problèmes de forme. Il fallait, pour chacun de ces groupes, déterminer des limites et une appellation, si l'on voulait éviter que le catalogue ne fût qu'un inventaire mécanique et sans vie. Il

serait souhaitable que les artistes puissent eux-mêmes soutenir de leurs conseils une telle entreprise. Avec toute la volonté d'objectivité possible, l'établissement d'un catalogue de ce genre reste une œuvre personnelle. C'est pourquoi je crois utile de commenter ici ma classification et les rapports que j'ai établis entre les diverses séries de cette œuvre.

Il s'avéra que Sophie Tæuber reprenait souvent un problème de forme, après l'avoir, parfois durant des années, abandonné pour un autre, qui s'était imposé à elle entre-temps. Pour fixer la chronologie de son évolution dans son ensemble, les dates d'apparition de chacun de ces problèmes sont les plus décisives. Les manifestations ultérieures d'un même problème ont été, dans le catalogue, subordonnées aux premières.

Les premiers travaux de Sophie Tæuber remontent à 1916. Ce sont des compositions planes, ordonnées selon une structure rigoureusement verticale-horizontale. Lorsqu'en 1916 Jean Arp fit la connaissance de Sophie Tæuber à Zurich, elle lui montra ses essais. Elle appliquait des conceptions semblables à toutes espèces de travaux, en broderie et en tissage, sans prétention artistique, mais avec une préoccupation morale très nette, et dont la fermeté, au témoignage de Jean Arp, l'impressionna et l'influença. Par la suite, Sophie Tæuber introduisit, dans le cadre des compositions verticales-horizontales, des figures animées, curvilignes. Souvent c'étaient, réduites à la ténuité de signes, des choses de l'existence extérieure: petits bateaux arborant des drapeaux, oiseaux, vases. Le signe «homme» est rare d'abord.

De tels signes ont eu la vie longue dans l'œuvre de Sophie Tæuber. On peut en retrouver la trace ici ou là dans ses travaux postérieurs.

Dans les gouaches au «pointillisme» libre de 1920 à 1921, dans les compositions en taches de couleur, apparaissent de vagues constellations, rappelant des figures de danse. Mais la plupart se contentent d'un rythme sans gestes, pures formes et couleurs. Ces œuvres font une impression joyeuse et d'une âpre santé. Sophie Tæuber les peignit pour tant durant une période d'incessante tristesse. Du point de vue génétique on les voit se

Compositions verticales-horizontales

Taches quadrangulaires en couleurs

118    119

1948. *Sophie. Taeuber-Arp* edited by Georg Schmidt. Designed by Max Bill. Published by Holbein-Verlag, Basel. Printed by Benteli AG, Bern — Bümplitz, Funke and Saurenmann, Zürich; Georg Rentsch Söhne, Olten-Trimbach. Bound by G. Wolfensberger, Zürich. 11¾″ × 8″. Text spread.

QUI Né le 24 mai 1899. IL Belge, de Paris. Aime EST les fugues Matelot à 21 ans. Atlantique Nᵉᵗˢ Plus tard, voyages en Amazonie, en Equateur aux Indes en Chine. Il est et se voudrait ailleurs, essentiellemᵉⁿᵗ ailleurs, autre. Il l'imagine. Il fauᵗ bien qu'il l'imagine

1942. *Le Rêve* by Henri Michaux. Designed, printed and published by Pierre Bettencourt. Edition limited to 100 copies. 4¾″ × 3¾″. Text page. The typeface is Peignot, designed by Cassandre.

## Swiss and French typography

French interest in typographic developments has been somewhat spasmodic, but a certain number of amateurs of printing have run their own private presses. From amongst these, Pierre Bettencourt and Pierre André Benoit have issued some interesting books. Henri Michaux's *Le Rêve* was published by Bettencourt in 1942, set in two weights of A. M. Cassandre's interesting, little-used typeface Peignot. This curious, half uncial is surprisingly successful, except for the large capital letters. It would have been more logical to have dispensed with these. Francis Picabia's *Parlons d'autre Chose* was published by Benoit in 1953. It is a pleasant book, set in Futura and with decorations by Picabia printed on a heavy grey Ingres paper.

72

ENSUITE
ON A UN MONDE DE CHOSES
À FAIRE, TANT QU'IL RESTE DE
LA CLARTÉ, SI BIEN QU'ON A
À PEINE LE TEMPS DE SE
REGARDER UN PEU.
LA CONTRARIÉTÉ POUR NOUS
DANS LA NUIT, C'EST QUAND
IL FAUT TRAVAILLER, ET IL LE
FAUT : IL NAÎT DES NAINS
CONTINUELLEMENT.

QUAND ON MARCHE DANS
LA CAMPAGNE, LUI CONFIE-T-
ELLE ENCORE, IL ARRIVE QUE
L'ON RENCONTRE SUR SON
CHEMIN DES MASSES
CONSIDÉRABLES . CE SONT
DES MONTAGNES ET IL FAUT

1942. *Le Rêve* text spread.

1953. *Parlons d'autre Chose* by Francis Picabia.
Designed, decorated and printed by Pierre André
Benoit. 7½″ × 5¾″. Edition limited to 75 copies.
Text and illustration spread printed in black on
grey Ingres paper.

Ne me posez pas de questions
parlons d'autre chose
parlons des lunettes mortes si vous voulez
Botticelli Piero della Francesca
                              ou Velasquez
ou d'une fille violée
              qu'un ramassis d'idiots pensent
                    qu'ils doivent plaindre

Vous rappelez-vous le vernis de mes tableaux
        ils étaient comme des miroirs
                    où à chaque moment
quelque chose peut surgir
        pour se confondre avec les oscillations
                    de mon cœur fatigué
qui ne sait plus aimer
              ni haïr
                    ni même se transporter
au-dessus des misères intimes

J'ai atteint le comble des souffrances

                    Francis Picabia

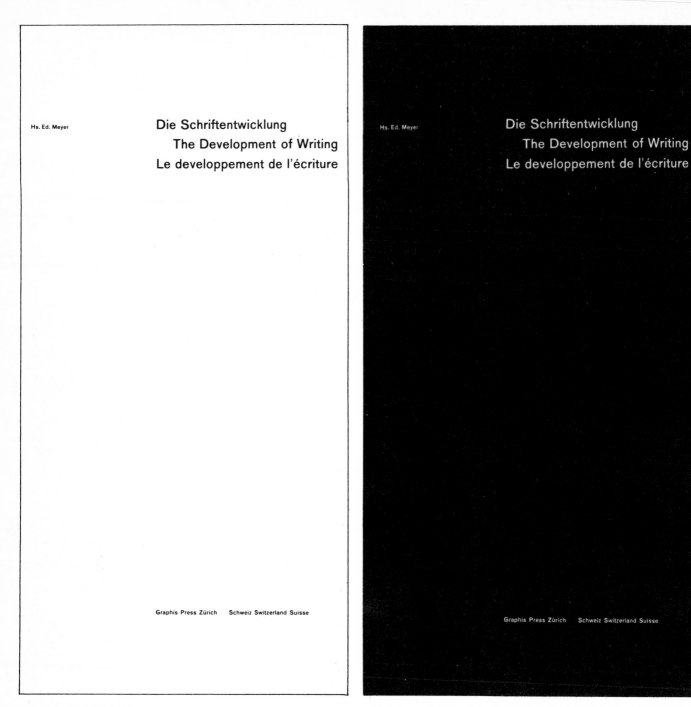

1958. *Die Schriftentwicklung* by Hs. Ed. Mayer.
Published by the Graphis Press, Zürich. Printed
by Bodmer and Leonardi, Zürich. $11\frac{5}{8}'' \times 6\frac{1}{8}''$.
Cover and title-page.

1958. *Laotse Tao Te King,* translated from the Chinese by Richard Wilhelm with a foreword by Jean Gebser. Designed by Max Caflisch. Published by Verlag Hans Huber, Bern and Stuttgart. Printed in Switzerland. 8″ × 4⅞″. Cover in black cloth with white paper label printed in black; and title-page.

## Swiss book design

Walter Herdeg at Zürich, with his *Graphis* magazine, has done much for the cause of modern design. Hans Meyer's *Die Schriftentwicklung* is an elegant, tall, crisp production, published by the Graphis Press in Zürich. An effective use is made of repeating the title-page design on the cover, but reversing to white on black. Hans Fischli, Director of the School of Arts and Crafts, Zürich, says in his preface to this book: 'The science of calligraphy points to the smallest detail and introduces the laws of order that are the basis of all creative activity, from the architecture of a cathedral to an advertisement in a newspaper'. This discipline is evident in all good printing, and particularly evident in Swiss typography.

Max Caflisch is a German book designer, working in Zürich, and in contrast with so many modern typographers, working in the English style. The main difference between a Caflisch book and those of his English and American opposite numbers is that his books are usually better produced, with better presswork, more precise setting and better-fitting bindings.

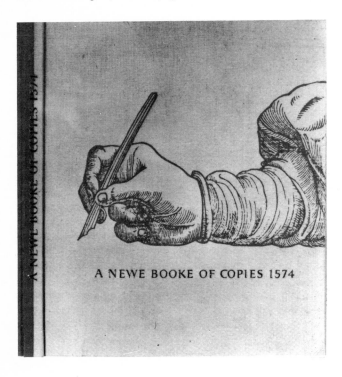

1959. *Die Neue Graphik* by Karl Gerstner and Markus Kutter. Published by Arthur Niggli, Teuffen AR, Switzerland. Printed by R. Weber AG, Heiden. Bound by Max Grollimund, Basel. 9⅛″ × 9″. Cover and contents page.

Gerstner and Kutter's *Die neue Graphik,* published in Switzerland in 1959, is one of the most interesting surveys of graphic design to appear since the last war. It is also a model example of clean layout, based on a grid structure. The book is set in German, English and French, in three unjustified columns, of 8 point Univers, to the page.

1959. *A Newe Booke of Copies 1574* edited by Berthold Wolpe, R.D.I. Designed, published and printed by the Lion and Unicorn Press at the Royal College of Art, London. 9½″ × 8½″. Cover in buff coloured cloth printed in orange and grey and blocked in gold, and title-page.

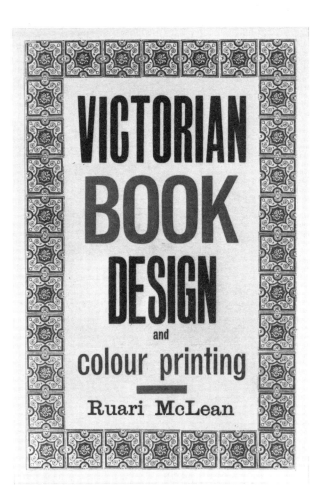

1963. *Victorian Book Design and Colour Printing* by Ruari McLean. Published by Faber and Faber, London. Printed by Shenval Press Ltd, London. $8\frac{1}{2}'' \times 5\frac{1}{4}''$. Jacket design by Ruari McLean printed in black, blue and brown.

1962. *Printed Ephemera* written, compiled and designed by John Lewis. Published and printed by W. S. Cowell Ltd, Ipswich. Distributed by Faber and Faber, London. $12'' \times 9\frac{1}{4}''$. Title-page printed in black and red.

## Allusive typography

The reprint of the Elizabethan writing book, *A Newe Booke of Copies*, was carried out at the Royal College of Art by the Lion and Unicorn Press, under the guidance of its editor, Berthold Wolpe. The completely traditional treatment was considered appropriate for a reprint of this nature. The case-binding had a solid orange printing over the back, continuing to the centre of the spine, and in spite of its cutting the title in half, this counterchange treatment made an effective-looking cover, though it called for some precision in the case making.

Ruari McLean's *Victorian Book Design* and my own *Printed Ephemera,* though on different subjects, covered in part the same period of time. The books were published within a year of each other, and we both turned to elongated Victorian sans serif typefaces for jackets, and in the case of *Printed Ephemera* for the title-page as well. There will, I think, always be a place for allusive typography.

The dichotomy of ideas about the design of books continued through the 1960's. *Die Neue Typographie* crystallizes in Germany, and even more so in Switzerland, into a precise rather mechanistic book style.

1963. *Schrift und Bild* compiled by Dietrich Mahlow. Designed by Wolfgang Schmidt. Published by Typos Verlag, Frankfurt-am-Main. Printed by Franz W. Wesel, Baden-Baden. $9\frac{1}{8}'' \times 9''$. Cover design printed in black on red paper-covered boards; and text spread.

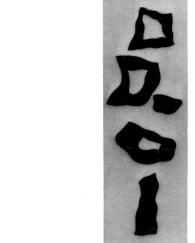

Typos Verlag

Im Zeichen wird die Wahrheit der Dinge und Gedanken durch den Menschen sichtbar, der in dem gleichen Strom mit ihnen schwimmt. Solche Zusammenfassung geistiger Vorgänge muß nicht an lesbare Schrift gebunden sein. Während diese Bindung in Ostasien möglich ist, weil die Schriftzeichen nicht Lautzeichen sind, sondern ihnen das Abbild zugrunde liegt, formt sich das westliche Zeichen frei von lesbarer Schrift. Damit ist es nicht nur nach der Seite der persönlichen Handschrift des Künstlers offen, sondern auch hinsichtlich seiner Bedeutung. Es geht nicht — oder es muß nicht von Erfahrungen, Empfindungen, Begriffen ausgehen, um dafür Symbole zu schaffen, sondern kann als Zeichenhaftes auch Vorstellungen erzeugen, die noch gar nicht vorhanden waren und die durch uns erst mit Sinn erfüllt werden müssen. Ihre Berechtigung und Schönheit finden diese Zeichen allein in der bildnerischen Sprache, aus der sie entstehen. Darin liegt das Geheimnis der Zeichen, immer wird in ihnen eine Bewegung sichtbar, die sich auf den Betrachter überträgt und ihn in Gefilde trägt, wo er sich staunend umsieht und sich fragt, warum er dort nicht schon längst zu Hause ist. Jedoch ehe er sich's versieht, wird er in neue Bahnen geworfen, bis er versteht, daß es um die Beschwörung der großen Kraft der Ungewißheit geht.

Grâce à l'homme, la vérité des choses et des pensées, emportées par le même torrent que lui, apparaît, visible, dans le signe. Une telle synthèse de phénomènes d'ordre spirituel n'a pas besoin d'être liée à une écriture lisible. Si, en Asie Orientale, cette liaison est possible, — les signes graphiques n'étant pas des signes phonographiques comme ceux de nos alphabets, mais des signes qui s'appuient sur une représentation —, le signe occidental se forme indépendamment de la lisibilité de l'écriture. C'est ainsi que, non seulement la graphie personnelle de l'artiste mais aussi la signification du signe achèvent de modeler ce dernier. Il n'est pas le fruit —, ou plutôt, il n'a pas besoin d'être le fruit d'expériences, de sensations, de concepts pour créer des symboles, sa qualité de signe peut également engendrer des représentations qui n'étaient pas encore présentes et qui ne parviennent à une signification que si nous leur en donnons une. Seul, le langage plastique d'où ils sont issus, confère justification et beauté à ces signes. C'est là que réside le mystère des signes: ils évoquent toujours un mouvement qui se transmet au spectateur et le transporte dans des sphères où son regard vagabonde, étonné, et où il se demande pourquoi il n'a pas découvert plus tôt cet univers familier. Et cependant, à peine s'est-il retourné, qu'il est déjà projeté sur de nouvelles voies, jusqu'à ce qu'il comprenne qu'il s'agit d'évoquer la grande force d'incertitude.

Willi Baumeister
Spitze Formen

38

Jean Arp
Constellation de six formes noires

39

1963. *The Typographic Book* by Stanley Morison and Kenneth Day. Published by Ernest Benn Ltd, London. Printed by the University Press, Cambridge; and the plates by L. van Leer and Co. Ltd, Amsterdam. 12″ × 9½″. Title-page engraved on the wood by Reynolds Stone, and printed in red. 9⅝″ × 6″ printed area.

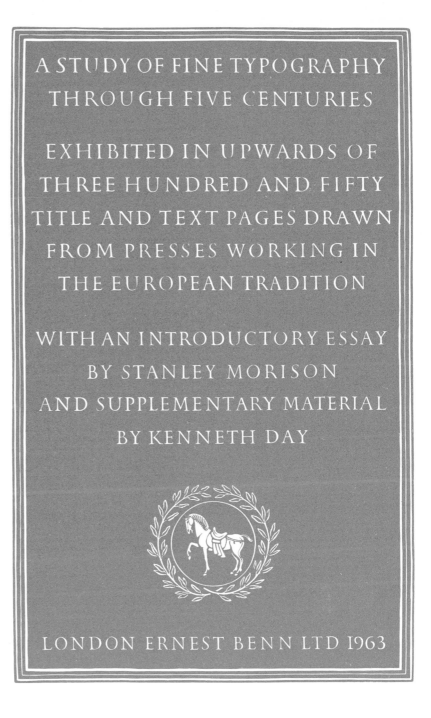

A STUDY OF FINE TYPOGRAPHY
THROUGH FIVE CENTURIES

EXHIBITED IN UPWARDS OF
THREE HUNDRED AND FIFTY
TITLE AND TEXT PAGES DRAWN
FROM PRESSES WORKING IN
THE EUROPEAN TRADITION

WITH AN INTRODUCTORY ESSAY
BY STANLEY MORISON
AND SUPPLEMENTARY MATERIAL
BY KENNETH DAY

LONDON ERNEST BENN LTD 1963

## German and English attitudes 1963

The cover of Dietrich Mahlow's *Schrift und Bild* makes an interesting comparison with one of the title-pages of Stanley Morison's *The Typographic Book.* Both books were published in 1963. The *Schrift und Bild* typography is by Wolfgang Schmidt; the engraving for the two title-pages for *The Typographic Book* (this is the second one) is by Reynolds Stone. The text pages show just as great a divergence of thought. *The Typographic Book* has a wide setting, thirteen words to the line of a large size of Monotype Bembo, the most classical of typefaces; and it is printed on a heavy antique paper. *Schrift und Bild* is narrowly set, six words in the line in a small size of Futura (the most machine-drawn of sans serif typefaces) and is printed on a coated paper.

1964. *Exercices de Style* by Raymond Queneau.
Illustrated by Jacques Carelman with typography
by Massin. Published for the Club Français du
Livre by Éditions Gallimard. 11″ × 8¾″. Text page
and cover.

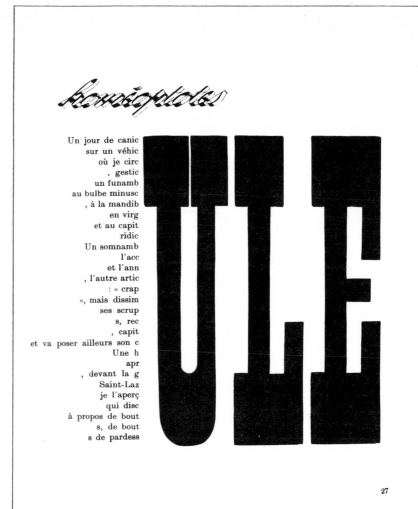

par Raymond Queneau, de l'Académie Goncourt. Edition nouvelle, revue et corrigée.
Avec 33 exercices de style parallèles, dessinés, peints et sculptés par Carelman et
99 exercices de style typographiques de Massin.          Gallimard.

### Raymond Queneau's typographic exercises

Raymond Queneau's *Exercices de Style* was published in a limited, illustrated
edition by Éditions Gallimard for the Club Français du Livre in 1964. It was
a most exciting, witty typographic frolic. Queneau's *Exercices de Style*, in
which he tells the same story in many ways and from many points of view, is a
perfect exercise for Jacques Carelman's typographic ingenuity. In whatever
typographic idiom a designer may work, his ultimate and sole justification is
to interpret, and if necessary clarify and point, his author's message. For-
tunately, there is still more than one way to do this. The two mainstreams of
book design, the German New Typography and the English Historic style,
may yet cross-fertilize each other. There is much that each can learn from the
other's approach.

## 3. THE INFLUENCE OF THE FRENCH *ÉDITIONS DE LUXE* ON COMMERCIAL BOOK PRODUCTION IN ENGLAND AND AMERICA

Since the beginning of this century, the most sumptuously illustrated books have come from France. The French have made a speciality of the picture book, particularly the *édition de luxe,* which bears little resemblance to its more restrained English or American counterpart. It is in one way an ancestor of the modern coffee-table book, which, beautifully produced though it may be, with its reproductions of great paintings or photographs of pretty gardens, is only art at second hand. The illustrated *édition de luxe* was, and still is, an excuse for graphically-minded painters and sculptors to express themselves in a new graphic medium. The expensive French limited editions, printed on hand-made paper, were often illustrated by the most illustrious of French contemporary painters. Such typographical virtues as these books may have possessed were of secondary consideration and were usually overwhelmed by the impact of the illustrations and the magnificence of their printing.

Ambroise Vollard, a Parisian art dealer, was one of the first publishers in this field of luxury picture books that were certainly not for children. Vollard issued his first book in 1900: Paul Verlaine's *Parallèlement.* For it Pierre Bonnard lithographed over a hundred illustrations, which were beautiful enough to stand on their own. Nevertheless this is a complete and lovely book. The lithographs, printed in a soft rose-sanguine, are a perfect foil for the superb presswork and for Claude Garamond's italic typeface, and are an integral part of the page. This book sets a standard of quality that Vollard's succeeding artists and printers were rarely able to equal.

*Parallèlement* was issued, following the French fashion, unsewn in Japanese paper covers, the intention being that the buyer would choose his own binding. But the choice of heavily tooled goat-skin and weighty boards would compress intolerably these ethereal pages; and for myself, I think they are best left free of such expensive constriction.

One of the reasons for the quality of these folios was Vollard's shrewd choice, not only of artists, but also of the craftsmen and printers who interpreted their work by wood engraving, lithography and etching.

Much has been written about these lovely books. Picasso's etchings for Buffon (printed by Lacourière), Georges Rouault's wood engravings and coloured aquatints for *Réincarnations du Père Ubu* and Segonzac's etchings for *Les Georgiques* have been reproduced again and again in reference books and periodicals. (This is the bedevilling effect of this age of endlessly repeated mechanical reproduction.) Because of this and because here we are primarily concerned with the design of books, and the place illustrations can play in this context, there would be little justification for dealing with them at length in these pages. Moreover the quality of the illustrations in these Vollard editions depended greatly on their direct methods of reproduction.

French painters turn freely to etching or lithography as an additional means of expression; and the great contribution made by France to the art of the modern book has been the willingness of her finest painters to move so naturally into the realms of book illustration.

In the years between the wars something of the exuberant quality of these books rubbed off onto the commercial publishers, who were cajoled, or perhaps inspired, by such painters as Fernand Léger in France and Paul Nash in England into publishing rather more colourful books than they otherwise might have done.

The publisher who contributed much to the production of books in this vein was the late George Macy, with his Limited Editions Club and Heritage Press editions in New York. This Book Club still continues with unabated vigour and produces twelve new volumes every year, illustrated, designed and printed by artists, designers and printers from many countries.

Je te veux trop rieuse
Et très impérieuse,
Méchante & mauvaise &
Pire s'il te plaisait,
Mais si luxurieuse!

Ah, ton corps noir & rose
Et clair de lune! Ah, pose
Ton coude sur mon cœur.
Et tout ton corps vainqueur,
Tout ton corps que j'adore!

Ah, ton corps, qu'il repose
Sur mon âme morose
Et l'étouffe s'il peut,
Si ton caprice veut!
Encore, encore, encore!

28

1900. *Parallèlement* by Paul Verlaine, illustrated by Pierre Bonnard with 108 lithographs printed in rose-sanguine and 9 wood engravings printed in black. Lithographs printed by Auguste Clot and the wood engravings by Tony Beltrand. Text printed by l'Imprimerie Nationale, Paris. 11⅞″ × 9⅝″. Illustration pages.

1928. *Bubu de Montparnasse* by Philippe with
etchings by André Dunoyer de Segonzac.
Published by Les Trents, Lyon. Illustration.

## The press book: France and England

Autographic methods of illustration are in common use in France and, until
recently, have been anything but common practice in England or America.
Since the time of Whistler, there have been few English artists whose etchings
could be compared in their directness and in their quality of drawing with
those of André Dunoyer de Segonzac. Sickert was one, and he never
illustrated a book. (One could compile an interesting dossier of real illustrators
who have never been commissioned to illustrate.)

Stephen Gooden's copper engraving is presented here to show the contrast
between the utterly different attitudes prevailing in the two countries. Segonzac's etchings are usually drawn straight to plate, without any preliminary
work. His etchings for *Bubu de Montparnasse*, for Vollard, are deliciously free
drawings, many of them executed at least in part *au grattoir*,[1] which gives
them something of the softness of a lithograph.

[1] With a scraping knife.

His picture of the girl sitting on the edge of a bed is a superb, yet most tentative

84

1933. *The Fables of La Fontaine* translated into English verse by Edward Marsh, with 12 engravings by Stephen Gooden. Published by Heinemann, London. Printed by the Windmill Press. 8⅜″ × 5½″. The engravings in this edition are reproductions and not printed from the original plates. Illustration: 'The Lion in Love'.

drawing, very lightly inked. No professional engraver or etcher would have been content with these tenuous lines. It is its utterly *unprofessional* quality that gives it its freshness.

In contrast with Segonzac's use of the etching needle, Stephen Gooden's meticulous copperplate engraving might seem somewhat laboured, though the medium is a severely testing one. Such engraving evokes the quiet satisfaction given by any piece of good craftsmanship. Gooden based his style on that of Wenceslaus Hollar, William Marshall and other seventeenth-century engravers. He even re-introduced the engraved title-page. This anachronistic attitude to illustration is one of the odd foibles of the English (and of the Germans); it is an attitude with which the French have little sympathy.

Engraving on copper is a medium well suited to book illustration, but it is little used nowadays, partly because of the difficulty of execution and partly because of the expense of intaglio printing.

1926. *Eclogae et Georgica* by Virgil. Illustrated
by Aristide Maillol. Published by Insel-Verlag
in Leipzig and published and printed by the
Cranach Press, Weimar. 13" × 10". Woodcut.

## The nude: Maillol and Picasso

Ever since Bonnard's exquisite *Parallèlement*, 'nudes' have been one of the
mainstays of the private press movement, not only in France, but also in
Germany and England. (A national Puritanism seems to have prevented this
happening in the U.S.A.) In 1913 the French sculptor, Aristide Maillol,
completed his illustrations for an edition of Virgil's *Eclogues* for Count Harry
Kessler. This work had been conceived in Greece in 1908, but was delayed
by the war and not published until 1926. It is a handsome book, though the
black line woodcuts, engraved by Eric Gill, give Maillol's nude studies a
somewhat stiff appearance.

MODERN PAINTERS AND SCULPTORS
AS ILLUSTRATORS

1936. *Modern Painters and Sculptors as
Illustrators* edited by Monroe Wheeler. Published
by the Museum of Modern Art, New York.
10″ × 7⅝″. Cover design from an etching by
Picasso from *Les Métamorphoses d'Ovide,*
published by Skira.

[2] *A History of Book Illustration* by David Bland.
Faber and Faber, London 1958.

The cover design for *Modern Painters and Sculptors as Illustrators* is from an
etching by Picasso, illustrating *Les Métamorphoses d'Ovide,* published by
Skira in 1931. This was the finest of Picasso's important illustrated books; he
repeated the same fluid line in a number of other books with classical texts.
David Bland draws attention to the erotic appeal of so many *éditions de luxe*
and quotes a writer in the *Times Literary Supplement* who was of the opinion
that quite half their sales depended on erotic, though rarely pornographic
appeal.[2]

1919. *La Fin du Monde* by Blaise Cendrars,
illustrated by Fernand Léger. Published by
Éditions de la Sirène, Paris. Set in Morland and
printed by Frazier-Soye in Montparnasse and the
stencil colour work by Ateliers de Richard,
Paris. 12½″ × 9⅞″. Title-page.

### Fernand Léger: Cubist and Dadaist

*La Fin du Monde* by Blaise Cendrars, illustrated by Fernand Léger, was
published by Éditions de la Sirène in Paris in 1919. This brown paper-
covered picture book, both Cubist and Dadaist in treatment, makes bold and
decorative use of letterforms.

The typography, in its roughness, is worthy of the Leadenhall Press; the book
is set in 24 point Morland and printed in a rich black with stencil colours. *La
Fin du Monde* was Léger's second book.

## 31 Décembre

Dieu le père est à son bureau américain. Il signe hâtivement d'innombrables papiers. Il est en bras de chemise et a un abat-jour vert sur les yeux. Il se lève, allume un gros cigare, consulte sa montre, marche nerveusement dans son cabinet, va et vient en mâchonnant son cigare. Il se rassied à son bureau, repousse fiévreu-

C'est le

1919. *La Fin du Monde.* Text spread.

Fernand Léger (1881–1955), mural painter and worker in stained glass, illustrated a number of books. His first was *J'ai tué,* also by Blaise Cendrars, published the year before *La Fin du Monde.* In 1921, Léger cut six woodcuts for André Malraux's *Lunes en Papier.* For the rest of his life he combined the activities of painting, designing and illustration with a catholic freedom. His last book, *Mes Voyages,* was published after his death with an introductory poem by Louis Aragon. Léger, though originally opposed to the Dadaists, incorporated many Dada elements into his *La Fin du Monde.*

89

ROMANCE A LA VIEILLE DAME
OU NATURE MORTE SENTIMENTALE

à Raoul Dufy.

L'AIR ENTRE PAR LE TROU DE LA SERRURE

Les quatres murs     mur     murent
          si las de t'attester ce qu'ils ont déjà vu
ICI PRÉVAUT LE MOTIF CŒUR

Flore et tenture dont la fanure est la raison
L'ombre des mannequins sentimentaux
                    manteaux à taille
          Sur capiton sensible à bergeries

56

1920. *Tour d'Horizon* by Marcel Willard.
Illustrated by Raoul Dufy. Published by Au Sans
Pareil, Paris. 7⅝" × 5⅝". Text spread and
illustration.

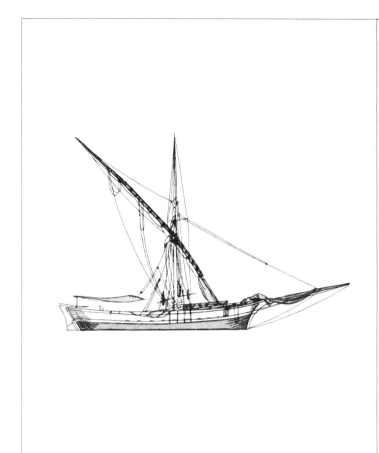

PLATE VII

## THE TARTANE

One of the largest vessels in the Mediterranean to-day still preserving the old Lateen sail. Although being slowly superseded, the Tartane were at one time well known, and ships with a similar sail plan are on record as 'Tartan' rigged: A curious point, possibly bearing on this, being the name of 'Dundee,' by which they are still known locally at St. Tropez.

They carry a jib, topsail, and the huge Lateen sail bent to a yard sometimes longer than the vessel herself. This yard or 'antenne' is hoisted by double tyes, as were yards in ships of the sixteenth century, and secured to the mast by a parral. Peak halyards are rove and a vang steadies the yardarm, the lower end being lashed to a short spar at the foot of the mast. Well suited by the light Mediterranean winds, they are engaged in all descriptions of coastal trade.

27

1926. *Sailing Ships and Barges of the Western Mediterranean and the Adriatic* written and illustrated by Edward Wadsworth. Published by Hazelwood Books, Frederick Etchells and Hugh Macdonald. Quarter-bound with a white cloth spine and orange paper-covered boards, blocked in gold. 12⅛" × 7¾". Text and illustration spread.

## The press book: France and England

Raoul Dufy (1877–1953), influenced by the Fauve painters, is best known for his colourful, short-hand calligraphic paintings of the Côte d'Azur, regattas, casinos and racecourses. Dufy illustrated a number of books, including lithographs for Apollinaire's *Le Poète Assassiné* in 1926 and etchings for *La Belle Enfant* for Vollard in 1930. His designs for Marcel Willard's *Tour d'Horizon* were produced for Au Sans Pareil in Paris and published in an edition of 325 copies in 1920. The illustrations for this typographically eccentric little book were a mixture of etchings and lithographs. Dufy's very free treatment of a sailing ship makes an interesting contrast with Edward Wadsworth's precise etching of a *tartane.* Wadsworth was a member of the Vorticist group and had a deep interest in ships; his book of etchings, *Sailing Ships and Barges of the Western Mediterranean and Adriatic*, is full of precise observation. His linocuts of First World War camouflaged ships are in a very different vein from these engravings.

1932. *Urne Buriall and the Garden of Cyrus* by
Sir Thomas Browne. Illustrated by Paul Nash.
Published by Cassell and Co. Ltd, London.
Printed by the Curwen Press, Plaistow. 12″ × 8¾″.
Illustration printed by collotype with stencilled
colours.

### The French influence in England

The most resolute attempt to combine the best of two worlds, the French
*édition de luxe* and the English typographic book was made by Desmond
Flower when, in 1932, he produced for Cassells an edition of Sir Thomas
Browne's *Urne Buriall and the Garden of Cyrus* with illustrations by Paul
Nash. This was very well printed by the Curwen Press with typography by
Oliver Simon. The collotype illustrations were hand stencilled. It is a beautiful

1931. *Seven Short Stories* by Walter de la Mare,
with illustrations by John Nash. Published by
Faber and Faber, London. Printed by
R. MacLehose and Co. Ltd, Glasgow. $8\frac{7}{8}$" × $6\frac{1}{4}$".
Illustration: 'The Bird of Travel' printed in line
and colour.

piece of work, though the illustrations, considering they come from a most
illustrious painter, seem just a little feeble.

John Nash illustrated in colour for Faber and Faber *Seven Short Stories* by
Walter de la Mare. His somewhat naïve drawings were reproduced by line
and coloured by the stencil process; the result is an attractive and pleasantly
fresh set of illustrations, published the year before his brother's *Urne Buriall*.

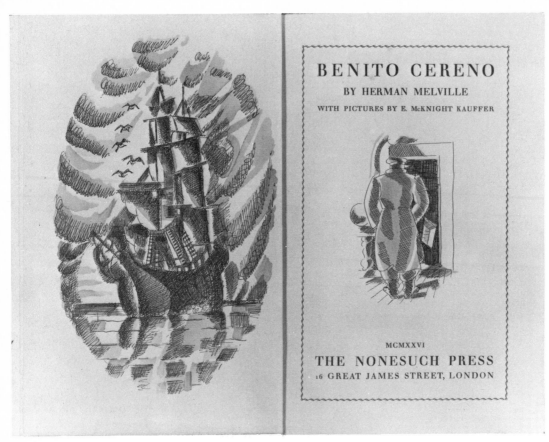

1926. *Benito Cereno* by Herman Melville.
Illustrated by E. McKnight Kauffer. Published by
the Nonesuch Press, London. Printed on a tinted
Van Gelder paper by the Curwen Press, Plaistow.
12″ × 7¾″. Frontispiece and title-page.

1929. *Elsie and the Child* by Arnold Bennett
with stencilled illustrations by E. McKnight
Kauffer. Published by Cassell and Co. Ltd,
London. Printed and stencilled by the Curwen
Press. 10″ × 7½″. Edition limited to 750 copies.
Chapter opening.

1928. *A Sentimental Journey* by Laurence
Sterne, with engravings by J. E. Laboureur.
Published by the Golden Cockerel Press.
9⅛″ × 5½″. Illustration.

*Opposite:*
1930. *Don Quixote de la Mancha* by Miguel de
Cervantes. Illustrated by E. McKnight Kauffer.
Published by the Nonesuch Press, London.
Printed by the Cambridge University Press.
9″ × 5⅝″. The illustrations are reproduced by
lithography with stencilled colours.

The influence of the French *Livres des Peintres* on English and American
private press books can be seen in productions where processes other than
letterpress have been used. The Nonesuch Press issued a number of illustrated
books. Mostly they were in the conservative English tradition, but there were
exceptions. In 1921, an American graphic artist, E. McKnight Kauffer, who
at that time lived in London, drew a series of stencilled designs for Herman
Melville's *Benito Cereno.* Eight years later, for Cassells, he drew a set of
coloured illustrations for Arnold Bennett's *Elsie and the Child*, which were
stencilled by the Curwen Press, the printers of the book. This attractive and
well-made edition was remaindered, like so many other nice books in the
1930's. Kauffer also used this stencilled technique for his coloured illustrations
for a two-decker Nonesuch edition of *Don Quixote*, where his modern
drawings sit somewhat incongruously alongside the evocative eighteenth-
century typography, and even more uncomfortably within the goatskin
covers. Kauffer's fame rests largely on his achievements as a poster artist, but
his book illustrations are still of interest.

The French painter-illustrators showed little interest in 'costume' illustration,
seeming happiest with either classical or contemporary themes. An exception
to this rule was J. E. Laboureur (1877–1943), who was a prolific illustrator.
Laboureur was a founder member of the Société des Peintres Graveurs
Indépendants and worked with the Cubists, although signs of this are not
very evident in this illustration for the Golden Cockerel edition of Sterne's
*Sentimental Journey* published in 1928.

1938. *High Street* by J. M. Richards. Illustrated with lithographs by Eric Ravilious. Published by Country Life Ltd, London. Printed by the Curwen Press, Plaistow. 9″ × 5¾″. Lithographed paper-covered board case-binding. Frontispiece and title-page.

1938. *High Street.* Illustration for the *Knife Grinder.*

In the 1930's something of the French attitude to book production and the use of autographic methods began to be felt in England by a few artists, of whom Eric Ravilious was one. Ravilious, inspired by Paul Nash, was as happy working in a number of different media as any French artist. He was as much at home on the lithographic stone as he was engraving boxwood or painting murals. In 1938, he collaborated with J. M. Richards, the editor of, *The Architectural Review* in producing a book called *High Street.* The illustrations were coloured lithographs of a variety of shop fronts, ranging from a cheese-monger to a clerical outfitter's and throwing in a knife-grinder for good measure. It is a delightful book, beautifully printed (once again by Curwen) and published by Country Life in an ordinary commercial edition.

1931. *Memoirs of an Infantry Officer* by Siegfried
Sassoon. Illustrated by Barnett Freedman.
Published by Faber and Faber, London. Printed
by R. Maclehose and Co. Ltd, Glasgow. 8⅝″ × 5¾″.
Lithographed cloth case-binding and text spread.

that night, so we were rewarded by a mention in the G.H.Q.
communiqué. '*At Mametz we raided hostile trenches. Our party
entered without difficulty and maintained a spirited bombing fight,
and finally withdrew at the end of twenty-five minutes.*' This was
their way of telling England. Aunt Evelyn probably read it
automatically in her *Morning Post*, unaware that this minor
event had almost caused her to receive a farewell letter from
me. The next night our Company was in the front line and
I recovered three hatchets and a knobkerrie from No Man's
Land. Curiously enough, I hadn't yet seen a German. I had
seen dim figures on my dark patrols; but no human faces.

The English illustrated book, as produced by the private presses, was nearly
always letterpress-printed, often with wood engraved illustrations. Purist
bibliophiles held out for a long time against the introduction of lithography.
One of the first English artists to change this was Barnett Freedman, an artist
who introduced a consummate craftsmanship to the art of book designing
and illustrating. He was technically a very skilful lithographer, influenced by
the nineteenth-century French trade lithographers rather than by the contemporary School of Paris. To some extent, his lithographic dexterity was a
limiting factor, yet within his imposed limitations, he achieved an extraordinary
technical consistency in his book illustration. His first important book was
Siegfried Sassoon's *Memoirs of an Infantry Officer* published by Faber in
1931; his most successful, Tolstoy's *War and Peace* (1938), for which he
lithographed the plates for George Macy's Limited Editions Club of New
York. Macy was a great admirer of Barnett Freedman's work, and offered him
much greater scope than any English publishers. Freedman drew lithographs
for four different titles for the Limited Editions Club. The first of these was
*Lavengro* (1935), which Macy wryly described as 'one of the ten finest
books we ever issued and one of the ten least popular'. In 1937, Freedman
illustrated *War and Peace* for Macy who became enthusiastic about these
lithographs. In the *Quarto-Millenary* of the Limited Editions Club, he wrote:
'Some illustrated books are destined for immortality: Botticelli's *Dante,*
Delacroix's *Faust,* Blake's *Book of Job,* Flaxman's *Homer.* To that illustrious
company I nominate Barnett Freedman's *War and Peace.*' Naturally enough
Macy asked Freedman to illustrate one of the twenty-seven volumes of the
monumental, Bruce Rogers-designed, edition of Shakespeare. Freedman
chose *Henry IV, Part I.* He had some odd bed-fellows amongst the other
illustrators, including Graham Sutherland (*Henry VI*), Boardman Robinson
(*King Lear*), W. A. Dwiggins (*The Taming of the Shrew*), Edward A. Wilson
(*The Tempest*) and Edy Legrand (*Hamlet*). Barnett Freedman's last book for
the Limited Editions Club was *Anna Karenina* (1951). Five years later George
Macy died, at the early age of fifty-six. By that time, he had published over
two hundred and fifty titles, introducing to a wide American public, something
of the French attitude to book illustration.

1938. *War and Peace* by Leo Tolstoy. Translated by Louise and Aylmer Maude. Illustrated with lithographs by Barnett Freedman. Designed by John Easton. Printed by R. MacLehose and Co. Ltd, Glasgow. Lithographs printed by the Baynard Press. Bound by Leighton-Straker. Published by the Limited Editions Club, New York. $8\frac{3}{4}'' \times 5\frac{7}{8}''$. Illustrations.

ENGLISH SCOTTISH & WELSH
LANDSCAPE
Verse chosen by
JOHN BETJEMAN and GEOFFREY TAYLOR

*Lithographs by* JOHN PIPER

Frederick
Muller

*Lithographs by* JOHN PIPER

1944. *English, Scottish and Welsh Landscape 1700–c. 1860.* An anthology of poetry chosen by John Betjeman and Geoffrey Taylor, with lithographs by John Piper. Designed and produced by Adprint. Published by Frederick Muller Ltd, London. Printed by the Curwen Press Ltd, Plaistow. Lithograph on the back and front of the cloth case-binding.

*Opposite:*
1945. *Soldiers' Verse* chosen by Patric Dickinson, With lithographs by William Scott. Produced by Adprint Ltd. Published by Frederick Muller Ltd, London. Printed by W. S. Cowell Ltd, Ipswich. 8¼″ × 5½″. Cover design and illustration.

1947. *Poems of Sleep and Dream* chosen by Carol Stewart. With lithographs by Robert Colquhoun. Produced by Adprint Ltd. Published by Frederick Muller Ltd, London. Printed by W. S. Cowell Ltd, Ipswich. 8¼″ × 5½″. Cover design.

In 1938, Walter Neurath, a Viennese publisher, settled in London. Within a few weeks he had established a book production (as opposed to publishing) unit, within the Adprint company. Here he offered a design, production, editorial and ideas service to publishers. As well as producing a number of sociological works, often in collaboration with his namesakes Otto and Marie Neurath, Walter Neurath created a wide-ranging and successful series called 'Britain in Pictures', published by Collins; and towards the end of the 1939–45 war, a series of anthologies 'New Excursions into English Poetry', published by Frederick Muller. These square-backed octavos were illustrated with lithographs by such artists as John Piper, William Scott and Robert Colquhoun. The jacket designs were also printed on the cloth covers. Of these books, *English, Scottish and Welsh Landscape*, with verse chosen by John Betjeman and Geoffrey Taylor and lithographs by John Piper, was probably the most successful. For these illustrations Piper used a limited range of sombre colours, with very effective results.

John Piper, who has done much distinguished work as a stage designer and in stained glass, has also illustrated or decorated a number of books. Amongst his best book illustrations were a fine set of prints for *Brighton Aquatints* in 1939.

In 1945, William Scott, a Scottish-born Ulsterman who had already achieved fame and recognition as a painter, lithographed the illustrations to *Soldiers Verse*, an anthology chosen by Patric Dickinson for this series. Two years later a young Scottish painter called Robert Colquhoun drew the lithographs for another anthology in the same series, called *Poems of Sleep and Dream*. This re-introduction in England of painters as illustrators was belated but welcome.

101

1936. *Green Mansions* by W. H. Hudson, with
illustrations by Miguel Covarrubias. Published
by the Heritage Press in New York and the
Nonesuch Press in London. Printed by the
Haddon Craftsmen and the Duenewald Printing
Corporation in New York. 9⅜" × 6⅜". End-papers
and line illustration.

## Book Club productions in America

In 1936 the Heritage Press published an interesting edition of W. H. Hudson's
*Green Mansions*. This romance of the Brazilian rain forests is a fairly stiff
proposition for an illustrator. In Miguel Covarrubias — a Mexican, Hudson
has found a sympathetic interpreter. His line illustrations are just such drawings as an Amerindian might have made and the colour illustrations and endpapers, though rather more sophisticated than the line drawings, still have a
primitive feeling. The reproduction, by four-colour offset, hardly does justice
to these decorative pictures. The cover repeats the jacket design and is
lithographed from an oil painting by Covarrubias. Like the endpapers it depicts
a jungle scene. These illustrations also give some indication of Covarrubias's
work as a mural painter. He has illustrated a number of books, including
*Mexico South* and *Island of Bali,* both published by Knopf and both written
by the artist.

*I found my Indian friends home again*

1936. *Green Mansions*. Full page coloured illustration.

1955. *Les Européens,* photographs by Henri
Cartier-Bresson. Published by Éditions Verve,
Paris. Printed by Draeger Frères. $14\frac{1}{2}'' \times 11\frac{3}{4}''$.
Cover design by Joan Miró, printed in four
colours.

I have *faute de mieux* had to leave bookjackets out of this survey. Where
jacket designs are printed on the cloth- (or paper-) covered boards, or on
drawn-on covers as in paperbacks, I think they do come within my self-
imposed limitations. Cartier-Bresson's book of photographs has such a cover.
This brilliantly colourful design is by Joan Miró. It is an interesting if unlikely
choice for the cover of a book of photographs.

1936. *Transition.* A periodical volume (no. 25). Edited by Eugène Joks. Published in New York. 8″ × 6″. Cover by Joan Miró, printed in black and blue.

### Painters as book designers and illustrators

Miró, a Spanish-born artist who has worked much in Paris, has brought an exceptional quality of colour to the books he has illustrated — a brilliance such as only Matisse had achieved before him. Miró has been both a Cubist and a Surrealist. His work is so individual that it would be difficult for any artist to follow him without being guilty of plagiarism. The cover for the periodical volume *Transition* was done in 1936, and in both these covers Miró's calligraphy adds an almost oriental quality to the designs.

Modern novels are rarely issued with illustrations. In 1950 Heinemann published an illustrated edition of *The Forsyte Saga,* which had been constantly in print since *The Man of Property*, the first of the trilogy, was published in 1920. Anthony Gross, an English artist who has lived and worked for a large part of his life in France, was commissioned to illustrate it. This was an unexpected but inspired choice, for here was a painter, who, like so many French artists, had worked in many media. The book was produced by two printers: the line illustrations, with the text, by one; the coloured plates, printed by offset, by another. The plates were reproduced from colour separations drawn by the artist on sheets of grained plastic, by which method subtle washes of colour could be printed without any screen or chalking. If only the text had been printed as satisfactorily as the coloured illustrations, this would have been a memorable piece of book production. As it is, it will stand as an example of what can be done when a graphically-minded painter turns his hand to illustration.

Soames in Park Lane

1950. *The Forsyte Saga* by John Galsworthy
with illustrations by Anthony Gross. Designed by
John Lewis. Published by William Heinemann
Ltd, London. The colour plates printed by
W. S. Cowell Ltd, Ipswich and the text by the
Windmill Press, Kingswood. $9\frac{1}{4}'' \times 6\frac{1}{2}''$.
Illustration: 'Soames in Park Lane'.

1956. *De Klokken van Chagall* by Bernard Majorick. Published and printed by Steendrukkerij de Jong and Co., Hilversum. $9\frac{5}{8}'' \times 9\frac{3}{4}''$. Lithographed by Chagall.

Romanticism takes different forms in different countries. It is a rare manifestation in France. In the case of Russian artists it nearly always has a religious significance. Marc Chagall, a Russian-born artist, came to Paris first in 1920 and was there associated with the Cubists. Michael Ayrton, writing some years ago about this artist, said, 'The intangible legend and religion of the Russian-Jew combined with the essentially tangible logic of French painting explains the strange chemistry of Chagall's art'.[3]

Chagall's three great works of illustration, Gogol's *Les Ames Mortes,* La Fontaine's *Fables*, and the *Bible* were all commissioned by Vollard. They were still unpublished when Vollard died, but the Parisian publisher Tériade came to the rescue and published the three books between 1948 and 1956. The illustration shown here is from a lithograph drawn by Chagall at Vence for Bernard Majorick's essay *De Klokken van Chagall* in 1956. Majorick wrote this essay because he was intrigued by the frequent recurrence of clocks in Chagall's work.

[3] Chagall: *Signature* No. 2 new series 1946.

107

1978 *Heureux qui comme Iris* written and
illustrated by Karine Huet and Yvon Le Corre.
Published by Gallimard, Paris. $12\frac{1}{4}'' \times 9\frac{5}{8}''$. Cover
and spread.

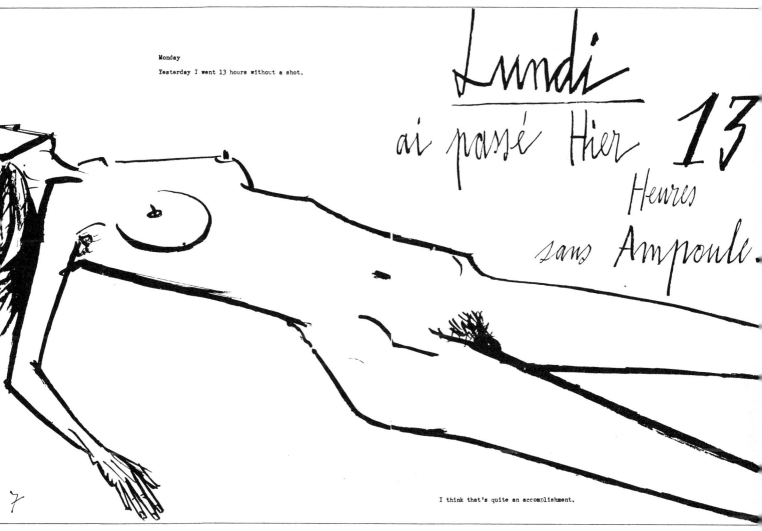

Monday

Yesterday I went 13 hours without a shot.

*Lundi*

*ai passé Hier* **13**

*Heures*

*sans Ampoule.*

I think that's quite an accomplishment.

1964–5. *Toxique* by Françoise Sagan, with illustrations by Bernard Buffet. Published by René Julliard in France, E. P. Dutton and Co., in New York and Souvenir Press in London. 12″ × 9¼″. Illustration: 'Yesterday I went 13 hours without a shot.'

4 '*Iris* restaurée par Charles Harker de Abberton, est un smack de moyenne dimension, construit avec peu de tirant d'eau dans le but de draguer les bancs d'huitres devant Bradwell . . . *Iris* n'est probablement jamais sortie de la Blackwater pendant les trois quarts de sa vie de travail. Si on les utilise comme yachts, les smacks de ce genre, tirant peu d'eau, ne sont pas des bateaux marin, à cause de leur franc-bord bas et de leur grand poids. Par grosse mer, il peuvent être très exposés, voire dangereux' John Lewis *Small Craft Conversion* 1972. Thus Yvon Le Corre was able to make me eat my words!

Something of the French attitude to illustration has rubbed off on the American and English books that I have described in this chapter, but only a little. The last word remains with France.

In 1964 René Julliard published 'a candid diary' of Françoise Sagan's nine days in a special clinic undergoing detoxification from morphine. Mlle Sagan showed this diary to an old friend, the painter Bernard Buffet. The result was *Toxique*, a brilliant series of pages, as effective in their calligraphy as in their spiky, urgent drawings of a tortured, naked girl. The cover, in its simplicity, is a masterpiece. It is a book that only France could have produced.

In the 1970s Yvon Le Corre, a French art teacher, bought the *Iris*, an old Colchester fishing boat which had been beautifully restored by Charles Harker.[4] As Le Corre was setting off for Brittany from the Blackwater river in Essex, Charles Harker said: 'Don't ask too much of her.'

Within a couple of years, Yvon Le Corre had sailed to the Mediterranean and across the Atlantic to Brazil, up to Grenada and Martinique and back to Brittany. *Heureux qui comme* Iris . . . *notes et dessins d'un voyage* is a description of those voyages, largely written by Karine Huet and designed and illustrated by Yvon Le Corre. It is a very French book with vivid illustrations and hand-written text wonderfully intermingled.

109

1921. *Ali Baba und die Vierzig Räuber.*
Lithographic illustration.

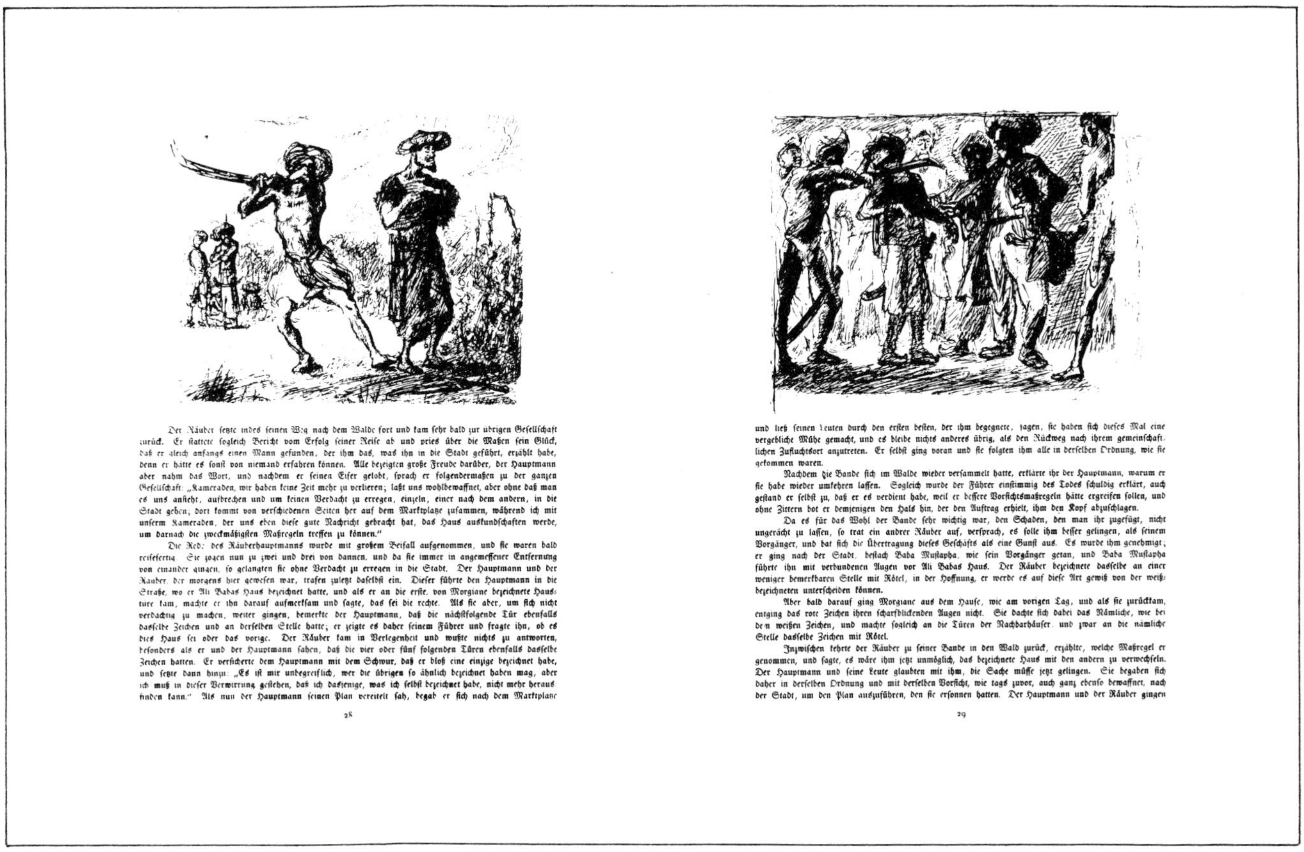

Der Räuber setzte indes seinen Weg nach dem Walde fort und kam sehr bald zur übrigen Gesellschaft zurück. Er stattete sogleich Bericht vom Erfolg seiner Reise ab und pries über die Maßen sein Glück, daß er gleich anfangs einen Mann gefunden, der ihm das, was ihn in die Stadt geführt, erzählt habe, denn er hätte es sonst von niemand erfahren können. Alle bezeigten große Freude darüber, der Hauptmann aber nahm das Wort, und nachdem er seinen Eifer gelobt, sprach er folgendermaßen zu der ganzen Gesellschaft: „Kameraden, wir haben keine Zeit mehr zu verlieren; laßt uns wohlbewaffnet, aber ohne daß man es uns ansieht, aufbrechen und um keinen Verdacht zu erregen, einzeln, einer nach dem andern, in die Stadt gehen; dort kommt von verschiedenen Seiten her auf dem Marktplatze zusammen, während ich mit unserm Kameraden, der uns eben diese gute Nachricht gebracht hat, das Haus auskundschaften werde, um darnach die zweckmäßigsten Maßregeln treffen zu können."

Die Rede des Räuberhauptmanns wurde mit großem Beifall aufgenommen, und sie waren bald reisefertig. Sie zogen nun zu zwei und drei von dannen, und da sie immer in angemessener Entfernung von einander gingen, so gelangten sie ohne Verdacht zu erregen in die Stadt. Der Hauptmann und der Räuber, der morgens hier gewesen war, trafen zuletzt daselbst ein. Dieser führte den Hauptmann in die Straße, wo er Ali Babas Haus bezeichnet hatte, und als er an die erste, von Morgiane bezeichnete Haustüre kam, machte er ihn darauf aufmerksam und sagte, das sei die rechte. Als sie aber, um sich nicht verdächtig zu machen, weiter gingen, bemerkte der Hauptmann, daß die nächstfolgende Tür ebenfalls dasselbe Zeichen und an derselben Stelle hatte; er zeigte es daher seinem Führer und fragte ihn, ob es dies Haus sei oder das vorige. Der Räuber kam in Verlegenheit und wußte nichts zu antworten, besonders als er und der Hauptmann sahen, daß die vier oder fünf folgenden Türen ebenfalls dasselbe Zeichen hatten. Er versicherte dem Hauptmann mit dem Schwur, daß er bloß eine einzige bezeichnet habe, und setzte dann hinzu: „Es ist mir unbegreiflich, wer die übrigen so ähnlich bezeichnet haben mag, aber ich muß in dieser Verwirrung gestehen, daß ich dasjenige, was ich selbst bezeichnet habe, nicht mehr herausfinden kann." Als nun der Hauptmann seinen Plan vereitelt sah, begab er sich nach dem Marktplatze

28

und ließ seinen Leuten durch den ersten besten, der ihm begegnete, sagen, sie haben sich dieses Mal eine vergebliche Mühe gemacht, und es bleibe nichts anderes übrig, als den Rückweg nach ihrem gemeinschaftlichen Zufluchtsort anzutreten. Er selbst ging voran und sie folgten ihm alle in derselben Ordnung, wie sie gekommen waren.

Nachdem die Bande sich im Walde wieder versammelt hatte, erklärte ihr der Hauptmann, warum er sie habe wieder umkehren lassen. Sogleich wurde der Führer einstimmig des Todes schuldig erklärt, auch gestand er selbst zu, daß er es verdient habe, weil er bessere Vorsichtsmaßregeln hätte ergreifen sollen, und ohne Zittern bot er demjenigen den Hals hin, der den Auftrag erhielt, ihm den Kopf abzuschlagen.

Da es für das Wohl der Bande sehr wichtig war, den Schaden, den man ihr zugefügt, nicht ungerächt zu lassen, so trat ein andrer Räuber auf, versprach, es solle ihm besser gelingen, als seinem Vorgänger, und bat sich die Übertragung dieses Geschäfts als eine Gunst aus. Es wurde ihm genehmigt; er ging nach der Stadt, bestach Baba Mustapha, wie sein Vorgänger getan, und Baba Mustapha führte ihn mit verbundenen Augen vor Ali Babas Haus. Der Räuber bezeichnete dasselbe an einer weniger bemerkbaren Stelle mit Rötel, in der Hoffnung, er werde es auf diese Art gewiß von der weißbezeichneten unterscheiden können.

Aber bald darauf ging Morgiane aus dem Hause, wie am vorigen Tag, und als sie zurückkam, entging das rote Zeichen ihren scharfblickenden Augen nicht. Sie dachte sich dabei das Nämliche, wie bei den weißen Zeichen, und machte sogleich an die Türen der Nachbarhäuser und zwar an die nämliche Stelle dasselbe Zeichen mit Rötel.

Inzwischen kehrte der Räuber zu seiner Bande in den Wald zurück, erzählte, welche Maßregel er genommen, und sagte, es wäre ihm jetzt unmöglich, das bezeichnete Haus mit den andern zu verwechseln. Der Hauptmann und seine Leute glaubten mit ihm, die Sache müsse jetzt gelingen. Sie begaben sich daher in derselben Ordnung und mit derselben Vorsicht, wie tags zuvor, auch ganz ebenso bewaffnet, nach der Stadt, um den Plan auszuführen, den sie ersonnen hatten. Der Hauptmann und der Räuber gingen

29

1921. *Ali Baba und die vierzig Räuber* (First edition 1903). Illustrated by Max Slevogt. Published by Bruno Cassirer, Berlin. Printed by W. Drugulin, Leipzig. 12¼" × 9¾". Text pages and line illustrations and title-page.

## 4. THE EFFECT OF GERMAN IMPRESSIONISM AND EXPRESSIONISM ON BOOK ILLUSTRATION

Ali Baba und die vierzig Räuber

Illustriert

von

Max Slevogt

Bruno Cassirer, Verlag
Berlin 1921

If this were a history of modern book production and illustration, an entire volume would be needed to do justice to German illustration, even from the time of Adolf Menzel and his great series of pen drawings for *Geschichte Friedrichs des Grossen*. Here, I can only attempt to show the work of a few artists who, since the turn of the century, have affected the general trend of European or American illustration.

From 1892 contemporary art in Munich had been represented by the Secession, which had established by the first decade of this century a form of German Impressionism. Max Slevogt and Lovis Corinth were its leaders. Both artists illustrated books, but Slevogt (1868–1932), who was both a painter and a lithographer, was the more prolific. Slevogt's lithography and pen drawings are full of lively action. In 1903 Bruno Cassirer published his *Ali Baba und die vierzig Räuber*, which was a mixture of line and half-tone drawings, all delightfully free. *Ali Baba* was reprinted a number of times; the illustrations on this page are reproduced from the 1921 edition. In 1908 Slevogt illustrated *Sinbad der Seefahrer* for the same publisher. Bruno Cassirer, and his cousin Paul, who was an art dealer, were amongst the first German publishers to make use of painter-illustrators. When Hitler came to power, Bruno Cassirer left Germany and settled in Oxford.

In the world of books, it is sad to think how many talented painter-illustrators have been neglected by publishers. One of the greatest illustrators who ever lived was the Norwegian Edvard Munch, who never illustrated a book. Munch made countless prints in every graphic process, from woodcuts, zincographs and etchings to lithographs. His woodcut *The Cry* would rank as one of the world's great book illustrations, if it had ever appeared in a book!

1911. *Tubutsch* by Albert Ehrenstein. Illustrated by Oskar Kokoschka. Published by Jahoda and Siegel, Vienna and Leipzig. 12¼" × 9¾". Title-page and illustration.

eines Cabkutſchers oder eines Karfiolſlowaken hülle, die Be=
kanntſchaft einer Kanalräumerin zu machen trachte und ihre
eheliche Treue einer Probe unterziehe...

Nein, das werde ich nicht tun, ich fühle nicht mehr die Kraft
dazu in mir. Der zweifelnde Blick des Hausmeiſters hat
meine ganze Energie hinweggenommen! Und als ich im
Schein des zuſammenſinkenden Wachsſtengels aus der Viſit=
karte, die auf der Tür meines Kabinetts mit ſepariertem Ein=
gang prangt, erſah, daß ich der Herr Karl Tubutſch war, da
ſagte ich leiſe, niedergeſchmettert, nichts als: „Scho wieder!"...

Oft in der Nacht fahre ich auf. Was iſt? Nichts, nichts!
Will denn niemand bei mir einbrechen? Alles iſt voraus=
berechnet. O, ich möchte nicht der ſein, der bei mir einbricht.
Abgeſehen davon, daß — meinen Stiefelknecht Philipp und
vielleicht noch ein Straßenverzeichnis ausgenommen — bei
mir nichts zu holen iſt, ich geſtehe offen und ehrlich: ich
kenne den Betreffenden zwar nicht im geringſten, aber ich
habe es auf den Tod des armen Teufels abgeſehen. Das
Federmeſſer liegt gezückt, mordbereit auf dem Nachtkaſtel.
Philipp, der Stiefelknecht, wacht wurfgerecht darunter...
will denn niemand bei mir einbrechen... ich ſehne mich nach
einem Mörder.

Wenn ich wenigſtens Zahnſchmerzen hätte. Ich könnte
dann dreimal „Abracadabra" ſagen, auch das heilige Wort
„Zip=zip" dürfte die gleiche magiſche Wirkung haben...
und wenn es mit den Schmerzen ſelbſt dann nicht beſſer
würde, möchte ich keineswegs zum Zahnarzt gehen, nein,
die Schmerzen hegen und pflegen, ſie nie erlöſchen laſſen,

21

1911. *Tubutsch* by Albert Ehrenstein. Illustrated
by Oskar Kokoschka. Published by Jahoda and
Siegel, Vienna and Leipzig. 8″ × 5¾″. Doublespread.

[1] *The Artist and the Book 1860–1960* [by Philip
Hofer and Eleanor M. Garvey], Museum of Fine
Arts, Boston, 1961.

## German expressionism

Oskar Kokoschka, born in 1896, an Expressionist painter of 'visionary and
symbolic humanism', had quite a considerable graphic output. In 1911 he drew
in pen the illustrations for Albert Ehrenstein's *Tubutsch*, which was published
in the same year by Jahoda and Siegel in Vienna, in a pleasant format with
handsome wide margins, and in a second edition by Insel-Verlag in 1919.
The *Tubutsch* drawings are typical of Kokoschka's work and indeed of the
whole German Expressionist movement.

Over the last few years there has been a revival of interest, particularly in the
U.S.A., in German Expressionism. Kokoschka has had a considerable influence
as painter, graphic artist and writer, on modern American art. He illustrated
some of his own books, including *Die Träumenden Knaben* which he wrote
and illustrated when he was only twenty-two. 'This book and Slevogt's *Sinbad*
(Berlin 1908) are the first important modern *livres de peintres* from east of the
Rhine.'[1]

1924. *Umbra Vitae* by Georg Heym. Illustrated
with 46 woodcuts by Ernst Ludwig Kirchner.
Published by Kurt Wolff. Munich. 9″×8⅛″. Cover
printed in black, yellow and green.

MIT DEN FAHRENDEN SCHIFFEN

Mit den fahrenden Schiffen
Sind wir vorübergeschweift,
Die wir ewig herunter
Durch glänzende Winter gestreift.
Ferner kamen wir immer
Und tanzten im insligen Meer,
Weit ging die Flut uns vorbei,
Und Himmel war schallend und leer.

Sage die Stadt,
Wo ich nicht saß im Tor,
Ging dein Fuß da hindurch,
Der die Locke ich schor?
Unter dem sterbenden Abend
Das suchende Licht
Hielt ich, wer kam da hinab,
Ach, ewig in fremdes Gesicht.

14

15

1924. *Umbra Vitae* by Georg Heym. Illustrated
with 46 woodcuts by Ernst Ludwig Kirchner.
Published by Kurt Wolff. Munich. 9″ × 6⅛″.
Text spread with woodcuts.

**Die Brücke**

Die Brücke, a group of artists founded in 1905, was influenced by Munch
and Gauguin, and by African and Pacific art. These artists would also seem to
have been natural book illustrators, both by the nature of German Expressionist
art, with its concern for the plight of humanity, and technically by their
excellence as wood engravers and print makers. Apparently an unhappy
group — sexually repressed and at variance with the world — they first showed
their distaste for the philistine German middle classes in an illustrated book,
*Odi Profanum Vulgus,* which has since disappeared.[2]

The animating force in Die Brücke was Ernst Ludwig Kirchner, strongly
supported by Emil Nolde and Karl Schmidt-Rottluff.

Kirchner, the most prolific graphic artist in the group, left over 1,600 prints.
His rather rugged woodcut technique was based on the mediaeval tradition
still practised in Southern Germany. Mediaeval German art, the woodcuts of
the fifteenth and sixteenth centuries, the tensions and obsessions in the work
of Dürer, Altdorfer and particularly Grünewald, all played a part in the
development of Die Brücke artists.

Kirchner's first woodcuts were Jugendstil in manner but soon the influence
of Edvard Munch changed their direction, so that they became powerfully
erotic, in the manner of so many of the Expressionists.

In 1924, eleven years after Die Brücke had been dissolved, Kirchner illustrated
Georg Heym's *Umbra Vitae* with woodcuts that were rough-hewn and brutal
in execution; the book is also interesting typographically, set throughout in a
heavy condensed sans serif, similar to Grotesque No. 9.

As far as I know, neither Nolde nor Schmidt-Rottluff illustrated any books.

[2] See *Expressionism* by Bernard S. Myers. Thames
and Hudson, 1963.

115

Unser Held, der keinerlei Gepäck hatte, stieg heimlich aus, ohne jemand ein Wort zu sagen, lief flink durch Marseille, immer von der Angst gepackt, das Kamel könne ihm folgen. Und er machte nicht eher Halt, ehe er nicht in einem Coupé dritter Klasse saß und der Zug gemächlich gegen Tarascon schuckerte...

Aber diese Sicherheit war trügerisch gewesen. Zwei Meilen hinter Marseille streckte alles die Köpfe aus den Wagen. Alles schrie und gestikulierte vergnügt. Tartarin seinerseits sah ebenfalls hinaus — und was sah er da? — Er sah das

Kamel, das unvermeidliche Kamel, welches in voller Karriere auf den Schienen hinter dem Bummelzuge herlief und leicht mit ihm Schritt hielt. Entsetzt schloß Tartarin die Augen und drückte sich in die Ecke des Coupés.

Er hatte gehofft, nach dieser verunglückten Expedition wenigstens inkognito nach Tarascon heimkehren zu können, aber die Anwesenheit dieses gottverdammten Vier=füßlers, der zudringlich war wie eine verliebte alte Jungfer, machte das unmöglich. Ein schöner Triumphzug das, weiß Gott! Kein Geld, kein Ruhm! Kein Löwe! Absolut nichts ... nur ein Kamel!

160

1921. *Die Abenteuer des Herrn Tartarin aus Tarascon* by Alphonse Daudet. Illustrated by Georg Grosz. Published by Erich Reiss, Berlin. 9″ × 6¼″. Illustration spread.

1913. *Tartarin von Tarascon* by Alphonse Daudet. Illustrated by Emil Preetorius. Published by Mundt and Blumtritt, Dachau. 7¾″ × 5″. Illustration.

### Georg Grosz and the 'New Objectivity'

In the Germany of the Weimar Republic grim attitudes were prevailing. Georg Grosz (born 1893), in company with the painter Max Beckmann, became an exponent of the 'New Objectivity'. Grosz, a left-wing Dadaist, was highly, perhaps hysterically critical of post-war Berlin. Many portfolios of his work were issued and in 1923 *Ecce Homo* was published. This extremely scarifying collection of drawings of bordels was confiscated by the police within a few months of publication. Grosz was brought to trial for publishing indecencies. In comparison with *Ecce Homo*, Grosz's illustrations to *Tartarin*, printed on a cheap wood pulp paper, were very mild but effective and witty; they made Preetorius's illustrations to the same book look rather dull.

1921. *Die Abenteuer des Herrn Tartarin aus Tarascon* by Alphonse Daudet. Illustrated by Georg Grosz. Published by Erich Reiss, Berlin. 9″ × 6¼″. Illustration.

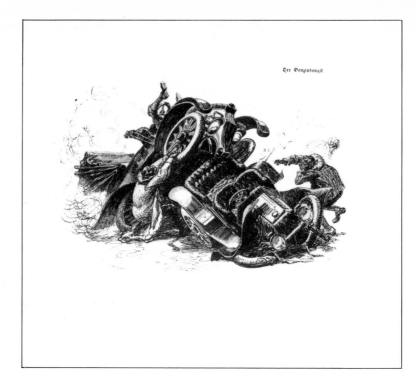

*c.* 1928. *Sammelalbum, alte und neue
Zeichnungen* by Heinrich Kley. Published by
Albert Langen, Munich. 13⅜″ × 10½″. Cover
printed in black on yellow cloth. Illustration:
'der Benzinhengit'.

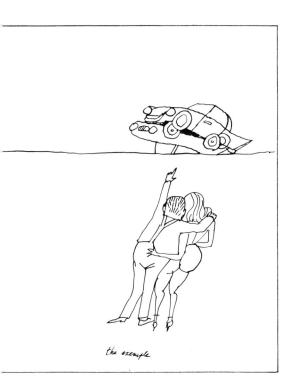

1964. *The Underground Sketchbook of Tomi Ungerer*. Illustration: 'The example'.

*Opposite:*
1964. *The Underground Sketchbook of Tomi Ungerer*. Published by the Viking Press and the Bodley Head. Printed by William Clowes & Sons Ltd, Beccles. 7" × 8⅜". Illustration without title.

## German pre-occupation with sex and violence

The drawings of Heinrich Kley appeared for a number of years in the periodical *Simplicissimus*. An album of his work was published by Albert Langen in Munich in the 1920's, though most of the drawings had appeared many years before. Kley's preoccupation with the sex-war, violence and the imbuing of mechanical contrivances with animal lusts is repeated in the work of Tomi Ungerer. *The Underground Sketchbook of Tomi Ungerer* (1964) certainly makes an interesting comparison with Heinrich Kley's *Sammelalbum* (*c.* 1925), though Ungerer, who is German born and New York domiciled, owes as much to Grosz as to Kley, particularly in his wobbly, sensitive line.

Minimax

*c.* 1928. *Sammelalbum* by Heinrich Kley. Illustration: 'Minimax'.

1920. *Kandide oder die beste Welt* by Voltaire. Illustrated by Paul Klee. Published by Kurt Wolff, Munich. 9¾" × 7¼". Printed by Spamersche Buchdruckerei, Leipzig. Text spread and illustrations.

## A comparison of *Candides*

Paul Klee (1879–1940), a Swiss of German-French parentage, was one of the key figures in modern European art, both as a member of *Der Blaue Reiter* group of painters in Munich and as a teacher at the Bauhaus. Klee's excursions into book illustration were slight. In 1920 he drew the lithographs for a limited edition of Curt Corrinth's *Potzdammer Platz, oder Die Nächte des Neuen Messias*; and in the same year Kurt Wolff published an edition of Voltaire's *Candide* with twenty-six illustrations by Klee. (This was re-issued by Pantheon Books in New York many years later.) These scratchy, slight little pen drawings were actually done in the years between 1906 and 1912. They make an odd marriage with the Fraktur typeface, and an even odder contrast with the English and American illustrated editions of *Candide*. Voltaire's *Candide* is certainly a much illustrated book. In 1922 Routledge in London and E. P. Dutton in New York published an edition, illustrated by Alan Odle, an English artist with a very quirky sense of humour and a Beardsleyesque, art nouveau line. This is an interesting, baroque production. In 1928 Rockwell Kent did the drawings for a Random House edition of the same book, Kent's line drawings being most carefully drawn to match the tone of the Garamond type.

This is an effective and well-balanced piece of book production; the actual illustrations are completely subordinate to the design as a whole; as with all the best of Rockwell Kent's work, the book, rather than the individual illustrations, is the important factor. The opposite could be said of Klee's *Kandide,* for in neither edition did his drawings receive adequate production.

1920. *Kandide oder die beste Welt* by Voltaire. Illustrated by Paul Klee. Published by Kurt Wolff, Munich. 9¾″ × 7¼″. Printed by Spamersche Buchdruckerei, Leipzig. Illustration.

*c.* 1922. *Candide or the Optimist* by F. A. M. de Voltaire (*sic*), translated by Henry Morley LL.D. Illustrated by Alan Odle. Published by George Routledge and Sons Ltd, London and E. P. Dutton and Co., New York. Printed by Headley Brothers, Ashford. 9¾″ × 7¼″. Illustration 'The Toilet of the Pope's Daughter'.

1930. *Candide* by Jean François Marie Arouet de Voltaire, translated by Charles Edmund Merrill, Jr. Illustrated by Rockwell Kent. Published by Random House, New York. These illustrations appeared two years earlier in the limited edition from the same publisher. 10¾″ × 7¼″. Tailpiece.

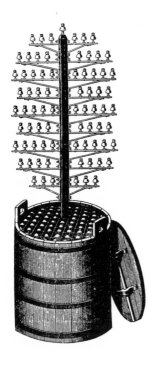

MAX ERNST

# LES MALHEURS DES IMMORTELS

révélés par

**PAUL ELUARD** et **MAX ERNST**

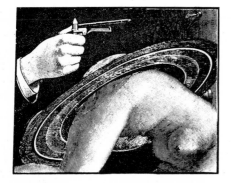

### MON PETIT MONT BLANC

La petite personne noire a froid. A peine si trois lumières bougent encore, à peine si les planètes, malgré leur voilure complète, avancent en flottant: depuis trois heures il n'y a plus de vent, depuis trois heures la gravitation a cessé d'exister. Dans les tourbières, les herbes noires sont menacées par le prestidigitateur et restent en terre avec les chauves et la douceur de leur chair que le jour commence à broder de nuages amers.

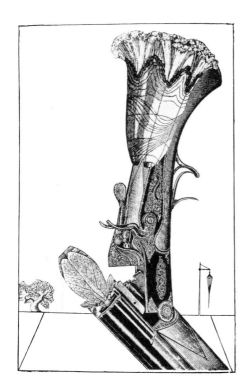

1922. *Les Malheurs des Immortels* by Paul Éluard and Max Ernst. Illustrated with collages by Max Ernst. Published by Librairie Six, Paris. 9½" × 7". Printed on a smooth cream Japanese paper and set throughout in a sans serif typeface. Frontispiece, title-page and text spreads.

### Surrealism and the book

Max Ernst, born in Cologne in 1891, was a founder member of the Cologne Dada Group. He established himself in the early 1920's as a Surrealist painter and showed himself as a master of Surrealist collage, the art of paste-and-scissors. Surrealism is not solely a perquisite of Max Ernst or of René Magritte, nor is it confined to them and the more vulgar manifestations of Salvador Dali. It occurs in the work of the Dadaists, and has had its English exposition in the books of Lewis Carroll and Edward Lear. Max Ernst, however, has produced books of exceptional interest. Paul Nash wrote nearly thirty years ago 'It is not for his alarming ability to horrify that Ernst wins our respect, it is for the intense poetical imagination working throughout all these conceptions'.[3]

With astonishing technical skill, Ernst has converted Victorian engravings into illustrations of often startling beauty. *Les Malheurs des Immortels,* which he produced in collaboration with Paul Éluard in 1922, adds a new dimension to the illustrated book, and shows how a 'directing intelligence' can cut and assemble pieces of type and out-dated engravings and make a coherent lively whole out of the disparate parts. *Les Malheurs des Immortels* was followed by *Histoire Naturelle* in 1926 and *La Femme 100 Têtes* in 1929, published by Éditions de Carrefour. Five years later came *Une Semaine de Bonté, ou les Sept Éléments Capitaux*, with over 150 Surrealist collages, from Éditions Jeanne Bucher, which was followed, in 1936, by *Rêve d'une Petite Fille qui voulut entrer au Carmel,* also published by Éditions de Carrefour.

A renewed interest in Dada and the lasting power of Max Ernst's work is bearing fruit in Germany. Günther Kieser, a practising graphic designer, was responsible for producing in 1962 the lively and amusing *Kriminal Sonette* by Ludwig Rubiner. Jens Rehn's *Das Neue Bestiarium,* published in 1963, has forty most haunting collage-cum-litho drawings by Marleen Pacha.

[3] Surrealism and the illustrated book. *Signature* (1st series No. 5, March, 1937).

123

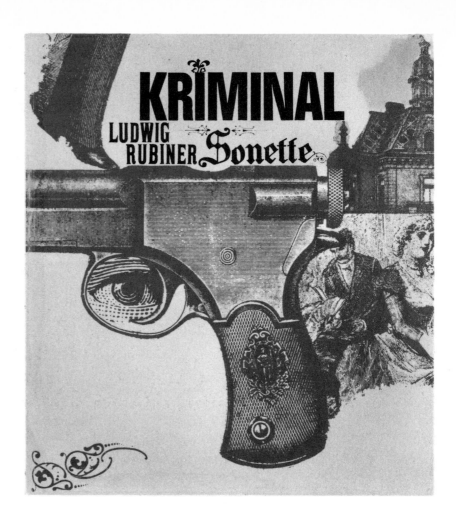

1962. *Kriminal Sonette* by Ludwig Rubiner,
Friedrich Eisenlohr and Livingston Hahn.
Designed and illustrated by Günther Kieser.
Published by Scherz Verlag, Stuttgart and printed
by Paul Robert Wilk. 7¾" × 6⅞". Case-binding
printed in black and purple on white cloth; text
and illustration spread.

Gold

FRED wird in einem braunen Tabakballen
Vom Hafen auf die Zollstation getragen.
Dort schläft er, bis die Schiffsuhr zwölf geschlagen.
Erwacht und schleicht sich in die Lagerhallen.

Am Gold-Depot, wo trunkne Wächter lallen,
Läßt er den kleinen Mörtelfresser nagen,
Bis wie beim Kartenhaus die Mauern fallen.
Dann lädt er Gold in einen Grünkohlwagen.

Als Bauer fährt er sächselnd durch den Zoll.
Doch dort verraten ihn zwei blanke Barren.
Berittne jagen den Gemüsekarren.

Fred sinnt verwirrt, wie er sich retten soll.
Da sitzt DER FREUND in hoher Eberesche
Und schießt ihm pfeiferauchend eine Bresche.

14

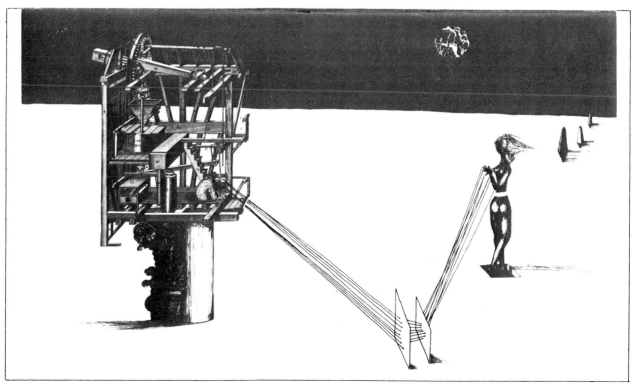

1963. *Das Neue Bestiarium* by Jens Rehn.
Illustrated with 40 offset-lithographs by Marleen
Pacha. Published and printed by the Eremiten-
Presse, Stierstadt Schloss, Sanssouris. $10\frac{7}{8}'' \times 6\frac{1}{2}''$.
Drawn-on and wrapped brown paper cover,
printed in black and designed by Günter Bruno
Fuchs. Collage by Marleen Pacha.

*c.* 1800. Vignetted bookplate engraved on the wood by Thomas Bewick.

1931. *The New Keepsake* illustrated by Rex Whistler and published by T. J. Cobden-Sanderson, London. Vignette.

## 5.  ENGLISH AND AMERICAN TRADITIONS IN ILLUSTRATION

It was not until the early days of the nineteenth century that a distinctive English style of illustration came into being. The literate public developed more quickly in this country than elsewhere because of Britain's pre-eminence in the industrial revolution. Demands for more and more books brought an impossible pressure on intaglio printers of illustrations. It became imperative to find a method of printing *adequate* illustrations at the same time as the text. This brought Thomas Bewick on to the scene; if it had not been Bewick, it would have been someone else. There were at that time plenty of wood engravers capable of cutting crude illustrations for chap-books and broadsides, but they were hardly of a high enough calibre to replace the artist-engravers working on steel and copper plates. Thomas Bewick was actually trained as an engraver on steel and copper. With inspired ingenuity he applied

1838. *The Adventures of Oliver Twist* by Charles Dickens, illustrated by George Cruikshank. Published by Chapman and Hall, London. Illustration: 'Mr Bumble and Mrs Corney taking tea'.

1939. *My Uncle Silas* by H. E. Bates, illustrated by Edward Ardizzone. Published by Jonathan Cape, London. Illustration: 'Finger wet, finger dry'.

1871. *Good Words*. A facsimile wood engraving
from a drawing by Arthur Hughes. Illustration:
'The Letter'.

1900. *Sartor Resartus* by Thomas Carlyle.
Illustrated by Edmund J. Sullivan. Published by
George Bell and Sons, London. Illustration.

exactly the same technique to the end-grain of boxwood, and with consummate skill he produced engravings that could be printed at the same time
as the type. As an artist-engraver, working to the limitations of letterpress
printing, he gave an incomparable example to hosts of engravers.

The technique of using vignetted engravings as head and tail pieces, as
Bewick did, also became a lasting and agreeable fashion in English book
design. A hundred years after Bewick's death, Rex Whistler, a master of the
*pastiche*, made use of the same technique; but as Bewick had substituted
boxwood for the copper plate, Whistler substituted the pen line and zinco for
burin and boxwood. Like Bewick, Whistler also formalized his landscapes in a
quiet, romantic vein.

George Cruikshank, one of the greatest of English illustrators, also made use
of the vignette, first with wood engravings (by another hand), and later with
etchings made by himself for a number of books. These included *Sketches by
Boz* (1834) and *Oliver Twist* (1837).

As the nineteenth century progressed, the copper or steel plate was finally
dropped in favour of the reproduction wood engraving, to avoid the expense
of a separate printing process. The influence of Cruikshank lay dormant until
an artist signing himself 'Diz' appeared on the scene in the late 1920's. This
was Edward Ardizzone, a very English artist of Italian decent, who was to
find in the compass of a small vignetted line drawing (and the process line
block) a perfect means of expression.

The fantastic dexterity of the nineteenth-century professional wood engraver
was no satisfactory substitute for the work of the artist's own hand, though a
formidable school of illustration making use of this reproductive process came
into being in the 1860's. The artists were either members of, or were heavily
influenced by, the Pre-Raphaelite movement. This tradition, established by
such artists as Arthur Hughes, was carried into the twentieth century by
Edmund J. Sullivan, a very skilful pen draughtsman, whose *tour de force* was
an edition of Carlyle's *Sartor Resartus.* In turn Sullivan's influence spread
through several generations of illustrators who were trained at Goldsmiths'
College School of Art where he taught for many years.

1866. *Mrs Caudle's Curtain Lectures* by Douglas
Jerrold, illustrated by Charles Keene. Published
by Bradbury, Evans and Co., London. Illustration:
'The black beetles came into the kitchen'.

1892. *Peter Ibbetson* edited and illustrated by
George du Maurier. Published by James Osgood,
McIlvaine and Co., London. Illustration:
'Bastard! Parricide!'

1891. *Cranford* by Mrs Gaskell illustrated by Hugh Thomson. Published by Macmillan and Co., London. Illustration: 'If you please, my love, will you call me Matilda'.

1893. *The Adventures of Sherlock Holmes* by A. Conan Doyle. Published by George Newnes Ltd, London. Printed by the Gresham Press, London and Chilsworth. Vignetted half-tone illustration by Sidney Paget.

1883. *Olde ffrendes wyth newe Faces* illustrated with hand-coloured woodcuts by Joseph Crawhall. Published in London by Field and Tuer, in New York by Scribner and Welford. Woodcut.

1922. *Poems from the works of Charles Cotton* illustrated by Claud Lovat Fraser. Published by the Poetry Bookshop, London. Printed by the Curwen Press, Plaistow. Headpiece.

There are other movements that have played a part in building up this English tradition in illustration. A recurring romanticism keeps cropping up. In the 1880's Field and Tuer at the Leadenhall Press produced a number of chapbooks, illustrated by Joseph Crawhall in the crude manner of the seventeenth and eighteenth centuries. Lovat Fraser picked up and made use of the same idiom in the years just before and after the First World War. Charles Keene's unmannered drawings were also an important influence in the late nineteenth century; interpreted by professional engravers and so much admired by Camille Pissarro, they had a lasting influence on certain English and American pen draughtsmen. George du Maurier, though by no means as fine a draughtsman as Keene, also played a part in establishing a style of illustration that endured for many years after his death. When du Maurier's drawings were freed from the hand of the trade wood engraver, as they were in *Peter Ibbetson,* their impact increased enormously. With the introduction of photomechanical reproduction and the line (or half-tone) block, artists such as Hugh Thomson and F. L. Griggs and the American Frederick Remington all made use of their emancipation from the trade engraver.

Though the invention of photo-engraving happened in 1860, the first English book illustrator to use the medium was Hugh Thomson, whose drawings for *Days with Sir Roger de Coverley* (which owed much to the American artist, E. A. Abbey) were reproduced from line blocks. These illustrations first appeared in 1886 in Macmillan's *English Illustrated Magazine* and were reprinted in book form in the same year. Thomson was a prolific illustrator; his books included *Cranford* and *The Vicar of Wakefield* for Macmillan's 'Cranford' series and various volumes in the 'Highways and Byways' series for the same publisher.

With the introduction in Philadelphia in 1896 of the Levy half-tone screen, the illustrator was finally freed from the limitations of line-block or interpretation wood engraving. Sidney Paget made good use of the half-tone process, for his vignetted illustrations for *The Adventures of Sherlock Holmes* — drawings that were originally published in the *Strand Magazine* and later reprinted in book form.

1902. *Ranch Life and the Hunting Trail* by
Theodore Roosevelt. Illustrated by Frederic
Remington. Published by the Century Co., New
York. Printed by the De Vinne Press. 10½″ × 7″.
Illustration and text spread.

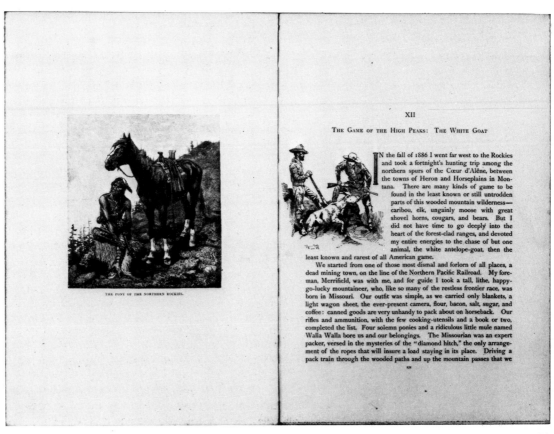

THE PONY OF THE NORTHERN ROCKIES.

XII

THE GAME OF THE HIGH PEAKS: THE WHITE GOAT

IN the fall of 1886 I went far west to the Rockies
and took a fortnight's hunting trip among the
northern spurs of the Cœur d'Alêne, between
the towns of Heron and Horseplains in Mon-
tana. There are many kinds of game to be
found in the least known or still untrodden
parts of this wooded mountain wilderness—
caribou, elk, ungainly moose with great
shovel horns, cougars, and bears. But I
did not have time to go deeply into the
heart of the forest-clad ranges, and devoted
my entire energies to the chase of but one
animal, the white antelope-goat, then the
least known and rarest of all American game.

We started from one of those most dismal and forlorn of all places, a
dead mining town, on the line of the Northern Pacific Railroad. My fore-
man, Merrifield, was with me, and for guide I took a tall, lithe, happy-
go-lucky mountaineer, who, like so many of the restless frontier race, was
born in Missouri. Our outfit was simple, as we carried only blankets, a
light wagon sheet, the ever-present camera, flour, bacon, salt, sugar, and
coffee; canned goods are very unhandy to pack about on horseback. Our
rifles and ammunition, with the few cooking-utensils and a book or two,
completed the list. Four solemn ponies and a ridiculous little mule named
Walla Walla bore us and our belongings. The Missourian was an expert
packer, versed in the mysteries of the "diamond hitch," the only arrangement of the ropes that will insure a load staying in its place. Driving a
pack train through the wooded paths and up the mountain passes that we

"Hark!" said Tom. "Listen—don't talk."

They waited a time that seemed an age, and then the same muffled boom troubled the solemn hush.

"Let's go and see."

They sprang to their feet and hurried to the shore toward the town. They parted the bushes on the bank and peered out over the water. The little steam ferryboat was about a mile below the village, drifting with the current. Her broad deck seemed crowded with people. There were a great many skiffs rowing about or floating with the stream in the neighborhood of the ferryboat, but the boys could not determine what the men in them were doing. Presently a great jet of white smoke burst from the ferryboat's side, and as it expanded and rose in a lazy cloud, that same dull throb of sound was borne to the listeners again.

"I know now!" exclaimed Tom;" somebody's drownded!"

"That's it!" said Huck; "they done that last summer, when Bill Turner got drownded; they shoot a cannon over the water, and that makes him come up to the top. Yes, and they take loaves of bread and put quicksilver in 'em and set

'em afloat, and wherever there's anybody that's drownded, they'll float right there and stop."

"Yes, I've heard about that," said Joe. "I wonder what makes the bread do that."

"Oh, it ain't the bread, so much," said Tom; "I reckon it's mostly what they *say* over it before they start it out."

"But they don't say anything over it," said Huck. "I've seen 'em and they don't."

"Well, that's funny," said Tom. "But maybe they say it to themselves. Of *course* they do. Anybody might know that."

The other boys agreed that there was reason in what Tom said, because an ignorant lump of bread, uninstructed by an incantation, could not be expected to act very intelligently when sent upon an errand of such gravity.

"By jings, I wish I was over there, now," said Joe.

"I do too," said Huck. "I'd give heaps to know who it is."

The boys still listened and watched. Presently a revealing thought flashed through Tom's mind, and he exclaimed:

"Boys, I know who's drownded—it's us!"

They felt like heroes in an instant. Here was a gorgeous triumph; they were missed; they were mourned; hearts were breaking on their account; tears were being shed; accusing memories of unkindnesses to these poor lost lads were rising up, and unavailing regrets and remorse were being indulged: and best of all, the departed were the talk of the whole town, and the envy of all the boys, as far as this dazzling notoriety was concerned. This was fine. It was worth while to be a pirate, after all.

As twilight drew on, the ferryboat went back to her accustomed business and the skiffs disappeared. The pirates returned to camp. They were jubilant with vanity over their new grandeur and the illustrious trouble they were making. They caught fish, cooked supper and ate it, and then fell to guessing at what the village was thinking and saying about them; and the pictures they drew of the public distress on their account were gratifying to look upon—from their point of view. But when the shadows of night closed them in, they gradually ceased to talk, and sat gazing into the fire, with their minds evidently wandering elsewhere. The excitement was gone, now, and Tom and Joe could not keep back

thoughts of certain persons at home who were not enjoying this fine frolic as much as they were. Misgivings came; they grew troubled and unhappy; a sigh or two escaped, unawares. By and by Joe timidly ventured upon a roundabout "feeler" as to how the others might look upon a return to civilization—not right now, but—

Tom withered him with derision! Huck, being uncommitted as yet, joined in with Tom, and the waverer quickly "explained," and was glad to get out of the scrape with as little taint of chicken-hearted homesickness clinging to his garments as he could. Mutiny was effectually laid to rest for the moment.

As the night deepened, Huck began to nod, and presently to snore. Joe followed next. Tom lay upon his elbow motionless, for some time, watching the two intently. At last he got up cautiously, on his knees, and went searching among the grass and the flickering reflections flung by the camp-fire. He picked up and inspected several large semicylinders of the thin white bark of a sycamore, and finally chose two which seemed to suit him. Then he knelt by the fire and painfully wrote something up-

⊲ 62 ⊳

⊲ 63 ⊳

## Frederic Remington and the English and American impressionist illustrators

Joseph Pennell, writing in *Pen Drawing and Pen Draughtsmen* in 1889 about the American artist Frederic Remington, together with the work of two other American illustrators, Arthur B. Frost and E. W. Kemble, said 'Nor has their work any of the slovenliness which characterizes so much English work of the same sort. . . All will fall under the English critics' ban because they are not pretty or beautiful; but they are more than this, they are real, and genuine realism was the one quality lacking in the brilliant Englishman of thirty years ago'.

Remington was a brilliant portrayer of the Far West. Though much of his work was done in wash, his pen drawings for Theodore Roosevelt's *Ranch Life and Hunting Trail*, published in 1888, were in an impressionist pen technique. He was a prolific painter and illustrated 142 books, including eight of his own. Remington (b. 1861 d. 1909) after a short period as an art student at Yale University (there was only one other art student there at the time), left his home in Up-State New York and made for the Far West. After working as cowboy, cook and ranch hand, he set about recording for posterity the life of the prairies and ranges, before the encroachment of the railways destroyed it. Remington, who possessed a photographic memory, rarely sketched from life, and some of these *Ranch Life* drawings almost look as if they were copied from photographs, so unformalized are the folds and creases in the cowboys' shirts or pants; their realism is certainly genuine enough. Another American artist, Donald McKay, forty years later carried this technique a step further in his illustrations for Mark Twain's *The Adventures of Tom Sawyer* (1930). Here a rather free line has the addition of a scattered green wash; and as this attractive book is printed on a tinted Van Gelder paper, the drawings blend in with the text most beautifully.

1930. *The Adventures of Tom Sawyer* by Mark Twain. Illustrated by Donald McKay. Published by Random House, New York. Printed by the Pynson Printers under the supervision of Elmer Adler. 10⅜" × 7¼". Illustration and text spread.

J. SHERIDAN LE FANU

# IN A GLASS DARKLY

With Numerous Illustrations
by
EDWARD ARDIZZONE

LONDON
PETER DAVIES
1929

1929. *In a Glass Darkly* by J. Sheridan Le Fanu, illustrated by Edward Ardizzone. Published by Peter Davies, London. Printed by the Cambridge University Press. 8½″ × 5¼″. Frontispiece and title-page; text and illustration spread.

and about in the house. She hummed tunes to herself, for a time; and then stopped and listened; and then resumed her work again. At last, she was destined to be more terrified than even was the housekeeper.

There was a back kitchen in this house, and from this she heard, as if coming from below its foundations, a sound like heavy strokes, that seemed to shake the earth beneath her feet. Sometimes a dozen in sequence, at regular intervals; sometimes fewer. She walked out softly into the passage, and was surprised to see a dusky glow issuing from this room, as if from a charcoal fire.

The room seemed thick with smoke.

Looking in, she very dimly beheld a

monstrous figure, over a furnace, beating with a mighty hammer the rings and rivets of a chain.

The strokes, swift and heavy as they looked, sounded hollow and distant. The man stopped, and pointed to something on the floor, that, through the smoky haze, looked, she thought, like a dead body. She remarked no more; but the servants in the room close by, startled from their sleep by a hideous scream, found her in a swoon on the flags, close to the door, where she had just witnessed this ghastly vision.

Startled by the girl's incoherent asseverations that she had seen the Judge's corpse on the floor, two servants having first searched the lower part of the house, went rather frightened upstairs to

inquire whether their master was well. They found him, not in his bed, but in his room. He had a table with candles burning at his bedside, and was getting on his clothes again; and he swore and cursed at them roundly in his old style, telling them that he had business, and that he would discharge on the spot any scoundrel who should dare to disturb him again.

So the invalid was left to his quietude.

In the morning it was rumoured here and there in the street that the Judge was dead. A servant was sent from the house three doors away, by Counsellor Traverse, to inquire at Judge Harbottle's hall door.

The servant who opened it was pale and reserved, and would only say that the Judge was ill. He had had a dangerous accident; Doctor Hedstone had been with him at seven o'clock in the morning.

There were averted looks, short answers, pale and frowning faces, and all the usual signs that there was a secret that sat heavily upon their minds, and the time for disclosing which had not yet come. That time would arrive when the coroner had arrived, and the mortal scandal that had befallen the house could be no longer hidden. For that morning Mr Justice Harbottle had been found hanging by the neck from the banister at the top of the great staircase, and quite dead.

There was not the smallest sign of any struggle or resistance. There had not been heard a cry or any other noise in the slightest degree indicative of violence. There was medical evidence to show that, in his atrabilious state, it was quite on the cards that he might have made away with himself. The jury found accordingly that it was a case of suicide. But to those who were acquainted with the strange story which Judge Harbottle

132

1939. *My Uncle Silas* by H. E. Bates illustrated
by Edward Ardizzone. Published by Jonathan
Cape, London. Printed by the Camelot Press Ltd.
$9\frac{7}{8}'' \times 7\frac{1}{4}''$. Illustration: 'A Funny Thing'.

Edward Ardizzone, one of the most talented of English illustrators, carried the
tradition of Cruikshank and Leech into the mid-twentieth century. With the
simplest of pen technique, a development of his method of watercolour drawings, he painted a thousand scenes; and all this without much resource to
period properties. When Ardizzone was illustrating Trollope's 'Barchester'
novels or *The Local* (a book about pubs), he established the period and the
place by the attitudes of the figures and by the subtlest characterization.
These drawings were something new in twentieth-century illustration, particularly at a time (in the '30's) when there was much mannered stuff about,
and it took the publishers some little time to realize that here was a *real* book
illustrator.

1947. *The Golden Asse of Lucius Apuleius*
translated by William Adlington. Illustrated by
Brian Robb and designed by Robert Harling.
Published by John Westhouse and printed by
W. S. Cowell Ltd, Ipswich. 7¼″ × 5½″. Illustrations.

battell, which you your selfe did appoint: for after that I felt the first
Arrow of cruell Cupid within my breast, I bent my bow very strong,
and now feare (because it is bended so hard) lest my string should
breake: but that thou mayst the better please me, undresse thy haire

and come and embrace mee lovingly: whereupon she made no long
delay, but set aside all the meat and wine, and then she unapparelled
her selfe, and unattyred her haire, presenting her amiable body unto
me in manner of faire Venus, when shee goeth under the waves of
the sea. Now (quoth shee) is come the houre of justing, now is come
the time of warre, wherefore shew thy selfe like unto a man, for I
will not retyre, I will not fly the field, see then thou bee valiant, see
thou be couragious, since there is no time appointed when our

56

¹ *Signature* II. N.S. 1950.

Ardizzone's first book commission was a handsome edition of Sheridan Le
Fanu's *In a Glass Darkly*, published in 1929 by Peter Davis (a publisher who
produced a number of well-designed illustrated books). Amongst the most
successful of Ardizzone's illustrated books (apart from his children's books)
are Anthony Trollope's *The Warden* and *Barchester Towers,* for the Oxford
University Press series, and *My Uncle Silas* by H. E. Bates, published in 1939.
The last, a book of bucolic and rather bawdy stories, is full of the most
lively drawings, each of which shows something of the painter's eye.

Brian Robb was a painter who, for a short period in his career, turned to
illustration as a complementary activity. His style as an illustrator varied
considerably. During the 1939–45 war, he served as Camouflage Officer to
Montgomery's 8th Army, and was with that redoubtable outfit from El
Alamein to the end of the Italian campaign. A little book of cartoons that he
drew at that time, called *My Middle East Campaigns,* shows one side of his
work; they are rather grotesque drawings that reveal a real understanding and
a clever and personal observation. Amongst the books he illustrated are
a somewhat archaic *Adventures of Baron Münchausen* (1947) and a delightful *Tristram Shandy* (1949). The *Golden Asse* drawings, done in 1947 at the
instigation of Robert Harling for John Westhouse, a now defunct publisher,
are splendid, rich drawings, discreetly erotic. Edward Ardizzone, as one
illustrator writing about another, said of them: '(they) have a truly classical
quality, one might say sculptural quality, which has been successfully
achieved by a loose, scribbly pen line with much attention to modelling'.¹

1942. *A Connecticut Yankee in King Arthur's Court* by Mark Twain. Illustrated by Warren Chappell. Published by Heritage Press, New York. Illustration.

1906. *Our Neighbours* by Charles Dana Gibson. Published by Charles Scribner's Sons in New York and John Lane in London. 11¾" × 17". Detail of illustration.

Charles Dana Gibson's books, lavish landscape folios of drawings of America's upper crust, were published in the first decade of the century. His intricate pen painting received kinder treatment from his blockmakers than it would today, for there were at the turn of the century still plenty of trained engravers, who by hand work gave precision to the zinc blocks. Gibson's fame today rests almost solely on his 'Gibson Girls', a type of American beauty he may well be said to have created.

Warren Chappell, an illustrator of some skill, was also a distinguished book designer, who studied type design at Offenbach under Rudolph Koch. In 1939 he designed the typeface Trajanus. Amongst the most successful books he illustrated are *A Connecticut Yankee at King Arthur's Court* (1942) for Heritage, and in 1939 a lively *Don Quixote* for Knopf. Chappell, like Donald McKay, is in the true tradition of American book illustrators – a tradition founded by E. A. Abbey, Howard Pyle, Charles Dana Gibson and, in particular application to Chappell's work, Pennell's trilogy – A. B. Frost, Frederick Remington and E. W. Kemble. Since the time of these father figures, a number of expatriated European artists have brought their disparate talents to enrich and sometimes muddy the stream. Coming from an older tradition, they have sometimes brought vulgarity rather than refinement to the native stock.
But there are other illustrators in the fine native tradition, such as James Daugherty and the painter Thomas Hart Benton. Daugherty's calligraphic draughtsmanship can be seen in *Courageous Companions* (see page 143) and Carl Sandburg's *Abe Lincoln Grows Up*.

1944. *Life on the Mississippi* by Mark Twain, illustrated by Thomas Hart Benton. Published by the Limited Editions Club, New York. Designed by Will Ransom and printed by William E. Rudge's Sons, New York. $9\frac{1}{2}'' \times 6\frac{1}{8}''$. Illustration of a sunken river steamer.

Thomas Hart Benton (b. 1889), a real 'mossback isolationist in art',[2] spent an unprofitable time studying in Paris, before returning to the U.S.A. to find his subject in the life of farming communities in the Middle West. Benton's painting technique was most curious; he made a painted clay model of his subject and then painted from that – a method reminiscent of the English painter Gainsborough, who used to make up little landscape models from pebbles, twigs and bits of parsley.

In 1942 Benton illustrated most vividly *Huckleberry Finn* for the Limited Editions Club, in a version designed by C. P. Rollins, which can more than stand comparison with the original edition illustrated by E. W. Kemble. Two years later he completed a further set of illustrations of Mark Twain's *Life on the Mississippi,* also for the Limited Editions Club.

Lynton Lamb was an impressionist illustrator with a real understanding of fine bookwork. For many years he acted as a consultant to the Oxford University Press, and at the same time practised as a painter and taught lithography at the Slade School of Art. For Oxford, he designed everything from prayer books to wrappers. His wrappers are most effective: economical in their means, often relying on only two workings, consisting of a flat background colour with whites reversed out and a black printing. For the same publisher he illustrated several books, including one of Anthony Trollope's political novels, for a series which Lamb himself designed. (The books in this series were illustrated by different artists, including Edward Ardizzone and Leonard Huskinson.) Lamb drew direct with the pen, with no preliminary working-up. I wrote some years ago about these drawings: 'These are illustrations of "things seen" by a man who observes keenly; and because he is, above all, so intensely interested in personality and character, and also has an abiding interest in the play of light on things and people and in those trappings and furnishings that give an authentic background of time and place, Lamb seems able to evoke naturally and thus successfully the true atmosphere of the author's *mise en scène*'.[3] Lamb was certainly not just a period illustrator; his own book *County Town* is full of the keenest open air observation. Joseph Pennell would have approved.

[2] See *300 years of American Painting.* Alexander Eliot. Time Inc. New York, 1957.

[3] Alphabet and Image 5. *The drawings and book decorations of Lynton Lamb.*

136

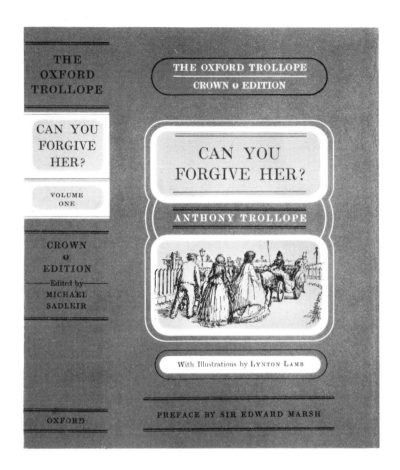

1948. *Can you Forgive Her?* by Anthony Trollope. Designed and illustrated by Lynton Lamb. Published and printed by the Oxford University Press. 8″ × 5″. Series jacket design, lithograph illustration and text spread with line illustration

MR. VAVASOR AND HIS DAUGHTER

seen John Vavasor at the only moment of the day at which he is ever much in earnest. All other things are light and easy to him,—to be taken easily and to be dismissed easily. Even the eating of the dinner calls forth from him no special sign of energy. Sometimes a frown will gather on his brow as he tastes the first half glass from his bottle of claret; but as a rule that which he has prepared for himself with so much elaborate care, is consumed with only pleasant enjoyment. Now and again it will happen that the cook is treacherous even to him, and then he can hit hard; but in hitting he is quiet, and strikes with a smile on his face.

Such had been Mr. Vavasor's pursuits and pleasures in life up to the time at which my story commences. But I must not allow the reader to suppose that he was a man without good qualities. Had he when young possessed the gift of industry I think that he might have shone in his profession, and have been well spoken of and esteemed in the world. As it was he was a discontented man, but nevertheless he was popular, and to some extent esteemed. He was liberal as far as his means would permit; he was a man of his word; and he understood well that code of by-laws which was presumed to constitute the character of a gentleman in his circle. He knew how to carry himself well among men, and understood thoroughly what might be said, and what might not; what might be done among those with whom he lived, and what should be left undone. By nature, too, he was kindly disposed, loving many persons a little if he loved few or none passionately. Moreover, at the age of fifty, he was a handsome man, with a fine forehead, round which the hair and beard was only beginning to show itself to be grey. He stood well, with a large person, only now beginning to become corpulent. His eyes were bright and grey, and his mouth and chin were sharply cut, and told of gentle birth. Most men who knew John Vavasor well, declared it to be a pity that he should spend his time in signing accounts in Chancery Lane.

I have said that Alice Vavasor's big relatives cared but little for her in her early years; but I have also said that they were

4

MR. VAVASOR AND HIS DAUGHTER

careful to undertake the charge of her education, and I must explain away this little discrepancy. The biggest of these big people had hardly heard of her; but there was a certain Lady

Macleod, not very big herself, but, as it were, hanging on to the skirts of those who were so, who cared very much for Alice. She was the widow of a Sir Archibald Macleod, K.C.B., who had been a soldier, she herself having also been a Macleod by birth; and for very many years past—from a time previous to the birth of Alice Vavasor—she had lived at Cheltenham, making short sojourns in London during the spring, when the contents of her limited purse would admit of her doing so.

5

1898. *London Types* by W. E. Henley. Illustrated
by William Nicholson. Published by William
Heinemann, London. 13″ × 11″. Cover design.
Coloured linocut illustration: 'Hammersmith'.

c. 1900. *The Man with the Hoe,* illustrated by
Howard Pyle. Published by Doubleday, Page and
Co., New York. Reproduced from *Modern Pen
Drawings, European and American*: Studio 1901.

1898. *London Types* by W. E. Henley. Illustrated
by William Nicholson. Published by William
Heinemann, London. 13″ × 11″. Cover design.

## The Romantic Movement in illustration

In English book illustration, romanticism made its appearance in the 1880's
with the chap-book productions of Field and Tuer, at the Leadenhall Press,
where Joseph Crawhall's amusing parodies of eighteenth-century broad-
sheets were happily wedded to battered old typefaces. William Nicholson, a
very talented painter, carried the same thought a stage further with his books,
*London Types, An Almanach of Twelve Sports* and *An Alphabet*, all published
in the same year, 1898. The illustrations were boldly cut in linoleum and hand-
coloured. The books had an immediate success. A contemporary reviewer
writing in the *St James's Gazette* said: 'You must turn to your best specimens
of Japanese colour-printing to get anything better than these boldly con-
structed blacks and reds. And what the Eastern world will gain by its delicacy
of outline or of tint, it will lose by comparison with the truth of modelling in
face and figure which is characteristic of this modern work'. Something of the
simplicity of these cuts is to be seen in the posters of the Beggarstaffs, the
pseudonym of William Nicholson and James Pryde.
In the same year, 1898, the Beggarstaffs carried their poster technique into
the illustrations for Edwin Pugh's book *Tony Drum.*
The American Howard Pyle had a lasting influence on American illustrators,
and particularly on the romantic illustrators such as N. C. Wyeth and Edward A.
Wilson. In his own lifetime and in his own country he was regarded as a
Colossus. Gleeson White, writing in 1897 in the special winter number of
*The Studio,* said: 'It is a matter of surprise and regret that Howard Pyle's
illustrated books are not as well known as they deserve to be in England . . .
anyone with artistic sympathy is completely converted to be a staunch admirer
of Pyle's work by a sight of *The Wonder Clock,* a portly quarto published by
Harper Brothers in 1894'. He is writing of the Dürer-influenced Pyle, and
compares him favourably with Walter Crane. Though the bulk of Pyle's work
was done for children, he illustrated a number of other books, including
Oliver Wendell Holmes's *One Horse Shay,* and, for Doubleday, Page & Co.,
*The Man with the Hoe* — which shows a marked Pre-Raphaelite influence.

139

## XIV

### I

Maud has a garden of roses
And lilies fair on a lawn ;
There she walks in her state
And tends upon bed and bower,
And thither I climb'd at dawn
And stood by her garden-gate ;
A lion ramps at the top,
He is claspt by a passion-flower.

### II

Maud's own little oak-room
(Which Maud, like a precious stone
Set in the heart of the carven gloom,
Lights with herself, when alone
42

1922. *Maud* by Alfred Lord Tennyson. Illustrated
by Edmund J. Sullivan. Published by Macmillan
and Co. Ltd, London. Printed by R. & R. Clark Ltd,
Edinburgh. 9" × 6". Text and illustration spread:
case-binding design blocked in silver on
white cloth.

Mention has already been made of Edmund J. Sullivan. He illustrated a
number of books in a romantic vein, including Carlyle's *History of the French
Revolution.*
In 1922, Macmillan published an edition of Tennyson's monodrama *Maud,*
with line illustrations by Sullivan which had been made some years earlier. It
is a charming piece of book making, with a pretty case. The illustrations, some
tinted, are as effective as those in *Sartor Resartus*, but freer and more dramatic.
The precise intricacy of the *Sartor Resartus* drawings matched Carlyle's
turgid prose; but this edition of *Maud* is high Victorian romanticism, half a
century out of context.
Sullivan, like Augustus John, another lyrical artist, lived out of his time
(possibly an English failing). But he was an artist of considerable erudition,

1915. *The Happy Hypocrite* by Max Beerbohm.
Illustrated by George Sheringham. Published by
John Lane, the Bodley Head, London. Printed by
Spottiswoode Ballantyne and Co. Ltd, London.
$10\frac{1}{8}'' \times 7\frac{1}{2}''$. Illustration: 'King Bogey' and chapter
opening initial letter.

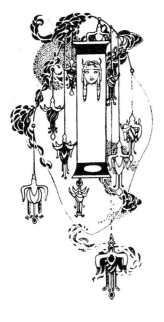

and as well as teaching wrote at length about pen drawing and illustration.
In his book *Line*, he has some salutary things to say about the importance of
the balance of illustration to type, and also of techniques, processes and paper.
After Nicholson's robust cuts and Sullivan's strong chiaroscuro pen work, the
romanticism of George A. Sheringham may seem a little watery. In 1915, he
illustrated Max Beerbohm's *The Happy Hypocrite* which was published by
John Lane. This book, which has a pretty, flowery cover, is a curious mixture
of coloured lithographs and decorative two-colour initials and line drawings.
Sheringham's softly tinted lithographs have an atmosphere of chintz and
pot-pourri. They marked the end of the golden days of pre-1914 England. They
also illustrated the gentler side of Max's evocative but usually astringent prose.

1924. *Iron Men and Wooden Ships*, illustrated with coloured woodcuts by Edward A. Wilson. Published by Doubleday, Page and Co., New York. 12″ × 8¾″. Coloured woodcut: 'Blackbeard'

The mantle of American romanticism has been most ably worn by Howard Pyle's pupils, N. C. Wyeth and Edward A. Wilson and by James Daugherty. Wyeth specialized in children's books, Wilson in stories of the sea. Wilson's illustrations for R. H. Dana's *Two Years before the Mast,* for the Lakeside Press, were reproduced from the artist's watercolours; for *Iron Men and Wooden Ships*, which Doubleday, Doran & Co. published in 1924, he used coloured woodcuts. The cut of Blackbeard here is a rather stiff illustration, but makes an interesting comparison with Claud Lovat Fraser's book, *Pirates,* published by Jonathan Cape in 1921, the year that very talented artist died. The full page illustrations to the *Pirates* were printed in black on sheets of richly coloured paper.

Lovat Fraser had an instinctive feeling for decorating book pages. He usually worked with a reed-pen, and often stencilled strong flat colours on to this rich framework. His colour sense can be appreciated from Haldane McFall's

## CAPTAIN JOHN RACKHAM, AND HIS CREW

JOHN RACKHAM was Quarter - Master to *Vane's* Company, till *Vane* was turned out for not fighting the French Man-of-War, and *Rackham* put in Captain in his place, which happened about the 24th day of *November*, 1718. His first cruise was among the *Caribbe* Islands, where he took and plundered several vessels. Afterwards, to the windward of *Jamaica*, he fell in with a *Madeïra* Man, which he detained till he had made his market out of her, and then restored her to her Master, suffering *Hosea Tisdel*, a tavern-keeper at *Jamaica*, whom he had taken among his Prizes, to go aboard her, she being bound for that Island.

Afterwards he sailed towards the Island

19

CAPTAIN JOHN RACKHAM

1921 *Pirates* with a foreword and illustrations by C. Lovat Fraser. Published by Jonathan Cape, London. $8\frac{1}{4}'' \times 6\frac{1}{4}''$. Text and illustration spread.

*Book of Lovat*, published by J. M. Dent in 1923. Fulsome though this may be as critical biography, it is a handsome piece of bookmaking greatly enriched with Lovat's colour designs.

James Daugherty's romantic drawing of Spanish galleons is from *Courageous Companions*, published by McKay. These are well designed illustrations.

1929. *Courageous Companions* by Charles J. Finger, illustrated by James Daugherty. Published by McKay, New York. Illustration: size $5\frac{1}{2}'' \times 6\frac{1}{4}''$.

1916. *Belgium* by Hugh Stokes, illustrated by
Frank Brangwyn. Published by Kegan Paul,
Trench, Trübner and Co. Ltd, London. Printed by
Spottiswoode Ballantyne and Co. Ltd, Colchester.
12″ × 9″. Illustration.

Frank Brangwyn (b. 1867 d. 1956), once reckoned as a giant amongst artists,
is today hardly remembered. His mural paintings, at one time covering acres
of wall space, now lurk in provincial galleries, his railway posters, heroic in
conception, re-appear almost apologetically in anthologies of commercial art.
His working career spanned over half a century and included working for
William Morris on tapestry designs. Brangwyn was already illustrating books
in the 1890's. In 1893 he worked on Robert Leighton's *The Wreck of the
Golden Fleece* for Blackie; in the next year, *The Cruise of the Midge* by Michael
Scott; and in 1896, S. R. Crockett's *Our Coast* for Chatto and Windus. Most
of his book illustration was of sea, ships and ports; his media ranged from oil
painting to pen drawing and wood engraving. His dark, sombre, often melo-
dramatic drawings will surely one day be appreciated again.
There has been an American tradition of sea painting based on first hand
observation that dates at least from the time of Winslow Homer, who used to

1930. *Moby Dick or the Whale* by Herman Melville. Illustrated by Rockwell Kent. Published by Random House in New York and by Cassell and Co. Ltd, London. Printed by R. R. Donnelley and Sons. 7" × 5⅜". Full page illustration.

[4] See *300 years of American Painting*. Alexander Eliot. Time Inc. New York, 1957.

work from an open ended shack down on the beach at Prout's Neck on the coast of Maine.[4] Rockwell Kent has had plenty of first hand observation of the sea. This illustrator, much of whose work has a kind of factory-production-line look about it, was a consummate book designer. His books have a unity; the rather mechanical looking illustrations, line drawings done in the manner of a steel engraving with evenly ruled lines to suggest receding tones in the sky, match the even lines of type. Kent's most interesting illustrations were drawn for his own travel books, but he has illustrated a number of other books, including an effective edition of Chaucer's *Canterbury Tales* in 1934 for the Garden City Publishing Co., New York. The full page illustrations for this book were of single figures, in Kent's simple engraved technique, printed in black and brown. Rockwell Kent is most widely known for his illustrations to *Moby Dick,* which was published first as a three-volume edition by the Lakeside Press, and in 1930 in a smaller format in one volume.

CHAPTER XXXVI                    THE QUARTER-DECK

[*Enter Ahab: Then, all*]

IT was not a great while after the affair of the pipe, that one morning shortly after breakfast, Ahab, as was his wont, ascended the cabin-gangway to the deck. There most sea-captains usually walk at that hour, as country gentlemen, after the same meal, take a few turns in the garden.

Soon his steady, ivory stride was heard, as to and fro he paced his old rounds, upon planks so familiar to his tread, that they were all over dented, like geological stones, with the peculiar mark of his walk. Did you fixedly gaze, too, upon that ribbed and dented brow; there also, you would see still stranger foot-prints —the foot-prints of his one unsleeping, ever-pacing thought.

← 230 →

But on the occasion in question, those dents looked deeper, even as his nervous step that morning left a deeper mark. And, so full of his thought was Ahab, that at every uniform turn that he made, now at the main-mast and now at the binnacle, you could almost see that thought turn in him as he turned, and pace in him as he paced; so completely possessing him, indeed, that it all but seemed the inward mould of every outer movement.

"D'ye mark him, Flask?" whispered Stubb; "the chick that's in him pecks the shell. T'will soon be out."

The hours wore on;—Ahab now shut up within his cabin; anon, pacing the deck, with the same intense bigotry of purpose in his aspect.

It drew near the close of day. Suddenly he came to a halt by the bulwarks, and inserting his bone leg into the auger-hole there, and with one hand grasping a shroud, he ordered Starbuck to send everybody aft.

"Sir!" said the mate, astonished at an order seldom or never given on ship-board except in some extraordinary case.

"Send everybody aft," repeated Ahab. "Mast-heads, there! come down!"

When the entire ship's company were assembled, and with curious and not wholly unapprehensive faces, were eyeing him, for he looked not unlike the weather horizon when a storm is coming up, Ahab, after rapidly glancing over the bulwarks, and then darting his eyes among the crew, started from his stand-point; and as though not a soul were nigh him resumed his heavy turns upon the deck. With bent head and half-slouched hat he continued to pace, unmindful of the wondering whispering among the men; till Stubb cautiously whispered to Flask, that

← 231 →

1930. *Moby Dick or the Whale* by Herman Melville. Illustrated by Rockwell Kent. Published by Random House in New York and by Cassell and Co. Ltd, London. Printed by R. R. Donnelley and Sons. 7″ × 5⅜″. Chapter opening with illustration and tailpiece.

This second version, a chunky little book (860 pages), was beautifully printed by R. R. Donnelley under the supervision of William A. Kittredge, at the Lakeside Press, Chicago. The drawings may be hard and mannered but it is still a stupendous piece of illustration. All the details of a working sailing craft were familiar stuff to Kent, and beyond this, there is a mystic streak that runs through his work, enabling him, if not to match Melville's magnificent prose, at least to give some pictorial substance to this allegory. Maybe no sperm whale ever reached to the stars as the one illustrated over the page does. Melville makes one feel it could and Kent has recaptured the mood.

Rockwell Kent's travel books began with *Wilderness*, a journal written on Fox Island, Alaska during the winter of 1918–19; his next book was *Voyaging* (1924), a description of a journey in a sailing boat southwards from the Straits of Magellan. These were succeeded half-a-dozen years later by *N by E* and in 1936 by *Salamina*. *N by E* was a most successful example of book design; within its limits, perhaps the most complete, well-balanced piece of book production ever to come out of the U.S.A. From its coarse sailcloth cover, clearly and boldly blocked with a forceful design of a compass rose, and its well-fitting case, to the excellent presswork and perfect balance of illustrations with type, *N by E* is an utterly professional piece of work. These Arctic or Antarctic climes suited Kent's way of drawing, or maybe he drew as he did because of those, cold, clear, bare land and seascapes.

*Godthaab*     [ I ]     *Late July*

IT IS but an hour or two before midnight and I am sitting on a hill above the little settlement of Godthaab. The sun has nearly set and the red beauty of its light is on the land.

I look over the rolling grassy hills of the foreground, at the stark mountains towering at my back; I look over the calm fiord toward far off peaks clear cut against the glowing sky. It is a breathless evening, breathless! And so profoundly beautiful that it is hard to bear alone. And from the settlement comes laughter and the dance music of the accordion.

So I descend to the village and go to the carpenter-shop where the dance is being held. Crowds of young Greenlanders are there; the place is packed. The girls dressed in their finest stand all in a row. They wear bright colored worsted caps, broad bead-work

∗ 189 ∗

1930. *N by E* by Rockwell Kent, designed and illustrated by the author. Published by Putnam, New York (after a Limited Edition from Random House) and by Cassell and Co. Ltd, London.

Printed by the Lakeside Press, Chicago. 8¼″ × 5⅝″. Case-binding, frontispiece, title-page and illustration page.

1893. *Goblin Market* by Christina Rossetti.
Illustrated by Laurence Housman. Published by
Macmillan and Co. Ltd, London. Printed by
R. & R. Clark, Edinburgh. $7\frac{1}{8}'' \times 4\frac{1}{8}''$.
Illustration spread and text page.

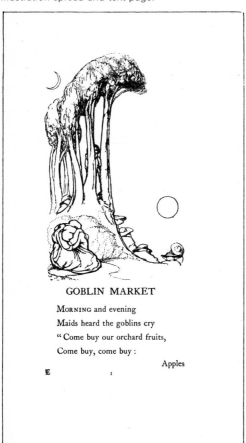

### GOBLIN MARKET

MORNING and evening
Maids heard the goblins cry
"Come buy our orchard fruits,
Come buy, come buy :
            Apples

## Art nouveau and decorative book illustration

Art nouveau had a marked influence not only on English book design but also, on English book illustration. In 1893–4, Laurence Housman, poet and artist, illustrated two books for Macmillan: *The End of Elfintown* by Jane Barlow and *Goblin Market* by Christina Rossetti. *Goblin Market*, mentioned on page 24, is an interesting, strange piece of book production. Housman's sister engraved, most skilfully, her brother's delicate, swirling lines, and R. & R. Clark printed them impeccably. There is a haunted feeling about them, in which the slack curves of art nouveau play some considerable part.

Other English illustrators working in an art nouveau manner included R. Anning Bell, T. Sturge Moore and Aubrey Beardsley. The latter, a brilliant artist (he was only twenty-five when he died), crammed a fantastic amount of work into the six years of his working life, from the time he left his job as an insurance clerk to his death in 1898.

During the short time he was working with the Guardian Life and Fire Assurance Company, Beardsley used to visit Jones and Evans's book shop just off Cheapside. Here he met Frederick Evans, who was most impressed both with the young man and with his drawings. Evans introduced him to the young publisher, J. M. Dent, and, the result was a contract for Beardsley to illustrate Malory's *Le Morte d'Arthur*. This was a tremendous task of illustration, for there were over three hundred and fifty separate drawings, one on almost every spread. Critics have usually dismissed Beardsley's *Le Morte d'Arthur* as immature, or even as hack work; yet if he had never illustrated another book, this edition of *Le Morte d'Arthur* could stand as a monument of decorative book illustration. Heavily influenced by the Kelmscott books of William Morris and to a lesser extent by Burne-Jones's illustrations, Beardsley already stands as a decorative master in his own right. The borders to his full page illustrations are as virile as Morris's, yet with a strong feeling of art nouveau. His figure

148

1894. *Le Morte d'Arthur* by Sir Thomas Malory.
Illustrated by Aubrey Beardsley. Published by
J. M. Dent and printed by Turnbull and Spears,
Edinburgh. 10″ × 7¾″. The illustrations are
reproduced from the second edition published
in 1909. Illustration spread; and chapter
opening decoration.

drawings, with their massed black and white spaces, are Japanese inspired,
yet possess some of the qualities of a Bonnard or a Lautrec poster. And
through all his work, there is that peculiar *fin de siècle* brooding quality; not
that the creatures of his imagination, unsexed or hermaphrodite, did not have
plenty to brood about.

In *Le Morte d'Arthur* Beardsley learnt his job, but the result is no bungling
student's work. Some of these designs (he never called his drawings
illustrations) stand as models of economy, none is impoverished.

A work that started almost in homage to Morris ended, as Sir Kenneth Clark
has said, as a macabre parody of the Kelmscott style.[5]

[5] From a lecture first given at the Aldeburgh
Festival in 1965.

1894. *Salomé* by Oscar Wilde, illustrated by Aubrey Beardsley. Published by Melmoth and Co., London. $8\frac{1}{2}'' \times 6\frac{5}{8}''$. The illustrations and sketch for the cover design are reproduced from the 1904 edition. This cover design was later used for *Under the Hill*, published by John Lane in 1904.

6 *The Life of James McNeill Whistler* by Elizabeth and Joseph Pennell.

The American artist and critic, Joseph Pennell, on first seeing Beardsley's work, wrote a glowing tribute in the first number of *The Studio*. The result of this was a commission from John Lane to illustrate Oscar Wilde's play *Salomé*. This, perhaps the most feeble of Wilde's plays, had enjoyed a *succès de scandale,* for Sarah Bernhardt was to have appeared in it before the play was banned. Beardsley's drawings, amongst the best he ever did, are a complete send-up; a witty, erotic commentary to Wilde's text.

*Salomé* resulted in Beardsley's appointment to the art editorship of *The Yellow Book* (see page 15) and after that, to *The Savoy*. The first number of this periodic volume included his drawings for his own rococo novel, *Under the Hill*; in the second number of *The Savoy*, appeared the first of his drawings for *The Rape of the Lock,* the forerunner of a most beautiful set of decorative pen drawings. If with *Le Morte d'Arthur* he had learnt his job, with the drawings for *The Rape of the Lock* he had reached a brilliant maturity, and all this within three years. The Pennells described how James McNeill Whistler, who had been no Beardsley fan, on seeing these drawings, turned to him and said, 'Aubrey, I have made a very great mistake — you are a very great artist'. And the boy burst out crying.[6]

Beardsley by this time was famous, though regarded by many as the very essence of decadence. As a consumptive, his desperate hold on life intensified his every action. His influences were mainly literary, and he was completely self-taught. Beardsley was the prince of decorators and I suppose a failure as an illustrator *per se*; his decorations overwhelmed, but how magnificently, his authors' texts.

In spite of Beardsley, or perhaps because of him, the art nouveau influence on English book illustration lasted for only a short time. One illustrator who was strongly affected by the movement was Robert Anning Bell, whose *The Tempest* (1901) is heavily decorated with art nouveau motifs and borders. By the First World War the movement had petered out.

1896. *The Savoy*. No. 2 an illustrated quarterly,
edited by Arthur Symons. Published by Leonard
Smithers, London. 10″ × 7⅝″. Illustration by
Aubrey Beardsley for *The Rape of the Lock*.

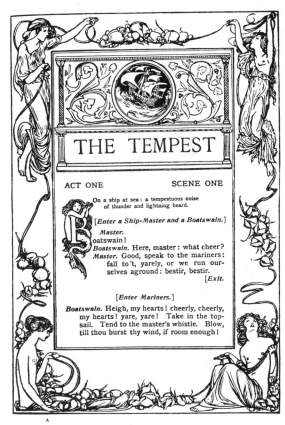

1901. *The Tempest* by William Shakespeare, decorated by Robert Anning Bell. Published by Freemantle and Co., London. Printed by T. and A. Constable, Edinburgh. 9½" × 6¾".

1923. *A Box of Paints* by Geoffrey Scott, illustrated by Albert Rutherston. Published by the Bookman's Journal, London. Printed by the Curwen Press, Plaistow. 9½" × 6¾". Illustration.

[7] *Modern Book Illustration in Great Britain and America.* Edited by C. Geoffrey Holme and published by The Studio, London and New York, 1931.

Albert Rutherston (brother of Sir William Rothenstein, one time principal of the Royal College of Art) was also an avowed decorator. His little, coloured line drawings, often of nubile young women, made charming decorations for *A Box of Paints*, a book of poems by Geoffrey Scott published in 1923, and for the Sitwells' *Poor Young People,* which the Fleuron published in 1925. This quarto was beautifully manufactured by the Curwen Press and contained sixteen coloured drawings by Rutherston.

Decoration, rather than illustration, has had only a precarious hold on English books and their publishers. Rex Whistler, however, made good use of mock-eighteenth-century architectural borders in many of his book jackets and in his splendid Cresset Press edition of *Gulliver's Travels* (1930).

This book is a most remarkable achievement. Here are pastiche eighteenth-century engravings, actually drawn by pen and reproduced and printed by flat-bed photo-gravure. The reproductions are printed in just the sepia colour an engraving would have and plate-sunk, to boot! The hand colouring at least is hand-coloured. Yet, though there is plenty for graphic purists to denounce, the result is one of the most handsome illustrated books ever to be printed in this country. And the illustrations are ravishing. The frontispiece to Volume 1 depicts a delightful scene outside a dockside, clapboard, bow-windowed pub, set in a rococo border of dolphins, spars and guns, supported by a mermaid and her merman. As this has been reproduced at least once before,[7] I have chosen a plate from Volume II illustrating *A Voyage to Laputa.* In all these illustrations, Whistler limited his colour (soft blues, pinks and yellows) to the scene within his architectural borders. These were left in monochrome. All Whistler's illustrations had a decorative quality, even the little vignetted head and tail pieces. One of the last books he illustrated was James Agate's *Kingdoms for Horses,* which Victor Gollancz published in 1936, and on the title-page of which is printed: 'With decorations by Rex Whistler'. No mention here of illustration.

The Lord Munodi
takes him in his chariot
to see the town of LAGADO.

Rex Whistler 1930.

1930. *Gulliver's Travels* by Jonathan Swift D.D. illustrated by Rex Whistler. Published by the Cresset Press and printed by the Oxford University Press. Edition limited to 195 copies on hand-made paper. Illustration: 'The Lord Munodi takes him in his chariot to see the town of Lagado' (From Volume II *A Voyage to Laputa*).

1934. *A.B.C. of the Theatre* by Humbert Wolfe, illustrated by Edward Burra. Published by the Cresset Press. Printed by Robert MacLehose and Co. Ltd, Glasgow. 9¾″ × 7⅜″. Cover and illustration spread.

32

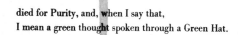

died for Purity, and, when I say that,
I mean a green thought spoken through a Green Hat.

1934. *Good Savouries* by Ambrose Heath
illustrated by Edward Bawden. Published by
Faber and Faber, London. Printed by
R. MacLehose and Co. Ltd, Glasgow. 7⅜″ × 4¾″.
Title-page.

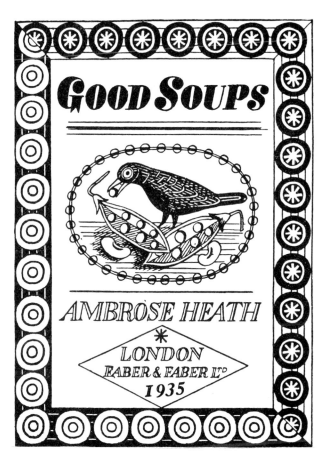

1935. *Good Soups* by Ambrose Heath illustrated
by Edward Bawden. Published by Faber and
Faber, London. Printed by R. MacLehose and Co.
Ltd, Glasgow. 7⅜″ × 4¾″.
Title-page.

1935. *Good Soups* by Ambrose Heath
illustrated by Edward Bawden. Cover design
from lino cuts printed in two colours.

That decoration and humour can go hand-in-hand can be seen in the work of both Burra and Bawden in England, and such artists as Ludwig Bemelmans and Artzybasheff in the U.S.A. As far as I know *A.B.C. of the Theatre* is Edward Burra's only excursion into book illustration; the rest of his working life has been devoted to painting, often religious painting, and always with a great intensity of feeling. His illustrations to Humbert Wolfe's witty lampoons are in a very different vein. There are slight shades of Georg Grosz in some of the drawings but the book as a whole is a success. It had decorated initials designed by Kathryn Hamill and was published by the Cresset Press in 1934. Edward Bawden has illustrated many books, ranging from *Good Food, Good Soups* and *Good Savouries* for Faber in the 1930's to an interesting *Gulliver's Travels* for the Folio Society, a fine edition of *The History of Herodotus* for the Limited Editions Club, and a beautiful set of lithographs of Portugal for *English as she is Spoke* for the Lion and Unicorn Press. He is not only a witty, satirical draughtsman but also a superb decorative craftsman, particularly in his handling of lino cuts. His title-pages for the Ambrose Heath cookery books, drawn fifty years ago, still stand as perfect examples of decorative economy, both in their simplicity of line and in the unfaltering use of the line block.

155

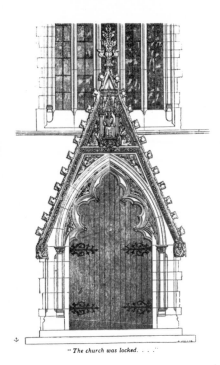

*Lines suggested by an advertisement in "The Guardian"*
*(The Broad Church newspaper)*

HE church was locked, so I went to the incumbent—
the incumbent enjoying a supine incumbency—
a tennis court, a summerhouse, deckchairs by the
walnut tree
and only the hum of the bees in the rockery.
" May I have the keys of the church, your incumbency ? "
" Yes, my dear sir, as a moderate churchman, I
am willing to exchange : light Sunday duty :
nice district : pop 149 : eight hundred per annum :
no extremes : A and M : bicyclist essential
same income expected."
" I think I'm the man that you want, your incumbency.
Here's my address when I'm not on my bicycle,
poking about for recumbent stone effigies—
14, Mount Ephraim, Cheltenham, Glos :
Rector St. George-in-the-Rolling Pins, Cripplegate :
non resident pop in the City of London :
eight fifty per annum (but verger an asset) :
willing to exchange (no extremes) for incumbency,
similar income, but closer to residence."

17

" *The church was locked.* . . . "

1937. *Continual Dew* by John Betjeman.
Published by John Murray, London. Printed by
William Clowes and Sons Ltd, London. 8″ × 5⅞″.
Illustration spread.

1938. *Pillar to Post* written and illustrated by
Osbert Lancaster. Published by John Murray,
London. Printed by Butler and Tanner Ltd,
Frome. 9¼″ × 6⅝″. Illustration: 'Gothic Revival'.

1939. *Homes Sweet Homes* written and illustrated by Osbert Lancaster. Published by John Murray, London. Printed by Butler and Tanner Ltd, Frome. 9¼″ × 6⅝″. Illustration: 'Art Nouveau'.

1933. *My Life and Hard Times* by James Thurber. Published by Penguin Books, Middlesex. Printed by Hunt, Barnard and Co. Ltd, London. 7″ × 4⅜″. Illustration: 'One night while doing the dishes . . .'

## Humour and genre

The master of *genre* illustration is Osbert Lancaster, the wittiest of all architectural draughtsmen. His *Pillar to Post* appeared in 1938 and *Homes Sweet Homes* in 1939, both published by John Murray. These books are a joy, leading one through a couple of thousand years of domestic architecture and manners, and enriching the English language with such styles as 'Stockbroker Tudor' and 'By-pass Variegated'. Osbert Lancaster's observation, apart from his wit, is acute, his sense of period almost faultless and his commentary profound.

John Betjeman's *Ghastly Good Taste* (1933) does very much in words what Lancaster does in pictures. The illustration 'the Church was locked . . .' comes from his 'little book of bourgeois verse', called *Continual Dew*. It is, quite apart from the quality of the verse, and its subject matter (which varies from architecture to church livings), a splendid Dada-Surrealist joke. It has a book-jacket by E. McKnight Kauffer, showing a dripping tap, a black-and-gold case-binding, which makes it look like a Victorian prayer book, and pages illustrated with the oddest selection of old engravings and modern drawings. If John Betjeman and Osbert Lancaster typify both English humour and English tradition, James Thurber's drawing (which needs no comment from me) can speak volumes for America and most fittingly bring this chapter — about English and American traditions in illustration — to a close.

1902. *Le Procurateur de Judée* by Anatole France illustrated by Eugène Grasset and engraved on the wood by Ernest Florian. 7½" × 5½". Black line woodcut.

## 6. THE WOOD ENGRAVING REVIVAL IN FRANCE AND ENGLAND

The belief in the importance of printing both type and illustration in the same operation was one of the factors in the wood engraving revival. This revival began in France, mainly through the work of trade engravers such as Beltrand, Froment, Bellenger and Florian. Maurice Denis was one of many French artist-illustrators who owed much to his engravers. For *Les Petites Fleurs* by St Francis of Assisi for Rouart et Watelin, he drew his designs on the woodblock and they were engraved by Jacques Beltrand. Paul Gauguin was one of the first artists actually to cut his own woodblocks – for his manuscript book *Noa Noa*. When he was in Paris in 1893, between his voyages to Tahiti, he showed his manuscript to the poet Charles Morice, and with Morice's help the text was published in *La Revue Blanche* in 1901 and, later in the same year, in a single volume.

Gauguin returned to Tahiti and began to enlarge and enrich his original manuscript with watercolour drawings, woodcuts and even a few photographs. From this manuscript, now in the Louvre, various facsimiles have been reproduced and printed. The woodcuts, of particular interest, are a very clear forerunner of the white line engraving that was such a feature of the twentieth-century revival of the craft. The French and English trade engravers were trained to produce black line engravings, by cutting away the wood up to the edge of the drawn black line. This is of course incomparably more difficult than white line engraving, and a denial of the proper use of a burin.

In the year 1902, the publisher Édouard Pelletan wrote in a foreword to *Le Procurateur de Judée*: 'Le livre est avant tout un texte. Le texte se manifeste par la typographie. Donc, le livre, est avant tout, une manifestation typographique . . .' These would hardly have been Vollard's sentiments, even though he brought his first book to the Imprimerie Nationale, who had been responsible for printing *Le Procurateur de Judée*; they were much nearer to the ideas of Ricketts or Morris, Updike or Rogers. French illustrated books, when Pelletan started publishing in 1896, were lacking what another French publisher, Léon Pichon, called 'any directing intelligence'. The woodcut or wood engraving had, by 1900, become an essential part of the typographic conception of a properly illustrated book. Morris's engraved decorations, Ricketts's cuts, Pissaro's coloured woodcuts were all partly responsible for

COMMENT SAINT FRANÇOIS, POUR UNE MAUVAISE PENSÉE QU'IL EUT CONTRE FRÈRE BERNARD, COMMANDA AUDIT FRÈRE BERNARD QUE TROIS FOIS LUI MARCHAT AVEC LES PIEDS SUR LA GORGE ET SUR LA BOUCHE

E très dévot serviteur du Crucifix, monsieur saint François, par l'âpreté de la pénitence et continuel pleurer, était devenu presque aveugle, et à peine voyait la lumière. Une fois entre autres il se partit du couvent où il était, et alla à un couvent où était frère Bernard, pour parler avec lui des choses divines : et venant au couvent, trouva qu'il était dans la forêt en oraison, tout élevé

*c.* 1907. *Les Petites Fleurs* by St Francis of Assisi illustrated by pen drawings on wood by Maurice Denis, engraved by Jacques Beltrand. Published by Rouart et Watelin, Paris.

158

*c.* 1900. *Noa Noa, Voyage de Tahiti* by Paul
Gauguin and C. Morice. Facsimile of Paul
Gauguin's manuscript, published in Dresden in
1926. Printed by Marée-Gesellschaft Druck.
13″ × 10″. White line woodcut.

the belief that only the raised surface of box or pearwood could match the
varied surfaces of fine typefaces. Félix Bracquemond in his *Étude sur la
Gravure sur Bois,* published in 1897, stressed the need for unity in a page,
which would only be attained by the woodcut, made up of clear whites and
rich blacks: no half-tones, no cluttering up the pages with ornament.
Bracquemond concluded, 'the fundamental constituent is the white of the
paper'.
The artists who first followed these precepts most faithfully were Raoul Dufy
and André Derain.

1909. *L'Enchanteur Pourrissant* by Guillaume
Apollinaire illustrated with 31 woodcuts by
André Derain. Published by Henry Kahnweiler,
Paris. Printed by Paul Birault. 10½" × 8". Woodcut.

In 1909 Derain illustrated with woodcuts *L'Enchanteur Pourrissant,* by
Apollinaire, which was published by the art dealer Henry Kahnweiler. This
was Kahnweiler's first publication; later he was to rival Vollard in the splendour
of his books and the quality of the artists he employed. *L'Enchanteur Pourrissant* was also Derain's first attempt at illustration. These bold, simple
designs were cut with a knife along the grain of a soft wood plank.
In 1911, Dufy engraved a vivid *Le Bestiaire,* also for Apollinaire. The original
edition of 122 copies sold badly[1] but two fascimile editions were produced

[1] On 3 May 1966 in a sale at Sotheby's of
'Modern French and German Illustrated Books', a
copy of this edition of *Le Bestiaire* was sold for
£1,800.

160

# LA CARPE.

Dans vos viviers, dans vos étangs,
Carpes, que vous vivez longtemps !
Est-ce que la mort vous oublie,
Poissons de la mélancolie.

1911. *Le Bestiaire ou Cortège d'Orphée* by
Guillaume Apollinaire. With 39 woodcut
illustrations by Raoul Dufy. Published by
Deplanche, Paris and limited to 122 copies.
Printed by Gauthier-Villars. 13″ × 10¼″.
Woodcut: 'La Carpe'.

later, the first (in a smaller format) by Éditions de la Sirène, Paris, in 1919; the
second by Éditions du Cap, Monte Carlo in 1956. The rich black prints of
animals were the forerunners of a great number of French, English and
American books illustrated in the same manner. Derain and Dufy could not
be contained for long by the black and white block, even though theirs was
pioneer work in the revival of wood engraving. Explosive, rich colour was to
be their means of expression.

1921. *Vénus et Adonis* by William Shakespeare with wood engravings by Roger Grillon. Published and printed by Léon Pichon, Paris. Text page and wood engraving.

1927. *Paradise Lost* by John Milton with woodcut illustrations by D. Galanis and initial letters by Anna Simons. Published by the Cresset Press. Printed at the Shakespeare Head Press, Oxford. 14″ × 10″. Designed by Bernard Newdigate. Opening page with wood engraving.

*c.* 1920. *Thaïs* by Anatole France. Woodcut illustration by Emile Charles Carlègle. Reproduced from *Carlègle* by M. Valotaire, published by Henry Babou, Paris. 5⅞″ × 4⅝″ size of illustration.

It is a curious fact, but it would seem that few if any of the English wood engravers were familiar with either Derain's *L'Enchanteur Pourrissant* or Dufy's *Le Bestiaire*. John Nash, a founder member (in 1920) of the English Society of Wood Engravers, in discussing this said, 'As far as I know none of us were aware that either Dufy or Derain had ever cut a block or illustrated a book. If one looked back at all, it was to Ricketts and Lucien Pissarro'.

In France many artists, of varying abilities, were soon willing and happy to cut and gouge the end grain of boxwood, or the side grain of pear or cherry. Émile Charles Carlègle, a Swiss who had lived in Paris since 1900, engraved an effective *Daphnis et Chloë* for Léon Pichon in 1913, which owing to the war was not published until 1919. Carlègle specialized in sinuous nudes, white bodies against dark backgrounds; the woodcut was the perfect medium for such modest eroticism.

Publishers who followed Pelletan's lead were Helleu et Sargent (with whom he was associated), Henry Babou and Léon Pichon. Their success was short lived, even on the paperback level with books such as the 'Livre de Demain' series, published by Arthème Fayard for two francs fifty centimes, illustrated by such artists as Hermann Paul, Roger Grillon, Guy Arnoux and Paul-Émile Colin. I can remember these yellow paper-covered books, thirty years ago, amongst the 'remainder' stocks of the Charing Cross Road booksellers. Pelletan's ideals, and his ideas of the 'typographic book', so un-French in their unexuberant attitude, survived his death by barely two decades.

c. 1925. *Mitsou* by Colette illustrated with wood engravings by Hermann Paul. Published by Arthème Fayard and Co., Paris. Printed by l'Imprimerie Bellenand. 9¼″ × 7⅜″. Cover design and woodcut

Covers for the paper-back series 'Le Livre de Demain'.

c. 1925. *La Bataille* by Claude Farrère illustrated with wood engravings by A. Roubille. Published by Arthème Fayard and Co., Paris. Printed by l'Imprimerie Bellenand. 9¼″ × 7⅜″. Cover design.

c. 1925. *Mitsou* by Colette; wood engraving by Hermann Paul.

1927. *The Chester Play of the Deluge* edited by
J. Isaacs with woodcut illustrations by David
Jones. Published and printed by the Golden
Cockerel Press. 12″ × 9½″. Wood engraving.

The book to encompass the work of artists such as Matisse or Rouault needs
almost to burst the bounds of book-making. There is no place here for the
subordination of such artists to the limitations of text or the wood block.

The revival of interest in wood engraving in England can be traced at least
as far back as the occasional periodical, *The Dial*, which was published by
Ricketts and Shannon between 1889 and 1897, and in which they showed not
only their own cuts, but also the work of Lucien Pissarro and T. Sturge Moore.
Another pioneer, working in Florence in the years before the First World War
was Gordon Craig who cut with the knife, along the grain of soft fruit wood,
the illustrations for *Hamlet* and *The Merchant of Venice*.

1924. *Genesis* with wood engraved illustrations by Paul Nash. Published by the Nonesuch Press – the first book from this press. Printed by the Curwen Press in an edition of 375 copies. 10½" × 7½". Wood engraving.

1927. *Poisonous Plants* by W. Dallimore, edited by Dr A. W. Hill, FRS. With wood engravings by John Nash. Published by Frederick Etchells and Hugh Macdonald, London. Printed by the Curwen Press, Plaistow. 12" × 7½". Wood engraving: 'The Horned Poppy'.

1924. *Directions to Servants* by Jonathan Swift D. D., with wood engravings by John Nash. Published and printed by the Golden Cockerel Press. 10" × 7½". Wood engraving: 'Directions to the coachman'.

In 1905, Noel Rooke who like his fellow-student, Eric Gill, had started engraving by this time, was appointed teacher of book illustration at the Central School of Arts and Crafts in London. It was not until 1912, after some opposition, that Rooke was permitted to teach the craft to his students, amongst them Robert Gibbings, who was later to play a great part in the movement, both by his own engraving and by his ownership of the Golden Cockerel Press.

In 1920, the Society of Wood Engravers was formed, amongst whose original members were Lucien Pissarro, Gordon Craig, Gill, Robert Gibbings and John Nash. (The last named, though inspired by his brother Paul to take up the craft, was self taught.)

But the commercial publishers in England were slow to make use of this perfect medium for book illustration, and it was left to the private presses to be the first to exploit this sudden burst of talent. In 1924 Paul Nash did a fine set of engravings for the Nonesuch edition of *Genesis*, which was set in Rudolf Koch's Neuland typeface, producing very much the effect of a block book.

In 1924 John Nash engraved some rather droll cuts for the Golden Cockerel Press edition of Swift's *Directions to Servants*, and two years later the same artist engraved twenty very fine illustrations for *Poisonous Plants,* which was printed by the Curwen Press. The attitude of both John and Paul Nash was similar to that of Derain and Dufy; they were of the modern movement, more interested in design than in representation. However, John Nash's obsession with flowers and plants gives an added authority to the engravings in *Poisonous Plants;* the 'Horned Poppy' is a vivid engraving, evoking in its background the windswept shingle banks of the North Sea. In 1927 David Jones, the Welsh painter, illustrated *The Chester Play of the Deluge* for the Golden Cockerel Press with appropriate and beautifully designed engravings.

1931. *Canticum Canticorum*. With wood engravings and initials by Eric Gill. Published by Insel-Verlag and printed by the Cranach Press, under the direction of Count Harry Kessler. Set in a version of Jenson's roman specially cut for the Cranach Press by E. P. Prince. $10\frac{1}{4}$" × $5\frac{1}{8}$". Wood engraving.

I cannot feel enthusiastic about Eric Gill's cuts for the Golden Cockerel's edition of *The Canterbury Tales,* which is spoilt by the insensitive post art nouveau vegetable forms that droop about the pages.

Gill's engravings for *Canticum Canticorum* for Count Harry Kessler's Cranach Press in Germany are, on the other hand, quite delightful. Gill had a healthy liking for the female body and was a very skilful engraver. Blair Hughes-Stanton, another artist interested in the human form, was working at the Gregynog Press in Montgomeryshire between 1931–4. Here he illustrated six books with wood engravings of a delicacy and fineness of line that was quite new to the craft – a delicacy that also made very considerable demands on his pressmen. I suppose that Hughes-Stanton and Gill were the best craftsmen in this English wood engraving revival, though Gill never attempted the intricacies that Hughes-Stanton took in his stride. The fineness of the latter's white line engravings has to be seen in the original, where they are printed on a smooth, cream-coloured Japanese vellum, with impeccable presswork, most sparely inked. No photographic process, however perfect, will reproduce these originals with complete fidelity.

SEINT Urban, with his deknes, prively
The body fette, and buried it by nighte
Among his othere seintes honestly.
Hir hous the chirche of seint Cecilie highte;
Seint Urban halwed it, as he wel mighte;
In which, into this day, in noble wyse,
Men doon to Crist and to his seint servyse.

WHAN ended was the lyf of seint Cecyle,
Er we had riden fully fyve myle,
At Boghton under Blee us gan atake
A man, that clothed was in clothes blake,
And undernethe he hadde a whyt surplys.
His hakeney, that was al pomely grys,
So swatte, that it wonder was to see;
It semed he had priked myles three.
76

1929. *The Canterbury Tales* by Geoffrey Chaucer, illustrated with wood engravings by Eric Gill. Set in Caslon Old Face. Published and printed by the Golden Cockerel Press in 4 volumes. 12" × $7\frac{1}{2}$". Text page with illustration.

ARCADES

1933. *Four Poems* by John Milton illustrated
with wood engravings by Blair Hughes-Stanton.
Published and printed by the Gregynog Press.
10″ × 6½″. Wood engraving: 'Arcades'.

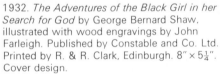

1932. *The Adventures of the Black Girl in her Search for God* by George Bernard Shaw, illustrated with wood engravings by John Farleigh. Published by Constable and Co. Ltd. Printed by R. & R. Clark, Edinburgh. 8" × 5¼". Cover design.

Title-page.

² *Graven Image*: John Farleigh, Macmillan, 1940.

During these years, only slight use had been made by English commercial publishers of the wood engraving process. In 1932, however, Constables had a tremendous success with Bernard Shaw's *The Adventures of the Black Girl in her Search for God*, with wood engravings by John Farleigh. These engravings, influenced to some extent by both Gill and Blair Hughes-Stanton and certainly inspired by his author, are Farleigh's best work. They were printed most faithfully from electros by R. & R. Clark.

Farleigh has described at length² the wonders of working with Shaw, who provided rough sketches for many of the illustrations. His description of Shaw's meticulous supervision of his work makes fascinating reading and makes one wish there were a few more authors who could and would take as much interest in the illustrations and production of their books.

Farleigh may not have been a *great* illustrator, but he was a very good craftsman and Shaw provided 'the directing intelligence'. Shaw, too, was a consummate craftsman, who surprisingly permitted his illustrator to order him about in turn, to the tune of asking him to write more copy to fill out a page here and there. This collaboration, like Tenniel's with Lewis Carroll, added a unique quality to this beautiful little book. The endearing little black girl was a figment of Farleigh's imagination, for he never used a coloured model.

*The Black Girl* is a model example of book planning. It all began with George Bernard Shaw writing to John Farleigh in 1932 in these words:

168

'Pavlov sitting on a crocodile': John Farleigh's engraving.

'Pavlov sitting on a crocodile': sketch by Shaw.

Whitehall Court
8th May 1932

Dear Sir,

As I am old and out of date I have not the privilege of knowing you or
your work. But Mr William Maxwell, of Clark's of Edinburgh, tells me that
you can design, draw and engrave pictures as part of a printed book, which,
you will understand, is something more than making a picture and sticking
it into a book as an 'illustration'. The idea is that you and I and Maxwell
should co-operate in turning out a good-looking volume consisting of the
story contained in the enclosed proof sheets (please hold them as very
private and confidential) and, say, a dozen pictures. Are you sufficiently
young and unknown to read the story and make one trial drawing for me
for five guineas? That is, if the job interests you.

faithfully,

G. Bernard Shaw

1932. *Twelfth Night* by William Shakespeare illustrated with wood engravings by Eric Ravilious. Published and printed by the Golden Cockerel Press. Engravings printed in sepia and grey. 13" × 9¼" page size. Wood engraving reproduced same size.

1938. *The Writings of Gilbert White of Selborne* edited by H. J. Massingham, illustrated with woodcuts by Eric Ravilious. Published by the Nonesuch Press. 10" × 6¼". Tailpiece same size.

*Opposite:*
1938. *Cirque de l'Étoile Filante* written and illustrated with etchings and wood engravings by Georges Rouault. Published by Ambroise Vollard, Paris. Etchings printed by Roger Lacourière, text and wood engravings by Henri Jourde. 17¼" × 13¼". Wood engraving by Georges Aubert.

³ The only comparable illustrated *Selborne* is the edition which John Nash illustrated for the Lutterworth Press in 1951, which was later issued with colour added to the plates by the artist, by the Limited Editions Club of New York in 1972.

Whilst the English artists of the wood-engraving revival were engaged in the crafts of wood cutting and wood engraving, there was a return in France to the use of the professional engraver. One of these, Georges Aubert, was responsible for the engravings in one of the greatest private press books. This was Georges Rouault's *Cirque de l'Étoile Filante*, published by Vollard in 1938. Rouault started work on the designs for this book in 1930. There were a number of coloured etchings and no less than eighty-two large, rich, dark textured wood engravings.

The sheer page size of the Vollard books (17¼ in. by 13¼ in. for the *Cirque*) makes most of the English private press books look a little insignificant. The work of the English artist, Eric Ravilious, is certainly *not* insignificant. His first attempt at illustration by wood engraving was in 1932 for an edition of Shakespeare's *Twelfth Night*. His most successful, the edition of Gilbert White's *Natural History of Selborne* in 1938. Ravilious had a very firmly-developed sense of design, an attribute he shared with his friend Edward Bawden, and which is evident in all his engravings.³

Douglas Percy Bliss, the author of the definitive work on the history of wood engraving, illustrated *Border Ballads* for Oxford University Press in 1925 with appropriate Scottish fervour. These ballads, which Bliss had selected, offered admirable scope for his engravings and the book as a whole was also a pleasant piece of design for which the engravings make effective headpieces. Robert Gibbings took over the management of the Golden Cockerel Press in 1924 and ran it for some years. A great, jolly, bearded giant of a man, he was a talented engraver, the strength of whose work is in the clearly defined contrasts of black and white. His method of working was somewhat unusual. He would draw a pen or scraper-board approximation of a woodcut and have this photographed on to the wood block. This preliminary work often showed marked weaknesses of drawing which largely disappeared as soon as he started engraving; it was as if his burin possessed qualities of draughtsmanship that his pen knew nothing about.

171

### LITTLE MUSGRAVE AND LADY BARNARD

*O wow for day!*
*And, dear, gin it were day!*
*Gin it were day, and I were away—*
*For I ha' na lang time to stay.*

I

As it fell on one holy-day,
  As many be in the year,
When young men and maids together did go
  Their matins and mass to hear,

II

Little Musgrave came to the church-door—
  The priest was at private mass—
But he had more mind of the fair women
  Than he had of Our Lady's grace.

III

The one of them was clad in green,
  Another was clad in pall,
And then came in my Lord Barnard's wife,
  The fairest amongst them all.

( 30 )

### JOHNIE ARMSTRONG

I

S U M speiks of lords, sum speiks of lairds,
  And sick lyke men of hie degrie;
Of a gentleman I sing a sang,
  Sum tyme called Laird of Gilnockie.

II

The King he wrytes a luving letter,
  With his ain hand sae tenderly,
And he hath sent it to Johnie Armstrang,
  To cum and speik with him speedily.

III

The Eliots and Armstrangs did convene;
  They were a gallant cumpanie—
' We'll ride and meit our lawful King,
  And bring him safe to Gilnockie.'

IV

' Make kinnen and capon ready, then,
  And venison in great plentie;
We'll wellcum here our royal King;
  I hope he'll dine at Gilnockie! '—

( 47 )

1925. *Border Ballads* selected, and with wood engravings, by Douglas Percy Bliss. Published by the Oxford University Press. Printed by the Westminster Press. 9¾″ × 6″. Illustrated pages.

1966. *Two Stories: Come and dine and Tadnol:*
T. F. Powys, edited by Peter Riley. Published by
R. A. Brimmell, Hastings. With wood engravings
by Reynolds Stone. 8″ × 5½″. Wood engraving,
same size.

1952. *The Four Gospels* with wood engraving
illustrations by Reynolds Stone. Published by
Penguin Books Ltd, Middlesex. Headpiece,
same size.

In 1929 Houghton Mifflin sent Gibbings off to Tahiti to collaborate on a book about that island with James Norman Hall. Gibbings spent four months there collecting material, by which time Hall had become so involved in the saga of *The Mutiny on the Bounty* that he had to back out. As a result of this Gibbings wrote the text of *Iorana*, his first serious attempt at authorship. This was the forerunner by many years of his autobiographical illustrated writings, such as *Blue Angels and Whales* (Penguin Books 1938) and the series of 'river' books for Dent, beginning with *Sweet Thames run softly* (1940). His last work was appropriately called *Till I end my Song* (1957).

Reynolds Stone was trained as a printer at the Cambridge University Press (as a university graduate apprentice). Whilst still at Cambridge he spent a couple of weeks at Eric Gill's home learning the rudiments of wood engraving. Since 1934, when he forsook printing, Stone has devoted his time to wood engraving and to cutting letters. His engraved letters are always exquisite pieces of craftsmanship and on these his reputation stands; but his engraving covers wider fields than letter cutting. He has engraved many attractive head and tail pieces, very much on a Bewick scale, including the cuts for the Penguin edition of the *Four Gospels*.

Joan Hassall is the daughter of John Hassall, famous illustrator and poster artist. She is a skilled engraver, with a feeling for period illustration. In 1937 she illustrated *Portrait of a Village* by F. Brett Young for Heinemann. In 1940, Harrap published a new edition of *Cranford* with engravings by Miss Hassall, including an interesting engraved title-page with a portrait of Mrs Gaskell, and in 1947 she followed this up with *Our Village* by Mary Russell Mitford, also for Harrap.

*Opposite left:*
1934. *Beasts and Saints* by Helen Waddell
illustrated with woodcuts by Robert Gibbings.
Published by Constable and Co. Ltd, London.
Printed by Charles Whittingham and Griggs Ltd,
London. 8″ × 6″. Woodcut.

*Opposite right:*
1932. *Iorana a Tahitian Journal* by Robert
Gibbings, with wood engravings by the author.
Published by Houghton Mifflin, Boston and
New York. 9″ × 6¼″. Wood engraving:
'Pandanus Grove'.

1940. *Cranford* by Mrs Gaskell illustrated with
wood engravings by Joan Hassall. Published by
Harrap. Wood engraving, same size.

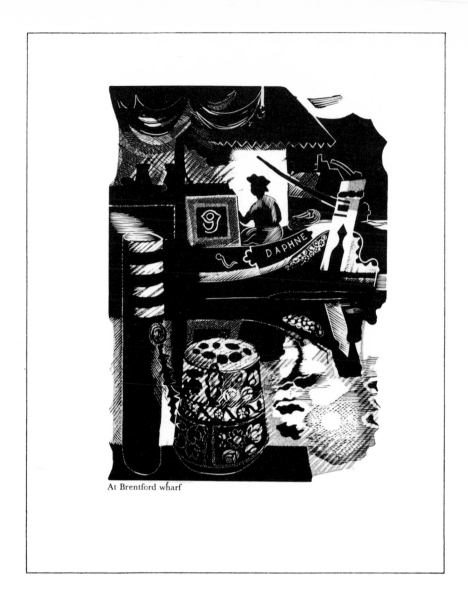

At Brentford wharf

1950. *Canals, Barges and People* by John
O'Connor with coloured wood engravings by the
author. Published by Art and Technics Ltd,
London. Printed by the Shenval Press. $8\frac{1}{4}'' \times 6\frac{3}{8}''$.
Coloured wood engraving.

The 1939–45 war broke the continuity of the English wood engraving revival.
The steam seemed to go out of the movement. Certainly during the time I was
teaching at the Royal College of Art (1950–63) there was only one notable
engraving student (David Gentleman). In the years before the war, the R.C.A.
had been a forcing house for them, when, in turn, the two Nashes and Eric
Ravilious were teaching there. John O'Connor was a pupil of Ravilious at that
time. One of the few notable books of engravings since the war is his *Canals,
Barges and People* written by the artist and designed by Robert Harling at
Art and Technics.

David Gentleman's first essay at wood engraving was in 1953. These
engravings were for a slim volume published by the Lion and Unicorn Press,
called *A Tale of Two Swannes*. His most ambitious book has been *The Swiss
Family Robinson* which was published by the Limited Editions Club, New
York, in 1963. These engravings had the addition of a second colour, which
had been hand drawn. In 1964 he illustrated *The Shepherd's Calendar* for the

174

MAY

Come queen of months in company
Wi all thy merry minstrelsy
The restless cuckoo absent long
And twittering swallows chimney song
And hedge row crickets notes that run
From every bank that fronts the sun
And swathy bees about the grass
That stops wi every bloom they pass
And every minute every hour
Keep teazing weeds that wear a flower
And toil and childhoods humming joys
For there is music in the noise

46

MAY

The village childern mad for sport
In school times leisure ever short
That crick and catch the bouncing ball
And run along the church yard wall
Capt wi rude figured slabs whose claims
In times bad memory hath no names
Oft racing round the nookey church
Or calling ecchos in the porch
And jilting oer the weather cock
Viewing wi jealous eyes the clock
Oft leaping grave stones leaning hights
Uncheckt wi mellancholy sights
The green grass swelld in many a heap
Where kin and friends and parents sleep
Unthinking in their jovial cry
That time shall come when they shall lye
As lowly and as still as they
While other boys above them play
Heedless as they do now to know
The unconcious dust that lies below
The shepherd goes wi happy stride
Wi morns long shadow by his side
Down the dryd lanes neath blooming may
That once was over shoes in clay
While martins twitter neath his eves
Which he at early morning leaves
The driving boy beside his team
Will oer the may month beauty dream
And cock his hat and turn his eye
On flower and tree and deepning skye

47

1964. *The Shepherd's Calendar* by John Clare
with wood engravings by David Gentleman.
Published and printed by the Oxford University
Press. 8" × 5". Text spread.

1964. *Peter Schlemihls Wundersame Geschichte*
by A. von Chamisso with wood engravings by
Imre Reiner. Published by Ars Librorum,
Frankfurt-am-Main. 8⅛" × 4⅞" page size, printed
on one side of the paper only. Pages folded and
uncut. Tailpiece: 3⅝" high.

Oxford University Press. This is an attractive book, with a set of most effective engravings, designed as headpieces to each month of the calendar, that give it a very agreeable scale. The engraving in no way overpowers the text.
This wood-engraving revival that started in France and flowered in England never made much headway in the United States. One or two expatriate German artists, such as Fritz Eichenberg and Hans Mueller, have engraved a number of illustrated books for the Limited Editions Club, but the medium has not been in much favour. Today it manifests itself in a livelier manner in Germany, Holland and Scandinavia, where the most potent influence has been Imre Reiner, a Hungarian trained in Germany and influenced to some extent by the German Expressionists. He is a completely cosmopolitan artist, utterly eclectic in his admiration for artists as diverse as Dürer and Bewick. Reiner has illustrated a number of books, making a most highly skilled use of multiple tool engraving. These include Goethe's *Novelle*, Voltaire's *La Princesse de Babilone* and Hugo von Hofmannsthal's *Andreas*.

1886. *Little Lord Fauntleroy* by Frances Hodgson
Burnett illustrated by Reginald B. Birch.
Published by Frederick Warne and Co., London.
Printed by Richard Clay and Sons, Bungay.
$8\frac{3}{8}'' \times 5\frac{3}{4}''$. Illustration: 'Are you the Earl?' said
Cedric, 'I'm your grandson. I'm Lord Fauntleroy'.

## 7.  THE ILLUSTRATION AND DESIGN OF CHILDREN'S BOOKS

Whatever the future may be for illustration generally, there will always be a place for it in children's books. Children's taste tends to be rather conservative; books that were old favourites when their parents were children often attract them. Whether fairy stories will have much of a hold in the space age may be doubted, but for younger children animal stories look a pretty safe bet. For older boys and girls, adventure stories may well be surpassed by stories of real adventure. Pirates and highwaymen may pale into insignificance when held up to comparison with moon dwellers and the activities of the modern criminal. And yet, I wonder. There seems to be an indefinite life ahead for the much loved little books of Beatrix Potter, and *Treasure Island* still 'holds children from play and old men from the chimney corner'.

If one looks back to the 1880's and '90's, English and American infants (or their mamas and nannies) were still happily turning over the pages of the picture books by Caldecott and Kate Greenaway, prettily printed in colour from wood blocks, most skilfully engraved by Edmund Evans. However, their tastes were changing; and in the late 1880's there was a spate of new successful children's books, many of them still in print today. I doubt if the American author Frances Hodgson Burnett has many readers for her *Little Lord Fauntleroy* (1886), though her charming *The Secret Garden* is still read widely.

In the 1890's boys still read R. M. Ballantyne's *The Young Fur Traders,* first published in 1856 as *Snowflakes and Sunbeams* (a singularly unpromising title that was quickly changed after the first edition).[1] The most successful writer of English school stories was an energetic young typefounder, by name Talbot Baines Reed, whose *The Willoughby Captains* and *The Fifth Form at St Dominic's* both appeared in 1887, and *The Cock House at Felsgarth* in 1891.

[1] *English Children's Books.* Percy Muir, Batsford, 1954.

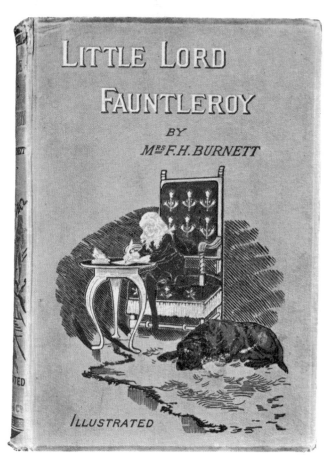

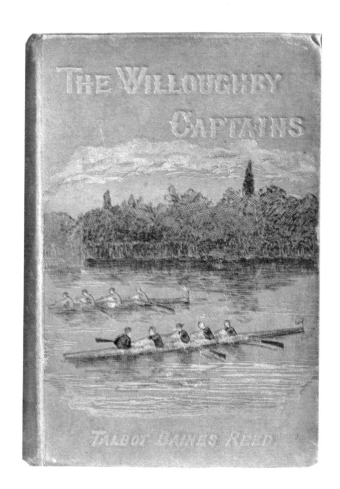

1886. *Little Lord Fauntleroy* by Frances Hodgson Burnett illustrated by Reginald B. Birch. Published by Frederick Warne and Co., London. Printed by Richard Clay and Sons, Bungay. $8\frac{3}{8}'' \times 5\frac{3}{4}''$. Case-binding, blocked in black, gold and brown on a grey cloth.

1887. *The Willoughby Captains* by Talbot Baines Reed illustrated by Alfred Pearse. Published by Hodder and Stoughton, London. Printed by Hazell, Watson and Viney Ltd, London. $7\frac{1}{4}'' \times 4\frac{3}{4}''$. Case-binding blocked in gold, black and colours on a grey cloth.

1894. *The Young Fur Traders* by Robert Michael Ballantyne. Published by T. Nelson and Sons, London. $7\frac{3}{8}'' \times 4\frac{7}{8}''$. Chromo-lithographed frontispiece and title-page by an anonymous artist.

1903. *With the British Legion* by G. A. Henty illustrated by Wal Paget. Published by Blackie and Sons, London, Glasgow and Dublin. $7\frac{3}{8}'' \times 5\frac{1}{4}''$. Half-tone illustration.

Ballantyne's staying power with his young readers, like Fenimore Cooper's and Marryat's a quarter of a century earlier, owed much to the authentic backgrounds of his books, and particularly of the Canadian arctic, for he had worked as a clerk in the Hudson Bay Company. Ballantyne also took a great deal of trouble over the illustrations for his books, preparing rough pen-and-wash drawings, with copious instructions for the engraver-illustrators.

Whatever one may think of *Little Lord Fauntleroy* as a story, it is certainly an attractive-looking book, with a prettily blocked cover and effective illustrations by the American Munich-trained illustrator, Reginald B. Birch. Joseph Pennell, writing in 1889, thought it was the best thing Birch had ever done.

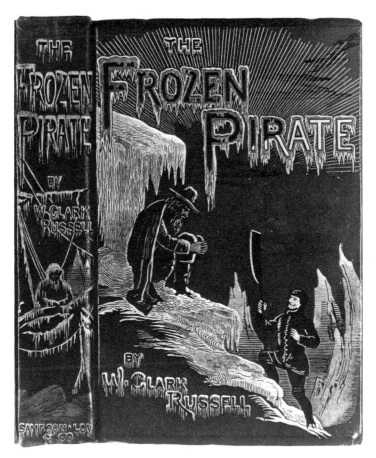

1888. *The Frozen Pirate* by W. Clark Russell illustrated by P. Macnab. Published by Sampson Low, Marston, Searle and Rivington, London. Printed by Gilbert and Rivington Ltd. $7\frac{3}{4}'' \times 5\frac{3}{8}''$. Case-binding blocked in gold and white on a dark green cloth. Scraper-board illustration.

## School and adventure stories

Most school stories are too subject to changing manners and times to outlive their period. The early successes in this field were *Tom Brown's Schooldays* (1887), and *Eric or Little by Little* (1858). *Tom Brown's Schooldays* was illustrated by Arthur Hughes and Sydney Prior Hall, and re-issued in 1896 with new illustrations by Edmund J. Sullivan. *Eric or Little by Little* by F. W. Farrar, first illustrated by the Dalziels, passed through thirty-six editions during Farrar's lifetime and, as Percy Muir said, 'achieved an immortality only of derision'.[2]

Most of Talbot Baines Reed's books appeared as serials in the *Boy's Own Paper,* which was published by the Religious Tract Society. His family had close connections with this pious body; but Reed's stories are anything but pious and his boys, drawn by Gordon Browne,[3] H. M. Paget and Alfred Pearse, are, unlike Dean Farrar's, very real boys. 'Between 1906 and 1952 no fewer than ten of his school stories were reprinted, including his first, *The Adventures of a Three Guinea Watch* (1880), and his last, *Tom, Dick and Harry* (1892).'[4]

G. A Henty followed Ballantyne as a writer of adventure stories. His books poured out in an apparently endless succession. He wrote something over ninety books for boys. These were illustrated by several artists, including Gordon Browne, H. M. Paget and Wal Paget – who illustrated, with wash drawings printed by half-tone, Henty's *With the British Legion* (1903). Nearly all these books had colourfully blocked or printed illustrations on their covers. *The Frozen Pirate* by W. Clark Russell is a good example of this kind of case-binding, and the illustrations for it by P. Macnab are an early example of the use of process half-tone, the plates showing considerable evidence of handwork. Until the '90's most children's books were illustrated by line, or line and wash reproduced by wood engraving. The intricately hatched wood blocks blended well with type, giving the books a most agreeable homogeneous quality. Chromo-lithography was widely used for books for young children, often with crude and garish colours, though the delicate title-page for *The Young Fur Traders* is an exception.

[2] *English Children's Books.* Percy Muir, Batsford, 1954.

[3] Gordon Browne was the son of Hablot K. Browne, the illustrator of so many of the novels of Charles Dickens.

[4] *Talbot Baines Reed*, Stanley Morison. Cambridge University Press, 1960 (privately printed). Also see P. M. Handover's article on Reed in *The Book Collector,* Spring 1963, with a list of his works.

1896. *Uncle Remus and his Friends* by Joel Chandler Harris illustrated by A. B. Frost. Published by James R. Osgood McIlvaine and Co., London. Printed by Ballantyne, Hanson and Co., London. 7½″ × 5″. Illustration.

1907. *The Tale of Tom Kitten* by Beatrix Potter. Published by Frederick Warne and Co. Ltd, London. 5½″ × 4″. Case-binding.

1904. *The Tale of Benjamin Bunny* by Beatrix Potter. Published by Frederick Warne and Co. Ltd, London. 5½″ × 4″. Illustration spread.

THAT wood was full of rabbit holes; and in the neatest sandiest hole of all, lived Benjamin's aunt and his cousins — Flopsy, Mopsy, Cotton-tail and Peter.

Old Mrs. Rabbit was a widow; she earned her living by knitting rabbit-wool mittens and muffetees (I once bought a pair at a bazaar). She also sold herbs, and rosemary tea, and rabbit-tobacco (which is what *we* call lavender).

15

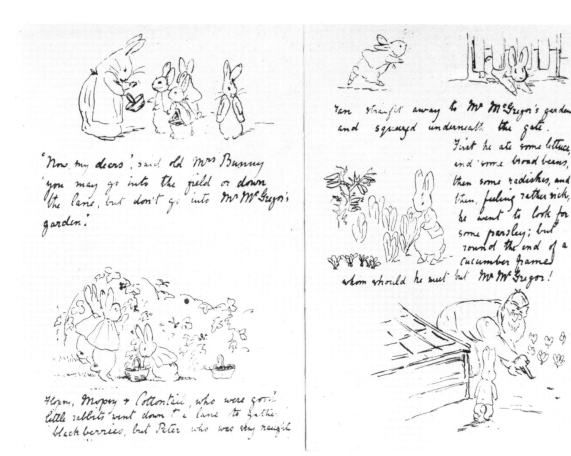

'Now, my dears', said old Mrs Bunny 'you may go into the field or down the lane, but don't go into Mr McGregor's garden.'

Flopsy, Mopsy & Cottontail, who were good little rabbits went down the lane to gather blackberries, but Peter who was very naughty

ran straight away to Mr McGregor's garden and squeezed underneath the gate.

First he ate some lettuce, and some broad beans, then some radishes, and then, feeling rather sick, he went to look for some parsley; but round the end of a cucumber frame whom should he meet but Mr McGregor!

1893. Facsimile of a letter to Noel Moore telling the original story of Peter Rabbit for the first time. Reproduced from *The Tale of Beatrix Potter* by Margaret Lane, published by Frederick Warne and Co., London and New York, 1946. Original size of letter $7\frac{3}{4}" \times 5\frac{1}{4}"$.

Beatrix Potter (b. 1866 d. 1943) was a natural illustrator. In her letters to her young friends, she expressed herself as freely by her drawings as in her words. That she should find such a perfect medium for her picture-stories in the three or four-colour half-tone medium is not surprising, for she was quite untutored in any of the autographic processes.

Beatrix Potter was also one of the first illustrators to make a really good use of this half-tone colour process. She was a 'natural', as a book designer as well as a book illustrator; with no training or printing experience she planned every detail of production and layout. Her first two books, *The Tale of Peter Rabbit* (1901) and *The Tailor of Gloucester* (1902), were printed at her own expense and privately published. General publication, in a revised form and with colour, followed, somewhat cautiously, from Frederick Warne who had previously rejected *Peter Rabbit*. *The Tale of Benjamin Bunny* came out in 1904 and *The Tale of Tom Kitten* in 1907.

The books were originally published at one shilling in paper-covered boards, and one-and-sixpence in a cloth binding. Both versions had a coloured illustration pasted down on the front cover.

Margaret Lane, in her excellent and most moving biography, extols Beatrix Potter's 'great sense of animal beauty, the imaginative truthfulness of her approach and her deeply felt beauty of the countryside'.[5]

Beatrix Potter's books are scaled carefully to a child's needs; they are little and they feel good. She had quite clear ideas of what a small child's book should be like. The books had to be about 5 in. by 4 in. with a coloured picture on every spread, and her text was always limited to no more than one or two simple sentences on each page. Beatrix Potter's rabbits, mice and hedgehogs, even if they are dressed up, are real animals; the illustrations have an intimate, close-up reality, a reality and a viewpoint familiar to any child's eye. Their appeal is just as great today as it was sixty odd years ago. Their anthropomorphism has had many followers and a few antecedents, such as various chapbook editions of Charles Perrault's *Puss-in-Boots*, or Joel Chandler Harris's *Uncle Remus*, published nearly half a century earlier than Beatrix Potter's books. A. B. Frost who illustrated *Uncle Remus* achieved as happy and indissoluble a union with his author as Tenniel had with Lewis Carroll. His animals, like Beatrix Potter's, were quite free from vulgarity.

[5] *The Tale of Beatrix Potter*. Margaret Lane, F. Warne.

1895. *The Blue Fairy Book* edited by Andrew Lang and illustrated by H. J. Ford and G. P. Jacomb Hood. Published by Longmans, Green and Co., London. Printed by Spottiswoode and Co., London. 7″ × 4¾″. Case-binding.

1895. *The Blue Fairy Book*, illustration by H. J. Ford.

1901. *Lion and Unicorn* by John Hassall. Reproduced from *Modern Pen Drawings: European and American*. 8″ × 11⅜″. Published by the Studio, London and New York.

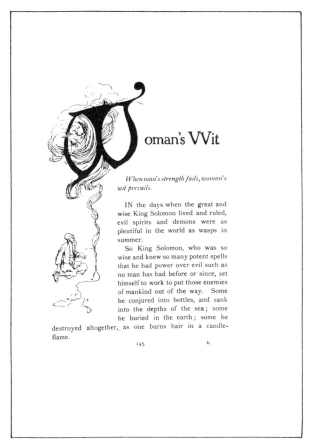

1896. *Twilight Land* written and illustrated by Howard Pyle. Published by J. Osgood McIlvaine and Co., London. Printed by Ballantyne, Hanson and Co., London. 8½″ × 5⅞″. Case-binding, chapter opening and illustration.

## Fairy stories

Andréw Lang's series of 'coloured' fairy books was the combined result of his great scholarship and much hard work on the part of his wife. Lang, who came from the border country and had been brought up in an atmosphere of legend and history, was not well served by his illustrators (H. J. Ford who illustrated many of his fairy stories was a feeble draughtsman). The books, however, were pleasantly produced and made a gay showing in their multiplicity of coloured covers. The 'Unicorn' drawing is by John Hassall, an English poster artist with a robust sense of humour – (his poster for the holiday resort of Skegness, of a bouncing fisherman, earned him wide fame). He also illustrated a number of children's books, many of pre-Tudor England. His work was influenced by Boutet de Monvel and other contemporary French illustrators. The 'Unicorn' drawing was done before 1900, but he was still at work in the 1930's. When I was a very young student, I visited him in his studio, which was just like a junk shop, there was so much bric-à-brac lying about. I can remember he showed me how to draw an ear!

Howard Pyle, an American artist who achieved a tremendous reputation in his lifetime, drew in a variety of styles, ranging from the stiff lines of a Dürer engraving to the sketchy impressionism of Daniel Vierge. His first successful book was *The Merry Adventures of Robin Hood*, which came out in 1883. *Twilight Land*, both written and illustrated by Howard Pyle, was first published in England in 1896, by Osgood McIlvaine, a publishing house with a record for producing interesting illustrated books. It is filled with amusing line illustrations, pleasantly set on the page with a lot of white space around them. The typography of the book, presumably by Pyle himself, is less successful; each chapter is headed with somewhat grotesque, very large initial letters and the title-page is decorated with rubrics.

Both *The Blue Fairy Book*, with 390 pages and *Twilight Land*, with 370 pages, really gave young readers something to get their teeth into. And with their heavily blocked, smooth blue cloth covers and gilded heads, they were books to treasure.

1900. *The Bunkum Book* by Aubrey Hopwood illustrated by Maud Trelawny. Published by Frederick Warne and Co., London and New York. Printed by Morrison and Gibb Ltd, Edinburgh. 9" × 11⅞". Illustration.

Undated. *Hauff's Fairy Tales* translated and adapted by Cicely McDonnell. Illustrated by Fritz Bergen. Published by Dean and Sons Ltd, London. 7⅛" × 5⅜". Case-binding.

'The parrot is a Polly Bird,
The Owl a Melancholly Bird,
But I'm the Cockiolly Bird,
And that's a Rara Avis!'

By the 1890's process engraving was in wide use, and the new generation of illustrators was only too eager to see its drawings appear unaltered by the hand of the trade engraver. (Amongst the illustrators of children's books, Howard Pyle was one of the first to make use of the four-colour half-tone.) However, the chromo-lithographers, particularly in Germany, France and the United States, were still very active, and continued to be so well into the twentieth century. *Hauff's Fairy Tales,* translated from the German by Cicely McDonnell, had a technically ingenious illustrated cover, lithographed and blocked in heavy relief; and Fritz Bergen's coloured drawings for it were also chromo-lithographed. *The Bunkum Book* by Aubrey Hopwood, the author of *The Sleepy King,* with chromo-lithographed illustrations after drawings by Maud Trelawny, is a strange, poetic creation, almost worthy of Lewis Carroll. The 'Cockiolly Bird' was a favourite in many British and American nurseries in the first decade of this century.

Florence and Bertha Upton's series of 'Golliwogg' books (there were ten of them) was also published in the United States and England at the beginning of the century. They are the most endearing inventions, very prettily lithographed. The text is hand drawn in an interesting art nouveau letter, so precisely done it could be mistaken for type.

Gordon Browne was a most versatile illustrator. As well as drawing the pictures for G. A. Henty's adventure stories and Mrs Ewing's books, he also illustrated several books for very young children, including an edition of *Rip van Winkle* in 1887. Twenty years later, he completed a set of watercolour drawings for *The Merry Tales of the Wise Men of Gotham.* This little book was chromo-lithographed sympathetically by Van Leer in Amsterdam, a printing firm of distinction which is still engaged in the printing of illustrated books.

1903. *The Golliwogg's Bicycle Club* by Bertha Upton with illustrations by Florence K. Upton. Published by Longmans, Green and Co., London, New York and Bombay. Printed by the Niagara Lithographic Co., Buffalo, New York. 8¾″ × 11⅛″. Illustration.

1907. *The Merry Tales of the Wise Men of Gotham* by F. J. Harvey Darton illustrated by Gordon Browne. Published by Wells Gardner, Darton and Co. Ltd, London. Printed by L. van Leer and Co., Netherlands. 7¼″ × 6½″. Cover and illustration.

"They all splashed into the water."

1905. *Rip van Winkle* by Washington Irving illustrated by Arthur Rackham. Published by William Heinemann, London, and Doubleday, Page & Co., New York. Printed by Richard Clay and Sons Ltd. 9⅞" × 7". Case-binding, illustration and title-page.

RIP VAN WINKLE

BY·WASHINGTON
IRVING
ILLUSTRATED·BY
ARTHUR·RACKHAM

LONDON: WILLIAM·HEINEMANN
NEW·YORK: DOUBLEDAY·PAGE·&·C°

As the twentieth century advanced, and with it the popular acceptance of the three- and four-colour half-tone process, the 'gift' book (virtually the 'Coffee Table' book for children) arrived on the scene, or at least on the nursery table. Arthur Rackham was the most successful English artist in this field; the muted tones and delicate tints of his water-colour drawings combined well with his strong feeling for the grotesque. The 'gift' books were really something for a child to receive. They were heavy and thick, with beautifully blocked covers, they often had a coloured illustration mounted on the front cover, and gilded heads, ornamental headbands and coloured end papers. Inside there would be colour plates, tipped-on to cartridge mounts and protected with tissue. These books were precious objects, to be looked at with awe and handled with care. Among those illustrated by Rackham were *Rip van Winkle* (1905), followed by *Peter Pan in Kensington Gardens* and *Alice in Wonderland*. W. Heath Robinson and his two brothers, and Edmund Dulac also made good use of 'process' and illustrated a number of 'gift' books. Heath Robinson's *The Water Babies* (1915) is full of pretty colour plates and whimsical line drawings, which owe just a little to Beardsley, and which were, at least to me when I was very young, much more acceptable than those in the Linley Sambourne edition. Violent prejudices can develop in one's tender years; I must admit that my affection for Heath Robinson's work may largely be governed by having had his *The Water Babies* and his own *Bill the Minder* (1912) in my nursery. He had a strange, innocent and very personal sense of humour which appeared in all his drawings; also, like Beardsley, he was expert at disposing of massed areas of white or black in his illustrations, as in the drawing here of Mr Grimes and Tom setting off at 3.0 a.m. on a summer's morning for Harthover Place. *Bill the Minder* is full of the strangest fancies, and just as in *The Water Babies,* there is the odd contrast of grotesque black-and-white drawings and very pretty watercolours. That the artist's name should have become a part of the English language has nothing to do with these illustrations. The term 'Heath Robinson' derives from a series of drawings he published in the 1920's in the weekly magazines — drawings of incredibly involved mechanical contrivances designed to solve the simplest problems.

186

## THE WATER BABIES

that that made up for his poaching Sir John's pheasants ; whereby you may perceive that Mr. Grimes had not been to a properly-inspected Government National School.

Now, I daresay, you never got up at three o'clock on a midsummer morning. Some people get up then because they want to catch salmon, and some because they want to climb Alps, and a great many more because they must, like Tom. But, I assure you, that three o'clock on a midsummer morning is the pleasantest time of all the twenty-four hours, and all the three hundred and sixty-five days ; and why everyone does not get up then, I never could tell, save that they are all determined to spoil their nerves and their complexions by doing all night what they might just as well do all day. But Tom, instead of going out to dinner at half-past eight at night, and to a ball at ten, and finishing off somewhere be-tween twelve and four, went to bed at seven, when his master went to the public-house, and slept like a dead pig, for which reason he was as pert as a game-cock (who always gets up early to wake the maids), and just ready to get up when the fine gentlemen and ladies were just ready to go to bed.

AND SOME BECAUSE THEY
WANT TO CLIMB ALPS.

6

ON THEY WENT.

1915. *The Water Babies* by Charles Kingsley illustrated by W. Heath Robinson. Published by Constable and Co. Ltd, London. Printed by Bradbury Agnew and Co. Ltd, London. 8¼″ × 6⅜″. Text and illustration spread.

1912. *Bill the Minder* written and illustrated by W. Heath Robinson. Published by Constable and Co. Ltd, London. 9⅝″ × 7⅛″. Printed by T. & A. Constable Ltd, Edinburgh. Illustration.

THE MUSICIAN

1935. *Fairy Tales and Legends* by Hans
Andersen illustrated by Rex Whistler. Published
by Cobden-Sanderson Ltd, London. Printed by
the Shenval Press and bound by the Leighton-
Straker Bookbinding Company Ltd. Page size
8″ × 5⅜″. Illustrations and case-binding.

*The Marsh King's daughter.*

From the 1890's the old favourites, *The Arabian Nights* and the stories of the
brothers Grimm and Hans Andersen, were meeting increasing competition in
the nurseries.

Jacob and Wilhelm Grimm's fairy tales were first published in England in
1823; the first Hans Andersen English translation appeared in 1846. Both
books have been through dozens of editions, with a variety of illustrators. The
best of the Grimm editions was probably the first English illustrated edition,
with George Cruikshank's vivid etchings, and the best Hans Andersen an
edition charmingly decorated by Rex Whistler and first published in 1935.

Whistler's Hans Andersen (which is still in print) is a pretty book, bound in a
green cloth cover,[6] lettered in gold, with an arabesque pattern, blocked in
pale yellow, the same pattern being used for the endpapers. For the illustrations, Whistler used scraper-board with great refinement.

[6] In some editions, the colour of the cloth and
blocking varied.

Gerda and Kay: *The Snow Queen.*

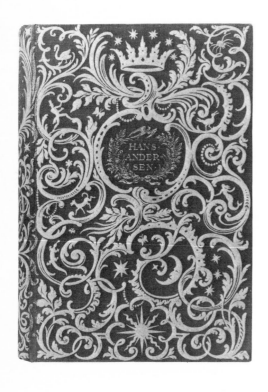

*Do you see yonder rock, & the large cave?
said the East Wind*

1935. *Fairy Tales and Legends* by Hans
Andersen illustrated by Rex Whistler. Published
by Cobden-Sanderson Ltd, London. Printed by
the Shenval Press and bound by the Leighton-
Straker Bookbinding Company Ltd. Page size
8″ × 5⅜″. Illustration: *The Garden of Paradise.*

# Wild·Animals·I·Have·KnowN

·and·200·Drawings·

by

Ernest Thompson Seton

NATURALIST·TO·THE·GOVERN-
MENT·OF·MANITOBA·AUTHOR·OF·
BIRDS·OF·MANITOBA
MAMMALS·OF·MANITOBA
ART·ANATOMY·OF·ANIMALS
TRAIL·OF·THE·SANDHILL·STAG
BIOGRAPHY·OF·A·GRIZZLY·
LIVES·OF·THE·HUNTED

Being the Personal Histories of
Lobo
Silverspot
Raggylug
Bingo
The Springfield Fox
The Pacing Mustang
Wully
and Redruff

PUBLISHED·BY·HODDER·&·STOUGHTON·LONDON·1920

1898. *Wild Animals I have Known* written and illustrated by Ernest Thompson Seton. Designed by Grace Thompson Seton. Published by Hodder and Stoughton, London. Printed by the Scribner Press, New York. $7\frac{7}{8}'' \times 5\frac{1}{2}''$. Title-page reproduced from the 1920 edition.

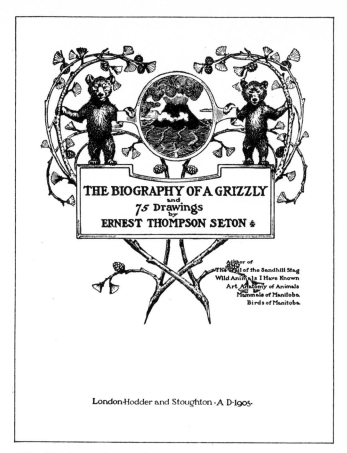

THE BIOGRAPHY OF A GRIZZLY
and
75 Drawings
by
ERNEST THOMPSON SETON

Author of
The Trail of the Sandhill Stag
Wild Animals I Have Known
Art Anatomy of Animals
Mammals of Manitoba
Birds of Manitoba

London·Hodder and Stoughton·A·D·1905·

1900. *The Biography of a Grizzly* by Ernest Thompson Seton. Published by Hodder and Stoughton, London. Printed in the United States by the De Vinne Press, New York. $7\frac{1}{2}'' \times 5\frac{3}{4}''$. Title-page reproduced from the 1905 edition.

1899. *The Trail of the Sandhill Stag* by Ernest Thompson Seton. Published by David Nutt Ltd, London. Printed by the De Vinne Press, New York. $7\frac{1}{2}'' \times 5\frac{3}{4}''$. Half-tone illustration.

## Animal stories

In 1898, just over two years before any of Beatrix Potter's books appeared, the first of a series of wild-life books by the American naturalist, Ernest Thompson Seton, was published. The attitude of this author and artist was very different to that of Beatrix Potter or A. B. Frost. He was certainly no anthropomorphist. Seton illustrated his stories of wild animals with most lively, realistic pen drawings and also with wash drawings. The animals jump and run and scutter through the pages of his books, which are themselves interesting pieces of design. They were conceived and laid out by his wife, Mrs Grace Gallantin Thompson Seton, with spacious, open cream-coloured pages, and wide margins, dotted with illustrations. Mrs Seton also drew out the most elaborate asymmetric title pages.

*Wild Animals I have Known* (1898), *The Trail of the Sandhill Stag* (1899), *The Biography of a Grizzly* (1900) and *Animal Heroes* (1905) were perhaps the most successful of Seton's works. *Wild Animals I have Known* and *Animal Heroes* were bound in a mossy green cloth and blocked in a darker green or in gold. Ernest Thompson Seton, who incidentally signed his drawings 'Ernest Seton-Thompson', was Naturalist to the Government of Manitoba. His books have endeared him to succeeding generations of American and English children. Though the main credit for their success must go to Seton's realistic approach to wild life and his easily read prose, his wife's part as designer of these most attractive-looking books was by no means negligible. Mrs Seton not only designed the books, but was also responsible for the general make-up and the literary revision. The feeling of space and air that runs through these books reflects something of Seton's writing about the 'Old-timers of the Big Plain of Manitoba', to whom *The Trail of the Sandhill Stag* was dedicated. This book was most beautifully printed by the De Vinne Press in New York.

## Badlands Billy

big and strong; the weaker must move out, and with them Yellow Wolf and the Dusky Cub.

Wolves have no language in the sense that man has; their vocabulary is probably limited to a dozen howls, barks, and grunts expressing the simplest emotions; but they have several other modes of conveying ideas, and one very special method of spreading information—the Wolf-telephone. Scattered over their range are a number of recognized "centrals." Sometimes these are stones, sometimes the angle of cross-trails, sometimes a Buffalo-skull—indeed, any conspicuous object near a main trail is used. A Wolf calling here, as a Dog does at a telegraph post, or a Muskrat at a certain mudpie point, leaves his body-scent and learns what other visitors have been there recently to do the same. He learns also whence they came and where they went, as well as something about their condition, whether hunted, hungry, gorged, or sick. By this system of registration a Wolf knows where his friends, as well as his foes, are to be found. And Duskymane, following after the Yellow Wolf, was taught the places and uses of the many

124

## Badlands Billy

signal-stations without any conscious attempt at teaching on the part of his foster-mother. Example backed by his native instincts was indeed the chief teacher, but on one occasion at least there was something very like the effort of a human parent to guard her child in danger.

The Dark Cub had learned the rudiments of Wolf life: that the way to fight Dogs is to run, and to fight as you run, never grapple, but snap, snap, snap, and make for the rough country where Horses cannot bring their riders.

He learned not to bother about the Coyotes that follow for the pickings when you hunt; you cannot catch them and they do you no harm.

He knew he must not waste time dashing after Birds that alight on the ground; and that he must keep away from the little black and white Animal with the bushy tail. It is not very good to eat, and it is very, very bad to smell.

Poison! Oh, he never forgot that smell from the day when the den was cleared of all his foster-brothers.

125

1898. *Wild Animals I have Known* written and illustrated by Ernest Thompson Seton. Published by Hodder and Stoughton, London. Printed by the Scribner Press, New York. 7½″ × 5½″. Dedication page and text spread.

This Book
Is Dedicated

To Jim

1931. *The Wind in the Willows* by Kenneth Grahame. Illustrated by Ernest H. Shepard. Published by Methuen and Co. Ltd, London. 8½" × 5½".
Illustration: 'Toad stared fixedly in the direction of the disappearing motor car'.

1926. *Winnie-the-Pooh* by A. A. Milne. Illustrated by Ernest H. Shepard. Published by Methuen and Co. Ltd, London. Printed by Jarrold and Sons Ltd, Norwich. 7⅞" × 4¾". Illustration spread.

30    WINNIE-THE-POOH

So he took hold of Pooh's front paws and Rabbit took hold of Christopher Robin, and all Rabbit's friends and relations took hold of Rabbit, and they all pulled together. . . .
And for a long time Pooh only said "*Ow!*" . . .
And "*Oh!*" . . .
And then, all of a sudden, he said "*Pop!*" just as if a cork were coming out of a bottle.

*The Wind in the Willows* by Kenneth Grahame, often described as 'the best-loved children's book of the twentieth century', was first published in 1908, with a rather improbable frontispiece by Graham Robertson.
Illustrated editions followed, the first by Paul Branson in 1913, the next by Nancy Barnhart in 1922 and a third by Wyndham Payne in 1927. It was not until 1930 that an illustrated edition appeared, with drawings by an artist whose work pleased the author. This was Ernest H. Shepard, who was really in sympathy with this whimsical story of Rat, Mole, Badger and Toad, and their doings on the upper reaches of the Thames. Kenneth Grahame died before Shepard had finished his drawings, but not before he had seen enough of the sketches to recognize his little animals as he felt they should be drawn, without any sense of caricature. Shepard's pen drawings for *The Wind in the Willows* are completely successful, except possibly for Mole, who is obviously a difficult subject; Toad is a masterly piece of characterization. Shepard is a most talented draughtsman, whose work has always been full of charm.
Shepard had previously illustrated Kenneth Graham's *The Golden Age* in 1928 and *Dream Days*, by the same author in 1930, both published by John Lane. *The Wind in the Willows* with his drawings, now in paperback form, has passed its 105th edition. The coloured illustrations that were added to a recent hard-backed edition are less successful.
A return to the not-so-real animal book was A. A. Milne's *Winnie-the-Pooh*, which was one of the great, popular successes of the 1920's. This and the succeeding books about Pooh and Christopher Robin were appropriately illustrated in delicate lines by Ernest H. Shepard. The immense success they had, called forth not only wonder but also psychological investigation from a later and less assured generation – an attitude foreshadowed by Dorothy Parker when she wrote in a review of one of these books: 'Here tonstant weader fwowed up'! In spite of the jibes, these were pretty books, nicely cased and blocked and charmingly illustrated.

192

1894. *Le Bon Roy Henry* by A. Hermant Job.
Published and printed by Alfred Mame and
Son, Tours. 8¾" × 10½". Illustration spread.

## A new look for children's books from France

One of the French contributions to the design and illustration of twentieth-century children's books has been to free the illustrator from the limitations of line blocks and four-colour process. The English publishers' almost total reliance on letterpress printing, at least up to the beginning of the Second World War, was one limiting factor, their lack of courage in this field an even more inhibiting one. The French since the early years of the nineteenth century have been much freer in their use of lithography, gravure, the intaglio processes, and later *pochoir* (the use of stencils) and even the *Jean Berté* process, where the illustrations were printed from rubber blocks with water-colour inks.

In France, by the end of the nineteenth century, lithography had almost completely usurped letterpress printing for the illustration of children's books. Boutet de Monvel's albums, *Nos Enfants, Jeanne d'Arc* and *Chansons de France*, were all illustrated in line and colour and printed by the lithographic press.

A. Hermant Job, the illustrator of *L'Épopée du Costume Militaire*, used the same methods of line and colour for his *Le Bon Roy Henry* (1894). Job, like so many French illustrators, was a very fluent, if literal, draughtsman. Some of his drawings in this book (particularly the one of the assassin François Ravaillac being torn apart by four horses, or the one of a distraught mother being served up with her own baby in a soup tureen, with a large pot of mustard to help it down), are pretty tough fare for the young. The same tradition in draughtsmanship can be seen in the work of Edy Legrand, particularly in his line and *pochoir* drawings for *Bolivar* and *La Fayette*.

In 1919, in rather a different vein, Edy Legrand wrote and illustrated *Macao et Cosmage,* for Éditions de la Nouvelle Revue Française. This was a large square book, printed in black line and stencilled colours, with a hand-written text. It is a gay, boldly drawn, colourful book, whose rather mannered drawings are very much of their time. *Macao et Cosmage* (page 197) was

193

Le 23 mai, comme elle se trouvait à Crespy, elle apprit que la ville de Compiègne était serrée de près par les Anglais et les Bourguignons. Elle s'y porta avec quatre cents combattants et entra dans la ville le 24, à la pointe du jour. Puis, prenant avec elle une partie de la garnison, elle attaqua les Bourguignons. Mais les Anglais vinrent l'assaillir. Les Français reculèrent. « Ne pensez qu'à férir sur eux, criait Jeanne, il ne tient qu'à vous qu'ils soient déconfits! » Mais Jeanne fut entraînée par la retraite des siens. Ramenés sous les remparts de Compiègne, les Français trouvèrent le pont levé et la herse baissée. Cependant, Jeanne, acculée aux fossés, se défendait toujours. Une troupe s'était jetée sur

1896. *Jeanne d'Arc* by M. Boutet de Monvel.
Published by E. Plon, Nourrit et Cie, Paris.
Gravure printed by Ducourtioux and Hulliard,
text by E. Plon. 9″ × 12⅝″. Illustration spread.

something quite new in cheap book production and made a lively contrast to insipid watercolours, printed in three- or four-colour half-tone or the repellent chromo-lithography still in use at that time. Nothing like this had appeared in England or the U.S.A.

One of the first French publishers to produce books of this kind for children was a Parisian printer called A. Tolmer, the author of *Mise en Page.*

In 1921, Tolmer published *Voyages et glorieuses découvertes des Grands Navigateurs et Explorateurs Français* (overleaf). It was vividly illustrated by Legrand and superbly printed by Tolmer with stencilled colours, the variety of these colours and their freshness and subtlety being quite beyond the photographic processes. One of the sadder developments in printing, is the loss of such simple methods; *pochoir* may yet be revived, but almost certainly only for costly and limited editions. In 1929 Tolmer published Edy Legrand's

elle. « Rendez-vous ! » lui criait-on. « J'ai juré et baillé ma foi à un autre qu'à vous, répondait la brave fille, et je lui tiendrai mon serment ! » Mais en vain elle résistait. Tirée par ses longs habits, elle fut renversée de son cheval et prise. Du haut des remparts de la ville, le sire de Flavy, gouverneur de Compiègne, assistait à sa capture. Il ne fit rien pour lui porter secours.

*Bolivar* and *La Fayette*, two attractive books in a landscape format. The drawings were in line, with transparent stencil colours, and the arbitrary placing of the colours and the sensitive line drawings combined to produce a pleasantly fresh effect. Legrand has a natural feeling for placing illustrations on a page. He has illustrated many books for children, including *Line en Nouvelle Calédonie* (1934) for Calmann-Lévy. A year later, in 1935, for the same publisher, he illustrated and designed Madeleine Ley's *La Nuit de la St Sylvaine,* in which the sensitive line of the earlier books had become a little stereotyped. However Edy Legrand over a long career has contributed much to French book illustration, and particularly to the illustration of children's books: *Grands Navigateurs* and *Macao* are far more inventive in their sweeping use of colour than almost anything that has appeared since.

1921. *Voyages et Glorieuses Découvertes des
Grands Navigateurs et Explorateurs Français* by
Edy Legrand. Published by A. Tolmer, Paris.
$14\frac{3}{4}'' \times 10\frac{3}{4}''$. Illustration.

...ILS PURENT TERMINER LA MAISON OÙ ILS VOULAIENT VIVRE..

1919. *Macao et Cosmage* written and illustrated
by Edy Legrand. Published by Nouvelle Revue
Française. Printed by Bellenand, Fontenay-aux-
Roses. Hand coloured by Saude. $13\frac{3}{8}'' \times 12\frac{1}{8}''$.
Illustration.

destiné à être promptement réprimé. La France,
qui n'avait jusqu'alors témoigné qu'une sym-
pathie très vive pour les insurgés, prit nettement
fait et cause pour les Américains.
Elle leur envoya sans tarder subsides
et munitions. Ce n'était pas encore
suffisant pour obtenir un résultat
définitif. La Fayette revint alors en
France pour solliciter de nouveaux
secours. Il fut fêté, acclamé, devint
un héros populaire. Il
représentait une idée
chère à la Nation.

*« Antoine l'Enragé » enlève à
l'assaut une forteresse réputée
imprenable.* Le roi le reçut
et l'écouta avec la
plus grande bienveillance, mais l'état
des finances et de l'armée française
empêchait le souverain de prendre
une décision. Habile diplomate,

*Combats à l'abordage.
Défaite des Espagnols sur l'Orénoque.*

au soleil. Beaucoup s'enfuirent. Il faut la flamme de Bolivar pour entraîner les plus
fidèles. Ces hommes à moitié nus, sortant de la forêt tropicale, se trouvent en
quelques jours au milieu d'un désert de glace. L'ascension prend vite l'aspect d'une
vision de cauchemar. Les précipices engloutissent des bataillons entiers.
La faim, la maladie déciment les soldats du Libérateur. Ils réussissent
cependant à traverser la montagne. Bolivar tombe à
l'improviste sur les Espagnols qu'il écrase à Boyaca.
La magnifique victoire de Carabobo le rendait maître
de la Colombie. Il va au Pérou. Admirablement secondé
par le général Sucre, il est vainqueur à Ayacucho (1824).
Il fait prisonnier le vice-roi, est nommé Président de
la République.
Bolivar remonte à cheval....
La Bolivie, l'Équateur sont affranchis....

*La traversée des Andes.*

Opposite:
1929. *Bolivar* written and illustrated by Edy
Legrand. Published and printed by Tolmer,
Paris. 8¼″ × 9⅝″. Cover and spread.

Opposite:
1929. *La Fayette* written and illustrated by Edy
Legrand. Published and printed by A. Tolmer,
Paris. 8¼″ × 9⅝″. Cover and spread.

1934. *Scaf le Phoque* by Lida with lithographed
illustrations by Rojankovsky. Published by
Flammarion, Paris, in the series Albums du Père
Castor. 8¼″ × 9″. Cover.

1934. *Panache l'Écureuil* by Lida with
lithographed illustrations by Rojankovsky.
Published by Flammarion, in the series Albums
du Père Castor. 8¼″ × 9″. Text and illustration
spread.

In the 1930's a Russian, called Feodor Rojankovsky, working in Paris, lithographed some colourful books for Flammarion. This series, called '*Albums du
Père Castor*', is still in print.

They were in a landscape format, similar to Legrand's *Bolivar* and *La Fayette*,
and were the forerunners of the English Puffin Picture Books. Rojankovsky
(he signed his work Rojan) was a skilful lithographer. His earlier books, such
as *Panache* (1934), were full of gay, lighthearted drawings of squirrels and
pine martens. His *Scaf* (1936) was a rather more ambitious book, with
exciting scenes of arctic seas and the Northern Lights, in which the animals
are still observed without sentimentality. His later work, drawn for American
publishers, has become somewhat vulgar.

Du matin au soir, ils
sautent et dansent sur les
branches. Ils se lancent des
pommes de pin, jouent à
cache-cache, se poursui-
vent comme des enfants.
Et leurs petits yeux vifs
luisent comme des perles
noires. Un beau jour, au
milieu de leurs jeux, Rouquette dit à Quick :

— Et maintenant
assez joué, mon petit mu-
seau. Il est grand temps
que nous nous occupions
de préparer un nid pour
nos enfants. Quelque
chose me dit qu'ils ne vont
pas tarder à naître. Notre
vieux gîte ne vaut plus

4

rien. Je veux que nos petits aient le plus beau nid du monde. Mais il
ne nous tombera pas du ciel! Cherchons. Je vais parcourir toute la forêt,
et que la fouine m'étrangle si je ne trouve pas ce qu'il nous faut! Viens
avec moi. Allons, viens vite!

Quick n'en avait aucune envie. Il aurait préféré continuer à jouer
avec Rouquette, mais elle avait l'air si décidé et si sérieux qu'il n'osa
pas protester. Les deux écureuils prirent leur élan. Sautant de branche en
branche, ils explorèrent la moitié de la forêt sans trouver d'arbre assez
commode pour y installer leur nid.
Celui-ci n'était pas assez haut; les
rameaux de celui-là étaient trop
clairsemés. Ils allaient, enfin, se dé-
cider pour cet autre, quand le vent
leur apporta la détestable odeur
de la fouine. Ils n'eurent pas besoin de renifler deux fois pour se
rendre compte que le terrier de leur
pire ennemie se trouvait juste au-
dessous d'eux. Hop! Hop! Hop!
En trois bonds, les voilà loin.

5

199

The country of the elephants faded from sight.
The balloon glided noiselessly along in the sky
and Babar and Celeste admired the view.
What a wonderful journey!
The air was warm, a light wind blew.
And there was the sea, the great blue sea.

1935. *Babar's Travels* written and illustrated by
Jean de Brunhoff. Published by Methuen and Co.
Ltd, London. Printed by W. S. Cowell Ltd,
Ipswich. 14⅛″ × 10⅛″. Illustration.

1937. *The Seven Simeons* written and illustrated
by Boris Artzybasheff. Published by the Viking
Press, New York and Cassell and Co. Ltd,
London. 11¼″ × 8¾″. Illustration.

## Author-illustrators

In 1934, the first of another successful series of children's books appeared
in Paris. This was Jean de Brunhoff's *The Story of Babar* which was later
published in England by Methuen. The large paged books (14¼ in. by 10¼ in.)
are colourful and gay, with rather naïve drawings, and a text written in a clear,
childish hand. The series continued with *Babar's Travels* and *Babar the King*;
and after Jean de Brunhoff's death, his son, Laurent de Brunhoff, took it
further, with some success.

There have also been a number of English authors of children's books, who
have illustrated their own works, including Rudyard Kipling (who drew the
pen drawings for his *Just So Stories*), Hugh Lofting (who illustrated the odd
doings of Dr Dolittle), and Arthur Ransome (who illustrated his books about
children and their exciting adventures in small boats). The fact that these
authors could hardly draw seems to have carried little weight with their
readers, who willingly accept their stiff, awkward drawings as being 'real',
because the author must have been there! The success even of an author-
illustrator like Edward Ardizzone, who really can draw, must depend at least
in part on this quality of authenticity.

Boris Artzybasheff's style has changed considerably over recent years. Thirty
odd years ago, he illustrated Padraic Colum's *Orpheus, Myths of the World*
with scraperboard drawings. His later work has, much to its advantage, been
reduced to an open, often evenly weighted line. For Heritage he has provided
yet another version of Balzac's *Droll Stories*, with amusing, rather ribald line
drawings. Artzybasheff's own book, *The Seven Simeons*, published by Viking
in 1937, is illustrated in line and colour. This is a beautiful piece of decoration.

200

1908. *Just So Stories for Little Children* written and illustrated by Rudyard Kipling. Published by Macmillan and Co. Ltd, London. Printed by R. & R. Clark, Edinburgh. 6¾″ × 4¼″. Illustration.

SCOTLAND YARD

1940. *The Big Six* written and illustrated by Arthur Ransome. Published by Jonathan Cape Ltd, London. Printed by the Alden Press, Oxford. 7⅞″ × 5¼″. Illustration.

"Rigged himself up like a tree"

1929. *Doctor Dolittle in the Moon* written and illustrated by Hugh Lofting. Published by Jonathan Cape Ltd, London. Printed by Butler and Tanner Ltd, Frome. 7¾″ × 5¼″. Frontispiece and title-page.

This was the beginning of many happy days.
Lucy loved the life at sea, especially as she had Tim there to tell her about everything. She made great friends with the second mate, and used to tidy his cabin and darn his socks.

*Mountainous seas a lee shore. Only a miracle could save us.*

This pleased him very much, as he was a bachelor and very

untidy. Often she and Tim would go to the galley, where the cook would tell them wonderful stories of his life at sea.

1938. *Tim and Lucy go to Sea* written and illustrated by Edward Ardizzone. Published by the Oxford University Press, London. Printed by W. S. Cowell Ltd, Ipswich. 10″ × 7⅛″. Illustrated pages.

Edward Ardizzone has been one of the most successful children's author-artists of this century. His first book in this vein was *Little Tim and the Brave Sea Captain*, published in 1936. A wildly improbable story, it is just the kind of dream a very little boy might have when, as a critic on the *New York Herald Tribune* said, 'he has his first sharp attack of sea fever'. This was followed by *Lucy Brown and Mr Grimes*, the story of a friendless old man, who was befriended by a very Victorian little girl. Both books are utterly charming and the successor that brings Tim and Lucy together, *Tim and Lucy go to Sea,* is even better. All have an open, hand-written text, and the artist has no compunction about using 'bubbles' when anyone is talking – as in the illustration here of a ship's cook sitting in his galley talking to the two enthralled children. Ardizzone has a genius for this kind of book, and it is no wonder that they have been equally popular on both sides of the Atlantic. The earlier books had a fine large format, were printed on only one side of the paper and were in colour throughout. The later ones and reprints of the earlier ones have a smaller page size and less colour.

Kathleen Hale's *Orlando* books, describing the adventures of a marmalade cat, have been much loved by children. The first appeared in 1939. The earlier illustrations were lithographed, the later ones were drawn on Plastocowell –

Every morning the Yellow Creature was placed in the front of the ship, where he looked lovely against the sparkling blue sea. Captain Slaughterboard would sit upon a barrel of rum, and watch the Yellow Creature for hours on end.

His pirates had to watch the Yellow Creature too, but they got rather tired of it sometimes..........

1945. *Captain Slaughterboard Drops Anchor*
written and illustrated by Mervyn Peake.
Published by Eyre and Spottiswoode, London.
$9\frac{1}{4}'' \times 7''$. Cover and text and illustration spread.

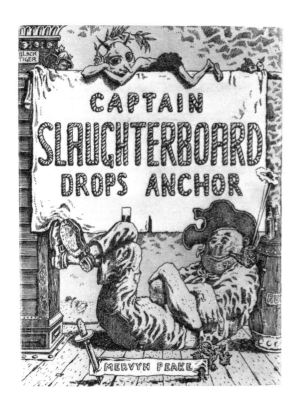

a technique similar to lithography in which the artist draws on a grained plastic sheet. The plastic sheet is then used in the same manner as a photographic positive, the image being printed down on to a deep-etched zinc plate, from which very big runs can be printed with no deterioration of the artist's original work.

Innumerable books for children appear every year, but few stand out from the general run of mediocrity. The ones that do, have, over recent years, mostly come from the United States of America and are the work of professional graphic designers who are taking time off in a less exacting field. There are, however, one or two books, apart from these, that are worth notice.

Early in the last war Mervyn Peake illustrated and wrote *Captain Slaughterboard Drops Anchor*. Unfortunately the edition was destroyed by enemy action. In 1945 Eyre and Spottiswoode reissued it, with flat coloured tints added by the artist to the plates. It was an impoverished edition, printed on wretchedly thin paper, but the drawings are fascinating, horrifying, yet within the scope of a child's imagination. These grotesque figures are the most extraordinary and poetic creations; and the book, I would have thought, is worthy of revival.

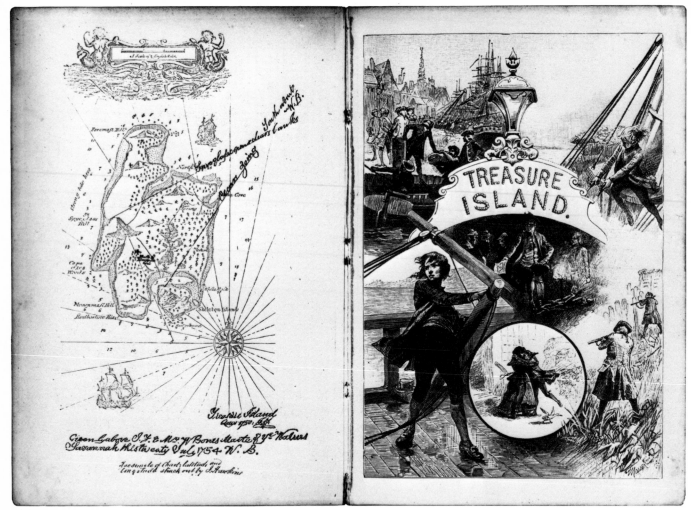

1885. *Treasure Island* by Robert Louis Stevenson illustrated by G. Roux and F. T. Merrill. Published and printed by Cassell and Co. Ltd, London. 7⅛" × 4¾". Title-page spread. Reproduced from the 1894 edition.

1911. N. C. Wyeth: 'All day he hung round the cove'.

## On re-hashing the classics

By 'classics', I mean books that have a continuing appeal to each new generation. Some are so dependent on their original drawings that there is little point in fresh illustrations; efforts to reillustrate *Alice in Wonderland*, for example, have proved singularly unsuccessful. However, there are books that benefit by new interpretations and fresh illustrations. Such a one is *Robinson Crusoe*. There have been innumerable illustrated versions, ranging from the charming Cruikshank wood-engravings of 1832 to Roger Duvoisin's agreeable pen drawings of 1946. *Tom Sawyer* and *Huckleberry Finn* are also renewed with fresh illustrations for each generation. But of all children's books Robert Louis Stevenson's *Treasure Island* would seem most successfully to lend itself to being illustrated over and over again. Its quality of appealing to adults as much as to children of each new generation — its extreme readability — cannot fail to stir any illustrator with a gleam of romance in his soul into once again re-enacting on paper the scenes on the *Hispaniola* and the quays of Bristol Docks, or Long John Silver wiping his blood-stained knife on a few blades of grass, or the horrific Blind Pew tapping his way into the Admiral Benbow Inn.

I have no idea how many illustrated editions of *Treasure Island* there have been since it was originally published in 1883, for it has been translated into many languages. Cassells were both printer and publisher of the first edition, which had no illustrations except the map. It was an agreeable little book, 7½ in. by 4¾ in., bound in a smooth dark blue cloth, the spine being blocked in gold.

Typographically it was not exceptional, but for a rather nicely displayed opening to the first chapter. The first illustrated edition, which appeared in

1911. *Treasure Island* by Robert Louis Stevenson illustrated by N. C. Wyeth. Published by Charles Scribner's Sons, New York. 9" × 6¾". Title-page printed in colour from trichromatic blocks.

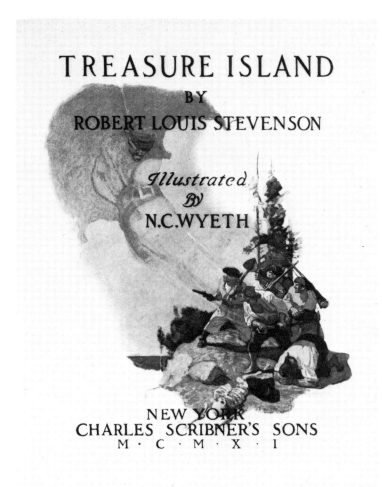

TREASURE ISLAND
BY
ROBERT LOUIS STEVENSON

*Illustrated By*
N.C.WYETH

NEW YORK
CHARLES SCRIBNER'S SONS
M · C · M · X · I

1929. *Treasure Island* by Robert Louis Stevenson illustrated by Rowland Hilder. Published and printed by the Oxford University Press, London. 9⅛" × 6½". Illustration: 'All day he hung round the cove or upon the cliffs with a brass telescope'.

the United States in 1884, published in Boston by Roberts Brothers, had four rather uninspired illustrations by F. T. Merrill. In 1885 the first French edition appeared, with a frontispiece and twenty-two full-page woodcut illustrations by Georges Roux.

In the same year the first English illustrated edition appeared, haphazardly combining the pictures from the French and American editions; the Merrill drawings were printed from zincos and Roux's twenty-two designs from woodcuts were engraved by Ladmiral, Bellenger, F. Moller and various other trade engravers.

It was not until 1899 that a new attempt was made to illustrate this story. In that year Wal Paget drew a fine set of illustrations for a new edition. Wal Paget, one of Henty's illustrators, was the brother of Sidney Paget, the first illustrator of the Sherlock Holmes stories.

Paget's illustrations for *Treasure Island* were reproduced by wood engraving, which gives to his, as it had to the French edition, a pleasant period charm. Paget's edition, however, was in a larger format than the 1885 edition, and was in Cassells' new uniform black binding which they used for all Stevenson's works. His illustrations set the scene pleasantly. To some extent they lack characterization, but this has been a common failing with all the *Treasure Island* illustrators, with one remarkable exception.

It might be reasonable comment to say that a romance like this needs in its illustrations little more than romantic or factual scene setting, and most of the editions shown here admirably answer this need. Between the publication of the Wal Paget edition and its going out of print in 1912 there was only one other illustrated *Treasure Island* of importance. This was published by

1927. *Treasure Island* by Robert Louis Stevenson illustrated by Edmund Dulac. Published by Ernest Benn Ltd, London. Printed by the Whitefriars Press Ltd, London. $9\frac{3}{8}'' \times 7\frac{1}{4}''$. Illustration: 'Black Dog disappears'.

1911. N. C. Wyeth: 'One last tremendous cut'.

1911. N. C. Wyeth: 'Tapping up and down the road in a frenzy' (*Below opposite*)

1899: Wal Paget: 'Now boy', he said, 'take me in to the captain'.

1949. *Treasure Island* by Robert Louis Stevenson illustrated by Mervyn Peake. Published by Eyre and Spottiswoode, London. Printed by the Chiswick Press, London. $8\frac{3}{8}'' \times 5\frac{1}{4}''$. Illustration: 'Now boy', he said 'take me in to the captain'.

THE BLACK SPOT. 35

And he gave it, as he spoke, a wrench, that made me cry out.

"'Now, boy,' he said, 'take me in to the captain'" (p. 34).

"Sir," said I, "it is for yourself I mean. The captain is not what he used to be. He sits with a drawn cutlass. Another gentleman——"

1899. *Treasure Island* by Robert Louis Stevenson illustrated by Wal Paget. Published and printed by Cassell and Co. Ltd, London. 7½″ × 5″. Illustration: 'He lay as we had left him . . .

1947. *Treasure Island* by Robert Louis Stevenson illustrated by John Minton. Published by Paul Elek Ltd, London. Printed in the Netherlands. 9″ × 5¾″. Illustration: 'He lay as we had left him'.

Scribner's in New York in 1911, with N. C. Wyeth's vigorous illustrations; his interesting title-page shows a group of frightened mutineers cowering below the ghost of Captain Flint. The illustrations, packed with action, are reproduced by four-colour half-tone and, of course, printed on coated stock, which is the penalty that illustrators who wished to work in colour had to pay. Books so illustrated immediately become books with plates; book design purists naturally enough object, but not so the generations of American schoolboys who must have delighted in such illustrations as the one of Billy Bones taking a tremendous swipe at the fleeing Black Dog, or that of 'Israel Hands and his companion locked together in deadly wrestle . . .' Wyeth's characters are sturdy specimens of humanity, filling their clothes well; the artist was obviously devoted to action rather than characterization, though his sense of atmosphere was acute. His portrait of Billy Bones standing on a misty Cornish cliff top and that of Pew 'tapping up and down the road in a frenzy' are both effective, even though the Admiral Benbow Inn looks a bit like a Cape Cod farmhouse.

In the late 1920's two interesting editions appeared within two years of each other. These were Ernest Benn's quarto, illustrated by Edmund Dulac, and Oxford University Press's large octavo, illustrated by Rowland Hilder. Both are handsome books, well printed and bound, the Dulac by Whitefriars Press, the Hilder by John Johnson at Oxford. Both made a full use of the four-colour process and both had a very slight scattering of pen-drawings in the text. There the similarity ends. Dulac, famous for his gentle, pretty watercolour illustrations to such books as the *Arabian Nights,* would seem a very odd choice for Stevenson's blood and thunder. Hilder, on the other hand, although a very young man at the time, had already achieved fame for his vigorous romantic draughtsmanship, particularly of ships and the sea.

Yet each book is in its own way successful. Dulac's curious, detached, air-view drawings of the Admiral Benbow and the *Hispaniola* add another dimension to Stevenson's story.

1963. *Treasure Island* by Robert Louis Stevenson illustrated by Peter Roberson. Published by the Folio Society, London. Printed by W. and J. Mackay and Co. Ltd, Chatham. $8\frac{3}{4}'' \times 5\frac{1}{2}''$. Illustration: 'Our little walk along the quays'.

*He made himself the most interesting companion*

1929. Rowland Hilder: 'He made himself the most interesting companion'.

WAL PAGET

1899. Wal Paget: 'Our little walk along the quays'.

Dulac's drawings may not be to the taste of every child, but there are some children who would enter his slightly magical world with eagerness. Hilder's strength comes over, both in the dramatic chiaroscuro and in his knowledge of sailing ships and how they worked. His *Hispaniola*, sailing full-and-bye across the end papers is a real topsail schooner, made of wood, rigged with Italian hemp and with heavy much-patched flaxen sails. This is in the Wyeth tradition and is splendid, vigorous stuff.

Another edition in the same vein was published by George Macy for his Limited Editions Club in New York in 1941, illustrated by Edward A. Wilson with watercolours and a lithographed chalk drawing of Long John Silver for the frontispiece. This particular illustration is a little slick and mannered, and the parrot looks like a crow; Wilson's earlier work was more appealing. Moreover, this *Treasure Island* was not intended for children, but for the subscribers of the Limited Editions Club.

In England, twenty years and another war later than the Dulac and Hilder editions, two more *Treasure Islands* appeared. In 1947 Paul Elek published a series of books which he called the Camden Classics. With the assistance of Denys Sutton, a remarkable short list of illustrated books was issued, including a *Wuthering Heights* with drawings by Anthony Gross, a *Jane Eyre* with lithographs by William Scott, a *Tom Sawyer* with drawings by Keith Vaughan and a *Treasure Island* illustrated by John Minton. This, as it proved from the publisher's point of view, ill-fated series was perhaps too good for its public. The typography, by Peter Ray, with asymmetric title-pages and heavy extended Grotesques for chapter headings was, for dear old England, ahead of its time; sadly enough, a mistake more costly in this conservative country than being behind the times. Looking at this *Treasure Island* now, it does not seem so advanced, with its pleasant if informal typography; but even so it makes a couple of recent editions of the book look a bit fusty. As for Minton's drawings, they are richly black with Minton's own kind of romanticism, for

208

Robert Louis Stevenson

**Treasure Island**

Introduction by H. M. Burton

*drawings by John Minton*

CAMDEN CLASSICS . PAUL ELEK . LONDON

1947. John Minton: Title-page and frontispiece: The Bristol quays.

1885. G. Roux. Illustration: 'I said goodbye to mother'.

he was at the peak of a brief flowering in the 1940's of romantic art in England.

John Minton's drawings match a certain sombreness in the story; they are atmospheric illustration, richly decorative, sultry and tropical, and once again there is little attempt at characterization. The latter charge certainly cannot be levelled at Mervyn's Peake's drawings done some two years later for Eyre and Spottiswoode. Here is a new *Treasure Island* and not a very comfortable one. To appreciate these illustrations it is best to rid one's mind of all previous ideas of how the book ought to be illustrated (though one or two of the scenes in Wal Paget's edition bear comparison). The pirates are dreadful evil old men, capable of terrible deeds. The quizzical expression on Silver's face does not hide the fearful potential of the man. As for Blind Pew, God help any poor boy if that old monster grabbed his arm in a lonely lane on a dark night. Mervyn Peake is the one illustrator amongst those I have mentioned here whose particular abilities have enabled him to dig below the surface of this adventure story, to find the characters that are lurking there. His curious foggy technique of drawing in dots also adds to the mystery of the scene.

Though at least two pleasant enough illustrated editions of this book have appeared since 1948, neither of them has added anything to widen one's appreciation. The Folio Society edition of 1963, illustrated by Peter Roberson, is an attractive piece of book production, and Roberson's drawings of the Bristol docks and of Long John Silver's back view are effective. Otherwise the illustrations are too thinly scattered. The same criticism applies to the equally well produced Nonesuch edition of the same year, illustrated by Robert Micklewright.

I picked *Treasure Island* as a random example for this brief comparative study. There are many other titles that would have done almost as well. As long as such stories are read by children, each succeeding generation will demand new editions and new illustrators to interpret the stories afresh for them.

1927. Edmund Dulac: 'The Apple Barrel'.

1885. G. Roux: 'I got bodily into the apple barrel'.

1963. Peter Roberson: 'The Apple Barrel'.

1929. Rowland Hilder: endpapers.

1949. Mervyn Peake: 'Cleansing his blood-stained knife the while upon a wisp of grass'.

1899. Wal Paget: 'Cleansing his blood-stained knife the while upon a wisp of grass'.

1963. Peter Roberson: Frontispiece.

Hunter brought the boat round under the stern-port, and
Joyce and I set to work loading her

1929. Rowland Hilder: 'Hunter brought the boat round under the stern-port'.

1911. N. C. Wyeth: 'About half way down the slope to the stockade, they were collected in a group'.

1963. Peter Roberson: Captain Silver. Blocked in dark blue on blue cloth. Case-binding.

1927. Edmund Dulac: 'Striking the Jolly Roger'.

CHAPTER XVI

*Narrative continued by the Doctor: How the Ship was Abandoned*

IT was about half-past one—three bells in the sea phrase—that the two boats went ashore from the *Hispaniola*. The captain, the squire, and I were talking matters over in the cabin. Had there been a breath of wind we should have fallen on the six mutineers who were left aboard with us, slipped our cable, and away to sea. But the wind was wanting ; and, to complete our helplessness, down came Hunter with the news that Jim Hawkins had slipped into a boat and was gone ashore with the rest.

It never occurred to us to doubt Jim Hawkins ; but we were alarmed for his safety. With the men in the temper they were in, it seemed an even chance if we should see the lad again. We ran on deck. The pitch was bubbling in the seams ; the nasty stench of the place turned me sick ; if ever man smelt fever and dysentery, it was in that abominable anchorage. The six scoundrels were sitting grumbling under a sail in the forecastle ; ashore we could see the gigs made fast, and a man sitting in each, hard by

123

1927. Edmund Dulac: Chapter opening with pen drawing of the stockade.

1949. Mervyn Peake: Captain Silver.

1911. N. C. Wyeth: 'For all the world, I was led like a dancing bear'.

1941. *Treasure Island* by Robert Louis Stevenson illustrated with water colours and a frontispiece lithographed by Edward A. Wilson. Published by the Limited Editions Club, New York. Printed by the American Book-Stratford Press, New York. 10½″ × 7″. Illustration: Captain Silver.

PART · 6

CAPTAIN · SILVER

1929. Rowland Hilder: Captain Silver.

wich zurück, kam wieder näher, um sich schließlich, zu meiner größten Überraschung und Bestürzung, auf die Knie zu werfen und die gefalteten Hände flehend zu heben.

Sogleich blieb ich wieder stehn.

»Wer bist du?« fragte ich.

»Ben Gunn«, erwiderte er, und seine Stimme klang heiser und unlenk wie ein rostiges Schloß. »Ich bin der arme Ben Gunn, ja, der bin ich, und drei Jahre lang habe ich mit keinem Christenmenschen gesprochen.«

Jetzt konnte ich erkennen, daß er ein Weißer war wie ich selber und seine Züge recht angenehm. Seinen Körper allerdings, soweit er entblößt war, hatte die Sonne dunkelbraun gebrannt, sogar seine Lippen waren schwarz, und seine hellen Augen blitzten seltsam widerspruchsvoll aus dem dunklen Gesicht. Von allen Bettlern, die ich gesehen oder mir je vorgestellt hatte, war dieser hier jedenfalls im König der Zerlumptheit. Seine einzige Hülle waren ein paar Fetzen aus altem Segeltuch, und dieses erstaunliche Flickwerk wurde durch ein System der verschiedenartigsten und unzusammengehörigsten Hilfsmittel zusammengehalten wie Messingknöpfe, Taureste und Schlingen von teerbeschmierten Gamaschen. Um den Leib trug er einen alten Ledergürtel mit Messingschnalle, das einzige ganze Stück an seiner Ausstaffierung.

»Drei Jahre!« rief ich. »Hast du Schiffbruch erlitten?«

»Nein, Maat«, sagte er. »Ausgesetzt!«

Davon hatte ich schon gehört, und ich wußte, daß es unter den Freibeutern als eine entsetzliche Strafe galt, wenn man den Missetäter mit etwas Pulver und Blei an Land setzte und auf irgendeiner fernen, verzweifelten Insel zurückließ.

»Vor drei Jahren ausgesetzt«, fuhr er fort, »und seither von Ziegen gelebt, von Beeren, von Muscheln. Wo auch ein Mensch ist, sage ich, muß er sich zu helfen wissen. Aber, Maat, mein Herz verlangt dringend nach christlichen Speisen. Hast du nicht zufällig ein Stück Käse bei dir? Nicht? Na ja, so manche lange Nacht habe ich von Käse geträumt – zumeist von gebratenem – und dann bin ich aufgewacht, und da war ich!«

»Wenn ich je wieder an Bord zurück kann«, sagte ich, »sollst du pfundweise Käse kriegen!«

Währenddessen hatte er den Stoff meiner Jacke betastet, meine Hände gestreichelt, meine Schuhe gemustert, und zwischen seinen Reden zeigte er immer wieder ein kindliches Vergnügen darüber, daß er sich einem Mitmenschen gegenüber sah. Doch bei meinen letzten Worten schaute er auf; etwas Verschlagenes trat in seinen Blick.

»Wenn du je wieder an Bord zurück kannst, sagst du?« wiederholte er. »Was heißt das? Wer sollte dich daran hindern?«

»Du nicht, das weiß ich«, erwiderte ich.

»Und da hast du's, wahrhaftig, recht!« er. »Na, du – wie heißt du eigentlich, Maat?«

»Jim.«

»Jim, Jim«, wiederholte er sichtlich erfreut. »Na, Jim, ich hab ein Leben geführt, so wüst, daß du dich schämen würdest, davon zu hören. Würdest du, zum Beispiel, glauben, wenn du mich anschaust, daß ich eine fromme Mutter gehabt hab?«

»Warum nicht?« erwiderte ich.

»Ja ja, sagte er, »und die hab ich gehabt – und wie fromm ist sie gewesen! Und ich war ein braver, frommer Junge und konnte meinen Katechismus so schnell herunterschnurren, daß man kein Wort vom andern unterschieden hat. Und das ist aus mir geworden, Jim! Mit Pennywerfen auf Grabsteinen hat's angefangen, jawohl, das war das erste, aber dabei ist's nicht geblieben. Und das hat meine Mutter mir auch gesagt, und alles hat sie prophezeit, jawohl, das hat sie, die fromme Frau. Aber die Vorsehung war's, die hat mich hierher geführt. Hier, auf dieser einsamen Insel, hab ich mir das alles zurechtgelegt, und jetzt bin ich wieder zurück bei der Frömmigkeit. Mich wirst du nicht dabei erwischen, daß ich auch nur einen Tropfen Rum trinke. Einen Fingerhut natürlich schon, auf dein Wohl, sobald ich Gelegenheit hab. Ich hab's mir zugeschworen, ich will ein braver Mensch sein, und meinen Weg dazu seh ich auch. Und, Jim«, er sah sich um und senkte die Stimme zu einem Flüstern, »ich bin nämlich reich!«

Jetzt war ich überzeugt davon, daß der arme Teufel in seiner Einsamkeit übergeschnappt war, und diesen Eindruck mußte ich wohl auch auf meinem Gesicht merken gelassen haben, denn er wiederholte seine Erklärung mit größtem Eifer.

»Reich! Reich! Ich sag's dir! Und noch was will ich dir sagen. Ich werde einen Mann aus dir machen, Jim. Ah, Jim, du wirst die Sterne dafür segnen, daß du der erste bist, der mich gefunden hat.«

Und nun senkte sich plötzlich ein dunkler Schatten über seine Züge, sein Griff um meine Hand verstärkte sich, und er hob drohend den Zeigefinger vor meine Augen.

»Sag mir die Wahrheit, Jim – das ist doch nicht Flints Schiff?« fragte er.

Da hatte ich einen glücklichen Einfall. Es kam mir in den Sinn, daß ich einen Verbündeten gefunden hatte, und so erwiderte ich ihm sogleich:

»Es ist nicht Flints Schiff, und Flint ist tot; aber da du mich doch fragst, will ich dir die Wahrheit sagen – es sind ein paar von Flints Leuten auf dem Schiff, und das ist das Unglück für uns andern.«

»Nicht auch ein Mann – mit einem – Bein?« keuchte er.

»Silver?« fragte ich.

»Ja ja, Silver«, rief er. »So hat er geheißen.«

»Er ist der Koch; und der Rädelsführer dazu.«

Noch immer hielt er mich beim Gelenk fest, und jetzt preßte er es mit schmerzhaftem Druck.

»Wenn es der lange John ist, der dich geschickt hat«, sagte er, »dann bin ich ein toter Mann, das weiß ich. Aber was wird aus dir? Was glaubst du?«

Da faßte ich einen raschen Entschluß, und statt einer Antwort erzählte ich ihm die ganze Geschichte unserer Reise und machte ihm auch klar, in welcher Patsche wir uns befanden. Mit größtem Interesse hörte er mir zu, und als ich fertig war, streichelte er mir den Kopf.

»Du bist ein guter Junge, Jim«, sagte er, »und jetzt seid ihr alle in die Gedränge gekommen, was? Na, ihr braucht nur Ben Gunn zu vertrauen – Ben Gunn wird's schon schaffen, er ist der rechte Mann dazu. Glaubst du, daß dein Squire sich freigebig zeigen wird, wenn ich ihm helfe? Wenn er doch in der Patsche sitzt, wie du sagst?«

Ich versicherte ihm, daß der Squire der großzügigste Mann auf Erden sei.

»Ja ja, aber verstehst du«, erwiderte Ben Gunn. »Ich meine damit nicht, daß er mir ein Tor zu hüten geben soll und mich als Lakai anziehen und was weiß; das ist's nicht, woran mir gelegen wäre, Jim. Ich meine, ob er sich dazu verstehn würde, mir, sagen wir mal, tausend Pfund von dem Geld zu geben, das jetzt schon so gut wie geborgen ist?«

»Ich bin überzeugt, daß er's täte«, sagte ich. »Alle sollten zu ihrem Anteil kriegen.«

»Und die Rückfahrt in die Heimat dazu«, fügte er mit schlauem Zwinkern hinzu.

42

hören konnten; und was das Klima anlangte, war der Doktor bereit, seine Perücke darauf zu verwetten, daß sie, auf dem Moorland gelagert und ohne Medikamente, keine Woche überstehn würden, ohne daß die Hälfte auf dem Rücken lag.

»Und so«, setzte er hinzu, »wenn wir nicht vorher alle erschossen worden sind, werden sie froh sein, mit dem Schoner das Weite zu suchen. Es ist immerhin ein Schiff, und vermutlich können sie damit auch wieder Freibeuterei betreiben.«

»Das erste Schiff, das ich je verloren habe«, sagte Kapitän Smollett.

Wie ihr euch wohl vorstellen könnt, war ich todmüde; und als ich endlich, nach langem Hin- und Herwälzen, einschlafen konnte, schlief ich wie ein Stück Holz.

Die übrigen waren schon lange wach, hatten bereits gefrühstückt und den Holzvorrat ungefähr um die Hälfte vergrößert, als ich durch Geräusch und lautes Reden geweckt wurde.

»Parlamentärsflagge«, hörte ich einen sagen; und gleich darauf einen Schrei der Überraschung: »Silver selber!«

Daraufhin sprang ich auf, rieb mir die Augen und lief zu einer Schießscharte an der Wand.

## SILVERS BOTSCHAFT

Da standen tatsächlich zwei Männer [a]ußerhalb der Palisade, und einer von ihnen wink[te] mit einem weißen Tuch; der andere, ke[in] geringerer als Silver höchstselbst, sta[nd] friedlich daneben.

Es war noch sehr früh am Morgen, u[nd] zwar war es der kälteste Morgen, an d[en] ich mich erinnern konnte, seit ich Engla[nd] verlassen hatte; die Kälte durchschauer[te] mich bis ins Mark. Der Himmel über u[ns] war hell und wolkenlos, und die Wip[fel] der Bäume schimmerten rosig in d[er] Sonne. Doch wo Silver mit seinem Spieß[ge]gesellen stand, lag alles noch im Schatte[n,] und sie wateten knietief im weißlich[en] Bodennebel, der in der Nacht aus de[m] Moor aufgestiegen war. Kälte und Neb[el] wußten, zusammengenommen, nichts G[u]tes vom Klima der Insel zu berichten. [Es] war offenbar ein feuchter, fieberbrütend[er,] ungesunder Erdenfleck.

»Bleibt im Haus, ihr Männer«, ordnete d[er] Kapitän an. »Zehn zu eins, daß dahin[ter] etwas steckt.«

Dann rief er den Freibeuter an.

»Wer da! Stehnbleiben, schieße[n] wir.«

»Parlamentärsflagge!« schrie Silver.

Der Kapitän war auf der Veranda vor d[er] Türe, hielt sich aber vorsichtig in Decku[ng] für den Fall, daß ein Schuß aus dem H[in]terhalt geplant war. Er wandte sich u[ns] und sagte zu uns:

»Der Doktor mit seiner Wache auf d[ie] Posten! Dr. Livesey, Sie gehen an d[ie] Nordseite, wenn ich bitten darf, Jim [an] die Ostseite, Gray nach Westen. Die a[n]dere Wache soll sämtliche Musketen lad[en.] Vorwärts, Leute, und geht gut acht!«

Dann wandte er sich wieder den Meutere[rn] zu.

»Und was wollt ihr mit eurer Parlame[n]tärsflagge?« rief er.

Diesmal war es der andere Mann, der an[t]wortete.

»Käp'n Silver will an Bord kommen, Si[r,] und die Sache ins reine bringen.«

»Käp'n Silver? Kenne ich nicht. Wer [ist] das?« rief der Kapitän. Und wir hörte[n,] wie er zu sich selber halblaut sagt[e:] »Gleich Käp'n? Der ist aber schnell ava[n]ciert!«

Jetzt antwortete der lange John selber.

»Ich, Sir. Die armen Burschen haben mi[ch] zum Käp'n gewählt, nachdem Ihr dese[r]tiert wart, Sir«, auf das Wort »desertie[rt]« legte er besonderen Nachdruck. »Wir si[nd] bereit, uns zu fügen, wenn wir zu ein[er] Einigung kommen können, und dan[n]

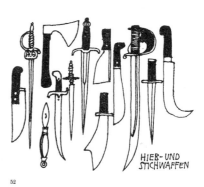

HIEB- UND STICHWAFFEN

52

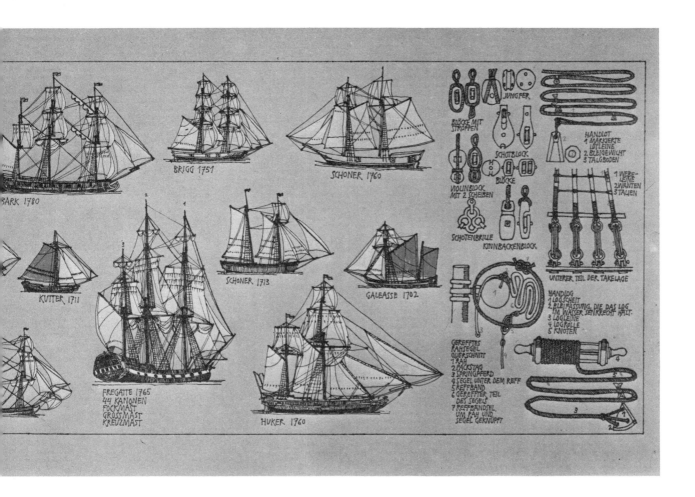

Labels within illustration:

BARK 1780
BRIGG 1751
SCHONER 1760
KUTTER 1711
SCHONER 1713
GALEASSE 1702
FREGATTE 1765
44 KANONEN
FOCKMAST
GROSSMAST
KREUZMAST
HUKER 1760

JUNGFER
BLÖCKE MIT STROPPEN
SCHOTBLOCK
VIOLINBLOCK MIT 2 SCHEIBEN
BLÖCKE
SCHOTENBRILLE
KINNBACKENBLOCK

HANDLOT
1 MARKIERTE LOTLEINE
2 BLEIGEWICHT
3 TALGBODEN

1 WEBE-LEINE
2 WANTEN STAUEN

UNTERER TEIL DER TAKELAGE

HANDLOG
1 LOGSCHEIT
2 BLEIFASSUNG, DIE DAS LOG IM WASSER SENKRECHT HÄLT
3 LOGLEINE
4 LOGROLLE
5 KNOTEN

GEREFFTES RAHSEGEL QUERSCHNITT
1 RAH
2 PACKTAG
3 SPRINGPFERD
4 SEGEL UNTER DEM REFF
5 REFFBAND
6 GEREFFTER TEIL DES SEGELS
7 REFFBÄNDSEL UM RAH UND SEGEL GEKNÜPFT

1964. *Die Schatzinsel* by Robert Louis Stevenson, illustrated and designed by Eleonore Schmid. Published by Rene Simmen, Zürich. Printed and reproduced by Käser Press and Graphischen Anstalt Freytag AG, Zürich. $10\frac{3}{4}'' \times 9\frac{3}{16}''$. Drawn-on cover of unbleached cardboard printed in black and orange. Cover printed in black and red. Plate printed on buff laid paper in black, white and orange. Text pages.

'Fünfzehn Mann auf des Totenmanns Kiste,
Jo-ho-ho und die Pulle Voll Rum
Teufel und Trunk bracht' die andern zur Ruhe
Jo-ho-ho und die Pulle voll Rum.'

In 1964, completely new ground was broken by a Swiss edition of Stevenson's book. This was *Die Schatzinsel*, published by Rene Simmen and illustrated and designed by Eleonore Schmid. This is a large square book, with drawn-on covers. The text is set in three columns and the illustrations are limited to vignetted line drawings of all the objects and the fauna that the reader might have encountered if he had shipped aboard the *Hispaniola*. Pistols, cutlasses, a compass and a sextant, turtles and fish, water kegs and meat casks, a sea-lion and a starfish are dotted through the pages. There are also a number of fold-out plates printed in black, white and orange on a buff laid paper. Among these are detailed plans of the *Hispaniola*, the sail plans of contemporary ships, and diagrams of a sailing vessel showing her running, reaching and sailing full and bye. There are also charts of Treasure Island and of the Caribbean, and the various flags used by such pirates of the Spanish Main as Bonnet, Rackham and Tew. There is only one figure drawing in the whole book and that is to show the costume of a seaman in 1750. This is an intriguing approach to illustration. It implies that Stevenson's imagery is quite sufficient and that the purpose of the illustration is to give substance and detail to the props that are the background to the story. The illustrations are completely factual, if freely drawn, renderings from contemporary source material. This almost scientific approach to illustration has, of course, been done before, by such artists as Gordon Macfie with his ship drawings for the Swedish publishers Tre Tryckare or William Fenton with his renderings of locomotives for Hugh Evelyn. The scope is considerable.

215

## The graphic designer's book

1953. *Mother Goose Riddle Rhymes* by Joseph and Ruth Low. Published by Harcourt Brace and Co., New York. Printed in the U.S.A. 8⅜" × 7". Cover design, title-page and text spread.

A new approach to the illustration of books, both in the United States and in England, has been brought about since the 1939–45 war by a number of graphic designers. Exasperated or plain bored by advertising graphics, they have turned their not inconsiderable talents to book production. Their books almost invariably have been for children, and as often as not they have written them themselves. As graphic designers, they have ranged from typographers to advertising art directors. Some, such as Ben Shahn and André François, have limited their graphic work to illustration or lettering. Shahn worked for many years as a litho-artist and François for advertising. And some (highly successful commercial designers on both sides of the Atlantic) have gone right back to base, to the hand press. Applying Morris's doctrine of the value of hand work, they have derived great benefit from the actual printing process, using it as a medium for experiment. Lively effects of overprinting are discovered in this way which are quite beyond the imagination of any artist whose techniques are limited to the drawing board and pots of paint.

Joseph Low, widely known as a designer of advertising work, record sleeves and book jackets, works in this manner and prints on a Colt's Armory Press

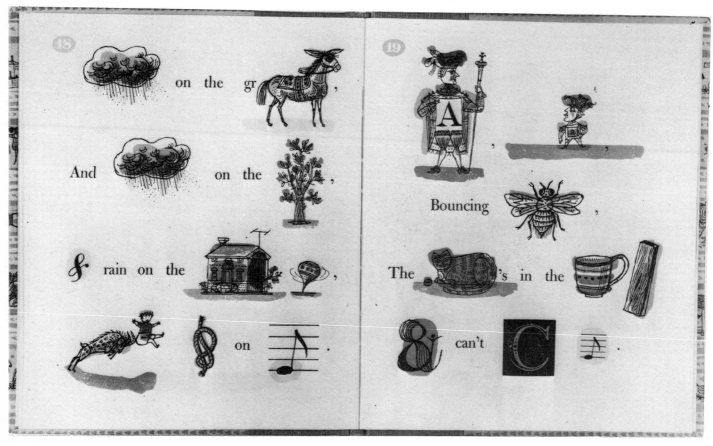

1942. *The Little Red Engine gets a Name* by
Diana Ross. Illustrated by Lewitt-Him. Published
by Faber and Faber Ltd, London. Printed by the
Baynard Press, London. 7¼" × 9¾". Illustration.

at his Eden Hill Press at Newton, Connecticut. He uses the press as a creative
tool, experimenting with type and wood or linocuts. His *Mother Goose Riddle
Rhymes,* a colourful book printed throughout in five colours, was published
in 1953 by Harcourt, Brace and Co. New York. It was preceded by his
*Rainbow Dictionary,* issued in 1947 by World Publishing with over 1,000
drawings in colour.

George Him was a formidable, successful and endearing figure in the English
graphic scene, with a wealth of graphic experience, who for some years
worked in graphic partnership with Jan Lewitt. They came from Poland to
settle in England in 1937, when their partnership was four years old, and the
work of Lewitt-Him cheered us through the days of the war. In 1942 they
turned from advertising to the production of a children's book, *The Little Red
Engine Gets a Name,* which was published in London by Faber and Faber.
The combination of such diverse personalities was most successful; *The
Little Red Engine* was a delicious book, naïve yet highly sophisticated. The
infusion of such continental talent provided a much needed shot-in-the-arm
to the design of English children's books. George Him, working on his own,
has illustrated some attractive children's books about 'Alexander the Giant',
written by Frank Herrmann. He has also illustrated *Two Plays for Puritans* and
*Zuleika Dobson,* both for the Limited Editions Club.

O Orang-utan

Sie maß die Beine des Reihers . . .

1960. *Stück für Stück* written and illustrated by Leo Lionni. German translation by James Krüss. Typography by Wolfgang Tiessen. Published by Friedrich Middelhauve Verlag, Cologne and Opladen. 11″ × 9¼″. Illustration spread.

*Opposite:*
1963. *Eulenglück* written and illustrated by Celestino Piatti. Published by Artemis Verlags-Aktiengesellschaft, Zürich. Printed in Switzerland by Sigg-Set, Sigg Söhne. 8¼″ × 11⅝″. Illustration.

1965. *Celestino Piatti's A.B.C.* Published by Artemis Verlag, Zürich and Ernest Benn Ltd, London. Printed in Switzerland. 8″ × 11½″. Illustration.

1956. *Les Larmes de Crocodile* written and illustrated by André François. Published by Robert Delpire, Paris. Printed by l'Imprimerie Savernoise. 3⁵⁄₁₆″ × 10″. Illustration spread.

The graphic designers whose work appears here have certainly brought fresh life to children's books over the last few years. The common factor running through all their books is the author-artist's reluctance to use more words than are absolutely needful; no doubt a natural enough reaction for graphic designers whose entire work is made up of finding new methods of visual communication. Though many of these graphic designers have been American, one of the most attractive books of recent years has come from an Italian-Swiss, Celestino Piatti, the author of *The Happy Owls*. Piatti has a brilliant decorative colour sense. He is one of the few living graphic designers whose work has the essential quality of communication, yet is intrinsically decorative as well. Another is the Amsterdam-born American, Leo Lionni, who is a painter, a graphic designer and an advertising man. The designs for *Stück für Stück* are cut from tissue-paper; the total effect is one of a dreamy softness, with moments of incisive colour, as in the sharp mustard yellow beak of the heron on this page. André François's *Les Larmes de Crocodile* completes the trilogy of animal books on this spread. François, one of the great advertising artists of this century, here turns his talents to a little book (3¼ in. by 10½ in.) suitable for a child's Christmas stocking.

...ut bien sûr trouver la bonne taille

Pas trop long, pas trop court, sinon le crocodile va

...otter dans la LONGUE CAISSE A CROCODILE;

1958. *Ounce, Dice, Trice* by Alastair Reid
illustrated by Ben Shahn. Published by Atlantic
Little, Brown and Co., Boston and Toronto.
Printed in the U.S.A. 10″ × 7⅜″. Jacket design.

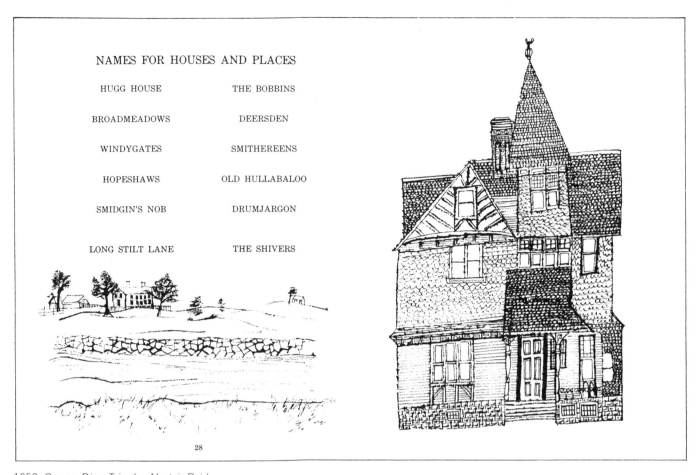

## NAMES FOR HOUSES AND PLACES

| | |
|---|---|
| HUGG HOUSE | THE BOBBINS |
| BROADMEADOWS | DEERSDEN |
| WINDYGATES | SMITHEREENS |
| HOPESHAWS | OLD HULLABALOO |
| SMIDGIN'S NOB | DRUMJARGON |
| LONG STILT LANE | THE SHIVERS |

28

1958. *Ounce, Dice, Trice* by Alastair Reid,
illustrated by Ben Shahn. Text spread.

Ben Shahn's stature as an artist and as a compassionate commentator on the human scene needs no boost from me. His children's books however have received scant notice, at least in this country, though the same qualities of humour, satire, gentleness and elegance are evident in all his illustrations for *Ounce Dice Trice* by Alastair Reid, published in Boston in 1958. He has interpreted Alastair Reid's 'treasure trove of sounds and images' in a delicious manner. The drawings of houses are particularly effective; he breathes life into bricks and mortar, clapboard and shingle. In *A Partridge in a Pear Tree*, published in 1951 by the Museum of Modern Art in New York, there is additional evidence of his completeness as a graphic artist, for accompanying the archaic drawings is the most beautifully lettered text. For nearly a quarter of a century, from 1913 to 1930, Shahn supported himself mainly by his work as a trade lithographer; and this vigorous discipline, instead of dulling his qualities as an artist, has given his work an unparalleled assurance, for here is an artist who is master of his craft. Ben Shahn's *Love and Joy about Letters* is one of the most handsome books of the last few decades. It is a book for all ages with page after page of his incomparable calligraphy.

WHO iS GOD?*WELL iT iS AN iNViSiBLE
PERSON AND HE LiVES UP iN HEAVEN*
i GUESS UP iN OUTER SPACE*HE
MADE THE EARTH AND THE HEAVEN &
THE STARS AND THE SUN AND THE
PEOPLE*HE MADE LiGHT HE MADE DAY
HE MADE NiGHT*HE HAS SUCH POWER-
FUL EYES HE DOESN'T HAVE MiLLiONS
AND THOUSANDS AND BiLLiONS AND HE
CAN STiLL SEE US WHEN WE'RE BAD*
HE STARTED ALL THE PLANTS GROWiNG*TO
ME i THiNK OF HiM WHO MAKES FLOWERS
& GREEN GRASS & THE BLUE SKY &
THE YELLOW SUN*GOD iS EVERYWHERE
& i DON'T KNOW HOW HE COULD DO iT

35

1963. *Love and Joy about Letters* by Ben Shahn
(English edition 1964). Published by Cory,
Adams and Mackay. Printed by Camera
Publishers, C. J. Bucher Ltd, Lucerne. 10″ × 13⅜″.
Text and illustration spread.

1951. *A Partridge in a Pear Tree* by Ben Shahn.
Published by Doubleday and Co. Inc., New York.
Printed by the Crafton Graphic Co., for the
Museum of Modern Art. 7¼″ × 8½″. Text spread.

ON THE SECOND DAY OF CHRIST-
MAS MY TRUE LOVE GAVE TO ME
TWO TURTLE DOVES AND A PARTRIDGE
                        iN
                        A
                        PEAR
                        TREE

1958. *Once there was a General* written and
illustrated by Tony Palladino. Published by
Franklin Watts. New York. Printed in the U.S.A.
$4\frac{1}{2}'' \times 5\frac{3}{4}''$. Text spread and cover.

**The graphic designer's book**

Tony Palladino's little book of woodcuts tells a moral tale about a general
whose rise to glory came to nothing but a field of daisies because he had no
wars! Tony Palladino is an Eastside New Yorker who practises as a designer
and illustrator. *The General* began as a single woodcut but slowly developed
into a complete and eminently satisfying story.

Then the general had many more cannons,

many more horses,

a lion. Then, I could trade my zoo for

a tall tower. (I might keep one rocking horse.) Then, in time, I could trade my tall tower for

1961. *A Balloon for a Blunderbuss* by Bob Gill and Alastair Reid. Published by Harper and Brothers, New York. Printed in the U.S.A. $10\frac{1}{2}'' \times 8''$. Text spread.

*A Balloon for a Blunderbuss* is another book by Alastair Reid, this time in co-operation with Bob Gill, an American graphic designer of great talent who works mostly in London.

*Blind Mice and other Numbers* is both written and illustrated with extreme economy by another talented American designer, Ivan Chermayeff. It is so sophisticated, that I imagine it may have more appeal to designers than to their children.

1961. *Blind Mice and other Numbers* designed and illustrated by Ivan Chermayeff. Published by Colorcraft, New York. Printed in the U.S.A. $10\frac{3}{4}'' \times 8\frac{1}{8}''$. Text spread.

Up until the eleventh hour on the Twelfth Night a baker's dozen days before Christmas.

40ty.                    end.

Borka was soon very friendly with the Captain, Fred and of course with Fowler. She coiled pieces of rope with her beak, picked up crumbs from the floor and helped in any way she could. In return she was given plenty of good food.

1963. *Borka, The Adventures of a Goose with no Feathers* written and illustrated by John Burningham. Published by Jonathan Cape. Printed by L. van Leer and Co., Amsterdam. $10\frac{1}{2}'' \times 8\frac{3}{8}''$. Text spread.

John Burningham's *Borka,* the first of a series of children's books by this English artist, had an immediate success. Burningham's books are delightful conceptions brilliantly carried out.

Ann and Paul Rand's *Sparkle and Spin* is another book about words. Paul Rand, who is a leading American artist-designer, here illustrates his wife's words with humour and beauty. The spread here from *Sparkle and Spin* brings this survey of designer-illustrators to a fitting close.

1957. *Sparkle and Spin* by Ann and Paul Rand. Published by Harcourt Brace and Co., New York. Printed in the U.S.A. $10'' \times 8\frac{1}{4}''$. Text spread.

Words are "Yes I will" and "No I won't," but they are polite too like please and thank you.

1960 *The Fatal Lozenge* written and illustrated
by Edward Gorey. Published by Astor, Honor Inc.,
New York and Ernest Benn, Tonbridge. 6″ × 5″
page size.
Illustration: 'The Proctor buys the pupil ices
                And hopes the boy will not resist
                When he attempts to practices vices
                Few people even know exist'.

The Proctor *buys a pupil ices,*

    *And hopes the boy will not resist*

*When he attempts to practise vices*

    *Few people even know exist.*

1964 *The Sinking Spell* written and illustrated by
Edward Gorey. Published by Ivan Obolensky Inc.,
New York and Ernest Benn, Tonbridge. 6″ × 5″
page size.
Illustration: 'It's gone beneath the cellar floor:
                We shall not see it any more'.

1973 *The Juniper Tree and Other Tales from Grimm* translated by Lore Segal and Randall Jarrell. Pictures by Maurice Sendak. Designed by Altha Tehon and Maurice Sendak. Translations copyright © 1973 by Lore Segal. Pictures copyright © 1973 by Maurice Sendak. Reprinted by permission of Farrar, Straus and Giroux, Inc. New York, and the Bodley Head, London. 6¾" × 5¼" page size. Illustrations: 'The Twelve Huntsmen' and 'The Three Feathers'.

Since the first edition of this book appeared old reputations have been confirmed and new reputations have been made in the field of children's books. As far as line illustrations go, I think the most significant artists have been Edward Gorey and Maurice Sendak, the most witty Quentin Blake and the most disturbing Ralph Steadman.

Edward Gorey was born in Chicago and graduated at Harvard. He has illustrated and published a number of little books that have as much appeal for adults as they have for children. Many of these have been gathered together and published in the U.S.A. by Putnam under the titles of *Amphigorey* and *Amphigorey Too*. The titles of such fantasies as *The Fatal Lozenge, The Curious Sofa, The Sinking Spell* or *The Pious Infant* (all published in the U.K. by Ernest Benn also) give some indication of this artist's taste for Victorian and *fin de siècle* subjects. Gorey has also illustrated books for other writers. A happy collaboration was with Polly Redford for *The Christmas Bower*, an enchanting book. Gorey's is certainly an original talent. His illustrations have an extra dimension. They give one the feeling that his characters are waiting for something awful to happen.

Maurice Sendak was born in Brooklyn of Polish descent. He has written and illustrated several books for children. His *Where the Wild Things Are* won the Caldecott Medal for Children's Books in 1964. It was published by Harper and Row in America and by the Bodley Head in Great Britain, later appearing as a Puffin Book and going through many editions. Sendak's 'Wild Things' are the most benign-looking monsters, at least to adult eyes. Maurice Sendak started thinking about illustrating Grimm's *Fairy Tales* before this book was completed, but it was not until 1972 that he began work on the actual illustrations. He forsook colour for pen drawing and with an intricate hatchwork of fine lines built up these tonal illustrations. A feature of his drawings is the stockiness of his figures and their large heads. (The head-to-body ratio is about 4.5:1.) The convention works and these are a haunting set of illustrations. The book was called *The Juniper Tree* and was impeccably designed by Altha Tehon and Sendak himself and published in two volumes in a slipcase.

1982 *Roald Dahl's Revolting Rhymes* illustrated by Quentin Blake. Published by Jonathan Cape, London. $10\frac{3}{4}'' \times 8\frac{1}{2}''$ page size. Illustrations: 'Cinderella' and 'Snow White and the Seven Dwarfs'.

Quentin Blake's deceptively free style conceals a very real talent. The drawings for Roald Dahl's *Revolting Rhymes* look as if they have been knocked off in a few moments. In fact they are the result of much thought. Quentin Blake is a Master of Arts and is the Head of the Department of Illustration at the Royal College of Art. He has also illustrated five other books by Roald Dahl – *The Enormous Crocodile, The Twits, George's Marvellous Medicine, The BFG* and *The Witches*.

Ralph Steadman's fame could rest on his work as a satirical cartoonist in *Private Eye, Punch* and *The Daily Telegraph*. His first successful venture into book illustration was for *The Young Visiters* by Daisy Ashford. In 1967 he illustrated an *Alice in Wonderland* for Dennis Dobson. These drawings are perhaps the most successful attempt to illustrate this book since Sir John Tenniel illustrated the original edition, with the possible exception of Mervyn Peake's. *Cherrywood Cannon,* a doom-laden tale by Steadman's Yugoslavian friend Dimitri Sidjanski, is revealed in all its apocalyptic horror by his brilliant drawings.

Unfortunately there is no space here to show the drawings of a number of contemporary artists who have done noteworthy work for children over the

1978 *Cherrywood Cannon* written and
illustrated by Ralph Steadman, based on a story
told to him by Dimitri Sidjanski. Published by
Paddington Press Ltd., New York and London.
12" × 9". Illustration: 'Stuffed the cannon full of
shot'.

last dozen years: illustrators such as Nicola Bayley, who illustrated *The Tiger Voyage* by Richard Adams with richly coloured studies of Victorian interiors, or Jill Barklem, a true successor to Beatrix Potter, with her detailed and wonderfully observed studies of the mice of *Brambly Hedge,* or Elisa Trimby whose book *Mr Plum's Paradise* has the kind of precise detail that children love, or Nancy Ekholm Burkert whose illustrations to an edition of *Snow White and the Seven Dwarfs* owe nothing to Disney. In her pictures Miss Burkert has created a magical version of the late Middle Ages that any child would want to return to again and again.

Monochrome reproduction could do little justice to Errol le Cain's richly coloured illustrations to Perrault's *Cinderella* or to Tomie de Paola's coloured pictures. A delightful book by de Paola is *The Clown of God* which he based on Anatole France's legend of the little juggler and the miracle with which he is involved. Trained as a painter, once a member of a religious order and now living in New Hampshire, Tomie de Paola has drawn on Renaissance sources for his illustrations to this touching little tale. This book reinforces my belief that no matter how beautiful the illustrations may be, unless there is a good story they have little appeal for children.

G

stands for Gnu, whose weapons of Defence
Are long, sharp, curling Horns, and Common-sense.
To these he adds a Name so short and strong,

That even Hardy Boers pronounce it wrong.

20

1899. *A Moral Alphabet* by H. Belloc with
illustrations by B.T.B. Published by Edward
Arnold, London. $8\frac{1}{4}'' \times 6\frac{1}{2}''$. Cover and illustration.

1930. *New Cautionary Tales* by H. Belloc, with
illustrations by Nicolas Bentley. Published by
Duckworth, London and printed by the Camelot
Press Southampton. $8\frac{3}{8}'' \times 6\frac{5}{8}''$. Doublespread.

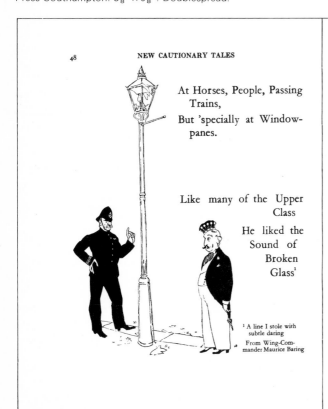

48     NEW CAUTIONARY TALES

At Horses, People, Passing
Trains,
But 'specially at Window-
panes.

Like many of the Upper
Class
He liked the
Sound of
Broken
Glass[1]

[1] A line I stole with
subtle daring
From Wing-Com-
mander Maurice Baring

FOR CHILDREN     49

It bucked him up and made him gay:
It was his favourite form of Play.
But the Amusement cost him dear,
My children, as you now shall hear.

JOHN VAVASSOUR DE QUENTIN had
An uncle, who adored the lad:

And often chuckled; "Wait until
You see what's left you in my will!"

D

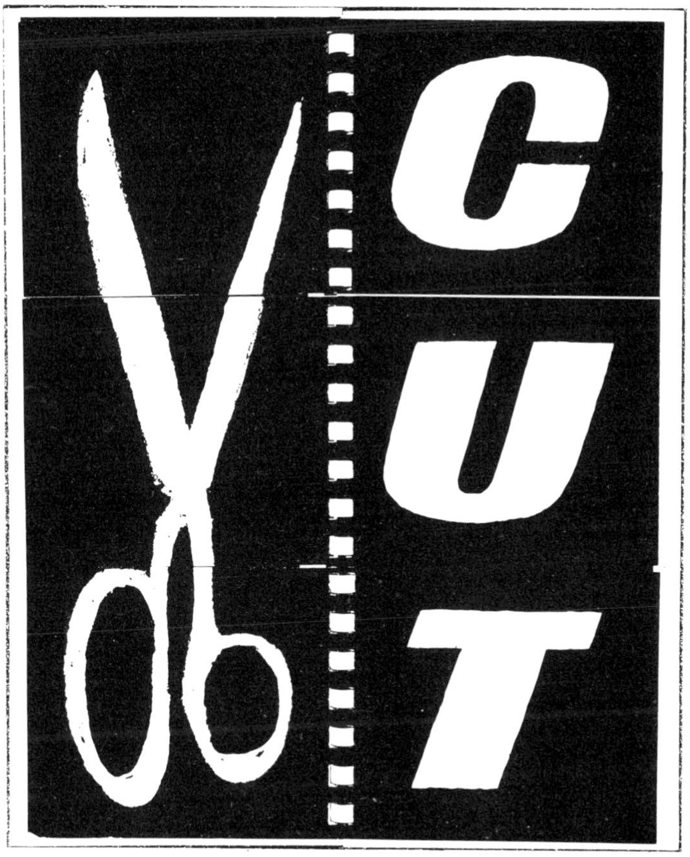
C
U
T

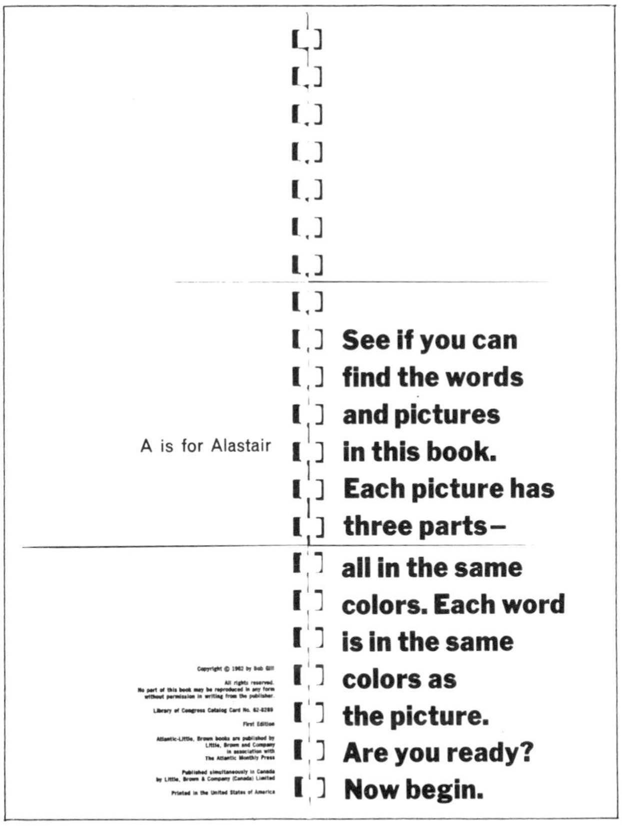
A is for Alastair
See if you can
find the words
and pictures
in this book.
Each picture has
three parts–
all in the same
colors. Each word
is in the same
colors as
the picture.
Are you ready?
Now begin.

1962. *A to Z* by Bob Gill. Published by Little, Brown and Co., Boston and Toronto. Printed in the U.S.A. $12\frac{1}{4}'' \times 5''$. Text and picture spreads. The book is cut horizontally into three sections.

**The sugared pill**

Children, understandably enough, have always regarded disguised attempts at instruction with a very proper horror. For a book to be successful in this way calls for considerable ingenuity on the part of the author. Alphabet books, which precede reading books, have provided an outlet for many illustrators, from Bewick to Walter Crane or B.T.B. to Celestino Piatti; Hilaire Belloc's *A Moral Alphabet* (1899) with illustrations by B.T.B. (Lord Basil Blackwood) is an acidulated plum rather than a sugared pill. The mood is set with:

> 'A stands for Archibald who told no lies,
> And got this lovely volume as a prize.'

and concludes with the searching moral:

> 'Idolatry, as you are well aware
> Is highly reprehensible. But there,
> We needn't bother, – when we get to Z
> Our interest in the alphabet is dead.'

The drawings are in open line and mark a kind of half-way stage between Edward Lear and Nicolas Bentley, who illustrated Hilaire Belloc's *New Cautionary Tales*.

The American graphic designer Bob Gill's *A to Z* (1962) uses the old parlour-game 'Heads, Bodies and Legs' technique for his alphabet book. The pages are cut horizontally into three and the intelligent infant is meant to sort out matching colours and words to make up the complete double spread of illustration and word. The book is Plastoic bound so lies flat when open.

1930. *1066 and all that* by W. C. Sellar and
R. J. Yeatman, illustrated by John Reynolds.
Published by Methuen and Co. Ltd, London.
Printed by the Mayflower Press, Plymouth.
$7\frac{1}{2}'' \times 4\frac{7}{8}''$. Illustration

7 Van Loon carried this little colour box everywhere. I remember in 1943 lunching with him at
the St Regis Hotel in New York. Something
occurred to him, he pulled his little box out of
his pocket, produced a minute brush, dipped it
into his glass of Chablis and painted a little scene
on the back of the menu.

In 1930 Walter Carruthers Sellar and Robert Julian Yeatman launched, with
the help of their publishers Methuen & Company, *1066 and all that, A
Memorable History of England*, on to an unsuspecting world. Sellar was a
Charterhouse master, Yeatman a successful advertising copy writer. They
co-opted John Reynolds, son of Frank Reynolds, art editor of *Punch*, to
illustrate their lampoon. The result of their collaboration was quite deadly!
English history after this witty send-up would never be quite the same again.
*1066 and all that* is more of a poisoned than a sugared pill.

Apart from *1066 and all that,* there have been many attempts to make history
more palatable for the young. The classic example of successfully sugaring a
pill was the late Hendrik Willem van Loon, a Dutch-American historian. Van
Loon had emigrated to the U.S.A. when still a young man. Ever afterwards
he lived in a nostalgic dream of past golden ages, and had an expatriate's
longing for the little fishing port of Veere on the island Walcheren where he
had once lived. Van Loon was a brilliant raconteur and once he had applied
this gift to his writing, he achieved an enormous public. His books bubbled
with endless anecdotes and often, I suspect, much inaccurate information.
Writing was not enough to contain this ebullient giant of a Dutchman, so he
decorated his books with very vital little drawings in colour and black and
white. He was anything but a skilled draftsman and his range of colours was
limited to primaries and a particularly virulent green. These colours came out
of a minute paint box, about two inches long, which he clipped to his thumb.[7]
His books have whetted the appetites of countless children and led them into
wanting to study more solid fare. The illustrations are an essential part of these
racy accounts of history and somehow, by the very fact that they come from
the author's hand, carry more authority than would the work of a separate,
even if more talented illustrator.

Enid LaMonte Meadowcroft's *Benjamin Franklin* shows a rather less frivolous
approach to the teaching of history. The illustrator of this handsome book is
Donald McKay, who a decade earlier had provided the drawings for the
Random House edition of *The Adventures of Tom Sawyer* (see page 131).
McKay's lively drawings are both pleasant and informative.

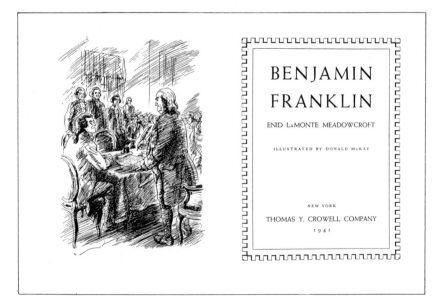

1941. *Benjamin Franklin* by Enid LaMonte
Meadowcroft illustrated by Donald McKay.
Published by Thomas Y. Crowell Co., New York.
$8\frac{3}{4}'' \times 6\frac{1}{2}''$. Frontispiece and title-page.

# VAN LOON'S
# LIVES

Being a true and faithful account
of a number of highly interesting meetings
with certain historical personages, from
CONFUCIUS and PLATO to VOLTAIRE
and THOMAS JEFFERSON, about whom
we had always felt a great deal of
curiosity and who came to us
as our dinner guests in a bygone year.
Written and illustrated by

## Hendrik Willem van Loon

1942
SIMON AND SCHUSTER
NEW YORK

1942. *Van Loon's Lives* by Hendrik Willem van Loon with illustrations by the author. Published by Simon and Schuster, New York. Printed in the U.S.A. 8⅜″ × 5¾″. Title-page spread and two illustrations.

*The Hospice of St. Bernard amidst the endless snows of winter.*

*They were playing Mozart's* KLEINE NACHTMUSIK.

1947. *The Arabs* by R. B. Sergeant, illustrated by
Edward Bawden. A Puffin Picture Book,
published by Penguin Books Ltd, Middlesex.
Printed by the Curwen Press Ltd, Plaistow.
7″ × 8⅝″. Illustration spreads.

'Puffin Picture Books' have been one of the most successful attempts at
producing cheap, popular educational books. The first of this lengthy series
of landscape shaped picture books came out in 1940, with the painfully
appropriate title of *War on Land.* Puffin Picture Books were published by
Penguin Books Limited, edited by Noel Carrington, and originally were printed
by W. S. Cowell Limited. These war time productions were an economical
printing of thirty-two pages, printed by offset in full colour on one side of the
sheet and black on the verso. The illustrations of the first Puffins were all
drawn direct to plate by such illustrators as James Holland, James Gardner
and S. R. Badmin. Later volumes included Richard Chopping's *Butterflies in
Britain* (Chopping is the artist who drew most of Ian Fleming's book jackets
for the James Bond stories); R. B. Talbot Kelly's *Paper Birds* and Paxton
Chadwick's *Wild Flowers.*

The format of the Puffin Picture Books was based on the kind of mass
produced illustrated children's books that were being produced in the Soviet
Union. They are also, of course, comparable to such French books as the
Flammarion Père Castor books and to the two Legrand publications, *Bolivar*

234

1964. *The Charge of the Light Brigade* by
Alfred Lord Tennyson, illustrated by Alice and
Martin Provensen. Published by the Golden
Press Inc, New York and Paul Hamlyn Ltd,
London. Printed in the United States of America.
7½" × 9¾". Illustration spreads.

and *La Fayette*. After the war, Puffins were given stiff covers. One of the most
attractive post-war volumes was *The Arabs*, with Edward Bawden's illustrations. The subject clearly appealed to the artist as Bawden had spent some
time as an official war artist during the 1939–45 war in the Middle East. It
is a splendidly decorative book.

Alice and Martin Provensen are amongst the most fertile and successful of
contemporary illustrators. In 1964 the Golden Press in New York and Paul
Hamlyn in London published their illustrated edition of Alfred Lord Tennyson's
*The Charge of the Light Brigade*. This book, in a Puffin format, is one of the
prettiest and wittiest pieces of illustration to appear for a very long time. The
drawings are comparable to an early illumination or to a Mogul painting.
The Provensens' have caught (as their blurb-writer so rightly says) 'the
rigidity, heroism and nobility of the most dramatic and useless battle of the
Crimean War'. Beautiful though the book is, it is strangely moving as well.
Their last illustration succinctly sums up the whole sorry business with a
quote from General Bosquet: 'C'est magnifique, mais ce n'est pas la guerre.'

235

1941. *The Battle of Britain* by David Garnett and
James Gardner. A Puffin Picture Book edited by
Noel Carrington. Published by Penguin Books
Limited, Harmondsworth, England and New York,
U.S.A. Printed by W. S. Cowell Ltd, Ipswich.
$7'' \times 8\frac{3}{4}''$. Cover design.

1941. *Guerra Terrestre* by James Holland.
A Puffin Picture Book edited by Noel Carrington.
Published by Penguin Books Limited,
Harmondsworth, England and New York, U.S.A.
Printed by W. S. Cowell Ltd, Ipswich. $7'' \times 8\frac{3}{4}''$.
Cover design.

1946. *Trees in Britain* by S. R. Badmin. A Puffin
Picture Book edited by Noel Carrington.
Published by Penguin Books Limited,
Harmondsworth, England and New York, U.S.A.
Printed by W. S. Cowell Ltd, Ipswich. 7″ × 8¾″.
Cover design.

1947. *Paper Birds* by R. B. Talbot Kelly. A Puffin
Picture Book edited by Noel Carrington.
Published by Penguin Books Limited,
Harmondsworth, England and New York, U.S.A.
Printed by W. S. Cowell Ltd, Ipswich. 7⅛″ × 8¾″.
Cover design.

## The Russian Churches

Russia had remained a Pagan country until the middle of the tenth century when its ruler, Prince Vladimir, determined to provide a more satisfactory religion for his people, investigated the religious practices of neighbouring countries, and made a study of the Hebrew, Greek, Roman and Mohammedan religions.

He despatched emissaries to consider each of these on the spot. The group that was sent to Constantinople, observing the ritual of the Greek Church reported so favourably, saying "they did not know whether they were on earth or in heaven," that Vladimir decided for the Greek Church and decreed that it be officially adopted throughout Russia. This decision accounts for the curiously Eastern appearance of the Russian Churches, such as S. Basil at Moscow, where the bulbous shapes terminating its octagonal features indicate Tartar origin and contact with the East.

30

*S. Basil at Moscow.*

1944. *Balbus* written and devised by Oliver Hill and Hans Tisdall. Published by Pleiades Books Ltd, London. Printed by McLagen and Cumming Ltd, London and Edinburgh. 10" × 8".

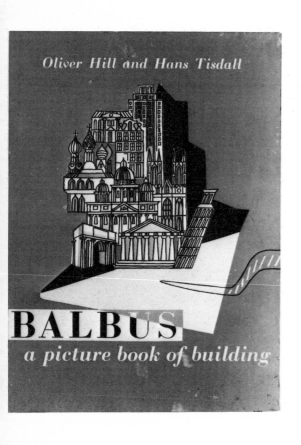

The world around us provides ample material for pictorial educational books. Only too often, the illustration and design of such books is very pedestrian. In 1940, Hans Tisdall, a German artist who had settled in England, collaborated with the architect Oliver Hill to produce a 'picture book of building', which they called *Balbus.* This was printed by the Edinburgh lithographers McLagan and Cumming. The illustrations are reproduced by chromo-lithography, with much use of mechanical stipple tints. This curious, old-fashioned technique is here used most effectively and the illustrations are brilliantly colourful.

Tisdall's was pioneer work. A book like *Geschichte der Schiffahrt,* published in Switzerland in 1962 by Éditions Rencontre and Erik Nitsche International, is now almost a commonplace. A visually articulated presentation and wide use of 'source' material for illustration are the basic ingredients for the modern popular educational books. The use of offset or gravure in place of letterpress has produced much more flexibility in the placing of half-tone or colour illustrations.

However effective 'source' material may be, original drawings are still needed. Nowadays there is a rather more scientific approach to the drafting of such subjects as architecture, furniture, ships, vehicles and locomotives. The English publisher Hugh Evelyn's 'coffee table' books of crisply drawn vintage motor cars are a manifestation of this attitude.

*Zeilend door de Eeuwen* (the Dutch edition of *Sailing Ships*) is an exquisite little book, originally published by Tre Tryckare, in Göteborg, Sweden. The drawings by Gordon Macfie are almost in the nature of a naval architect's elevation and sail plan. They are printed on a mottled khaki-coloured Ingres paper. The effect of an off-white printing for the sails, against the coloured, textured paper is both subtle and effective.

238

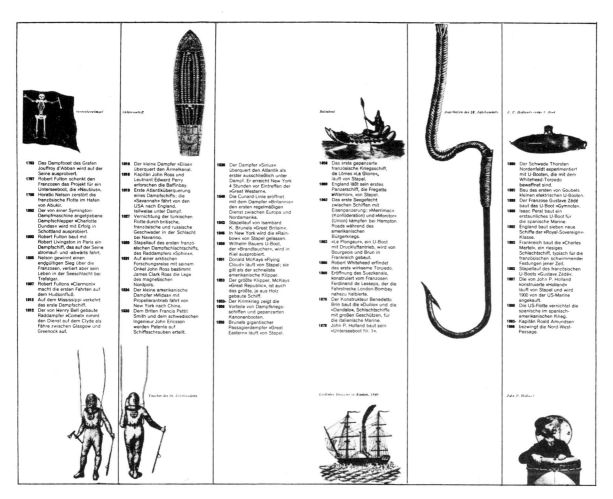

1962. *Geschichte der Schiffahrt* by Courtlandt Canby, translated by Elinor Lipper. Published by Erik Nitsche International. Printed by Heliogravure Centrale S.A., Lausanne. $10\frac{3}{8}'' \times 6\frac{1}{2}''$. Cover and spread.

1964. *Zeilend door de Eeuwen* by Sam Svensson illustrated by Gordon Macfie. Published by P. N. Kampen & Zoon, Amsterdam. $7\frac{1}{2}'' \times 7\frac{1}{2}''$. Illustration printed in black, white and yellow ochre on a tinted Ingres paper.

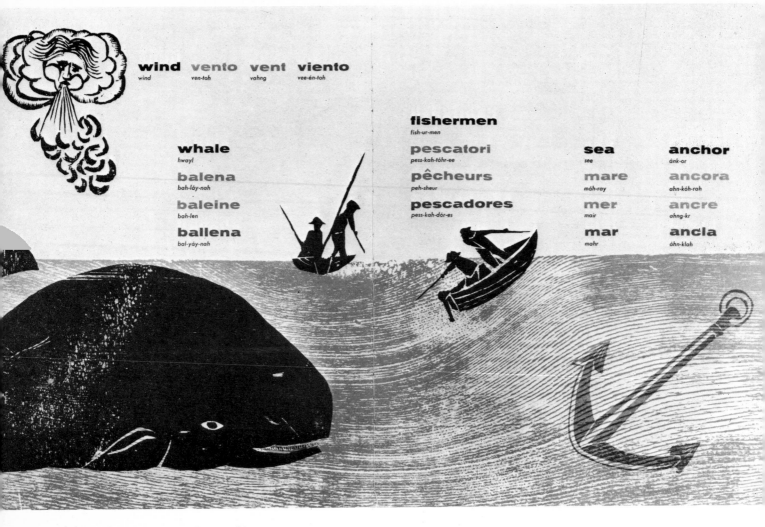

wind    vento    vent    viento
wind     ven-toh  vahng   vee-én-toh

fishermen
fish-ur-men

whale
hwayl

pescatori
pess-kah-tóhr-ee

sea
see

anchor
ánk-or

balena
bah-láy-nah

pêcheurs
peh-sheur

mare
máh-ray

ancora
ahn-kóh-rah

baleine
bah-len

pescadores
pess-kah-dór-es

mer
mair

ancre
ahng-kr

ballena
bal-yáy-nah

mar
mahr

ancla
áhn-klah

1955. *See and Say* written and illustrated by
Antonio Frasconi. Published by Harcourt Brace
and World Inc, New York. Printed in the U.S.A.
10⅜″ × 8¼″. Spread.

The publishers of school books have been slow to make use of good illustration and design, and by good, I mean illustration and design that do not merely
decorate, but help to elucidate and point a text. A fine example of this is
Antonio Frasconi's *See and Say,* which was published in 1955.
Frasconi wrote in this book, 'I was brought up in a family where more than
one language was spoken . . . the idea that there are many nationalities speak-
ing many languages is to me one of the most important for a child to
understand.'
The book is illustrated with coloured woodcuts, the text is in four languages,
each printed in a different colour, black for English, blue for Italian, red for
French and green for Spanish. The result is one of the most appealing and
colourful 'readers'.
Antonio Frasconi was born in Uruguay of Italian parentage and now lives in
Connecticut.

1968 *Bauhaus*. Royal Academy of Arts
Exhibition Catalogue prepared by Wulf
Herzogengrath and designed by Herbert Bayer
and Peter Wehr. 8⅝″ × 8¾″. Cover design by
Herbert Bayer.

It is not altogether inappropriate to end this educational section with the cover
of a catalogue commemorating one of the most influential educational estab-
lishments of this century. Fifty years after the Bauhaus was founded, Herbert
Bayer, one of the most distinguished students to come out of the school, was
one of the instigators of the Bauhaus Exhibition, which was sponsored by the
Federal Republic of Germany. The catalogue for the Royal Academy showing
of the exhibition in London was designed by Herbert Bayer and Peter Wehr.
The handsome cover is Bayer's own work. The catalogue itself makes no
pretence at elegance. It is, on the other hand, a highly informative document.

1936. *A Passage to India* by E. M. Forster.
Published by Penguin Books Ltd,
Harmondsworth. Printed by Wyman and Sons
Ltd, London. 7⅛″ × 4¼″. Original cover and series
design by Edward Young.

1939. *The Story of Mankind* by Hendrik Willem
van Loon. Published by Pocket Books Inc.
Printed in the U.S.A. 6⅜″ × 4 1/16″. Cover design.

## 8. THE PAPERBACK EXPLOSION AND THE DESIGN OF THE MODERN BOOK

During the first half of the twentieth century, the first significant paperback publishers were Penguin Books in Great Britain and Pocket Books in America. Sir Allen Lane founded Penguin books in 1935, and Robert de Graaf, in association with three directors of the publishers Simon and Schuster, started Pocket Books in 1939. The Penguin story has been fully documented, and much has been written about 'the American paperback explosion'.[1] Our concern here is only with the design of these books and the effect their design has had on the appearance of hard-cover books. Paperbacks began as cheap reprints of hard-cover books. (I am here not taking into account the pulp market, with its cheesecake and blood and thunder covers.) The kind of soft cover books we are considering began in Leipzig in 1841 when Baron von Tauchnitz started on his huge series of reprints (over 5,000 titles) of American and English authors. They were squarish (6½ in. by 4⅝ in.) books with white paper covers, printed in black. The titles, set in a mixture of typefaces, were enclosed in a fine rule border with floral corner pieces. They were well printed on quite tolerable, if uncut, pages. Their format and cover remained virtually unchanged for ninety years when a modest restyling took place. It was then given a second new look when the firm was merged with its rival, the Albatross Library in 1936, which had been founded in 1932 in Hamburg by J. Holroyd-Reece, Kurt Enoch and Max Christian Wegner.

The Albatross Library produced the first really good-looking paperbacks. Their covers were designed by Giovanni Mardersteig, the owner of the Officina Bodoni in Verona and one of the greatest of private press printers. The Albatross covers were very simple designs with seven different background colours to differentiate crime, love, travel, biography, psychology, novels and essays, plays and poetry, humour and short stories.

Mardersteig also used the same colour system for his re-design of the Tauchnitz covers when Albatross absorbed the Leipzig firm. The Tauchnitz and Albatross paper-covered books, originally intended for British travellers to while away interminable hours in *wagons lits* and then to throw away, became rather less ephemeral, for they were pleasant books to handle and ideal for reading in bed (whether a *couchette* or a four-poster).

Penguin's first designer was Edward Young. He followed the Albatross format, a convenient one for the pocket. The Penguin cover was a supremely successful design. It was horizontally divided into three panels, a panel of orange at the top and bottom and a white panel between, with the title set in two weights of Gill Sans. Edward Young also drew the penguin trade mark. By that time, in the early 1940's, when he had joined the Navy, Penguins had become a feature of English life and had briefly opened up a new bookselling outlet, through Woolworth 6d. Stores, who at the beginning were their staunchest supporters. By the mid-thirties various English and American publishers had made tentative forays into the paperback market. Most of them retired hurt. In 1929, Charles Boni had started his Paper Books. These attractive books, designed by Rockwell Kent and published at half a dollar, were offered on a subscription basis of twelve titles a year. Perhaps as a result of this, they failed. Alfred Knopf started his Borzoi Books in the 1930's. They were issued in both hard and soft covers and had an almost identical cover design and format for their paperbacks as the Albatross Library.

[1] *The Paperback*. A paper read to the Double Crown Club by Dr Desmond Flower, published by Arborfield Products Ltd, London, 1959, 'Penguin Panorama', by P. G. Burbidge and L. A. Gray in *Printing Review* No. 72. Autumn 1956.

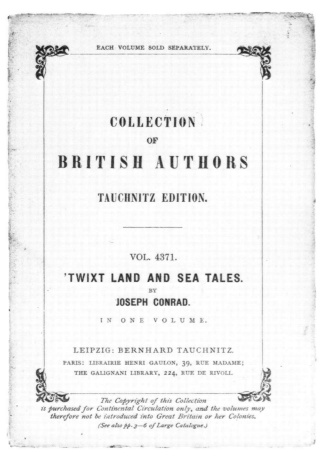

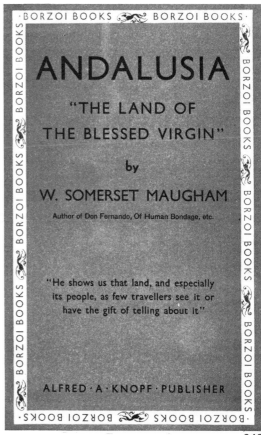

1912. *'Twixt Land and Sea Tales* by Joseph Conrad. Published and printed by Bernhard Tauchnitz, Leipzig and Paris. $6\frac{3}{8}'' \times 4\frac{1}{2}''$. Cover.

1932. *Bernard Shaw* by Frank Harris. Published by the Albatross Modern Continental Library, Hamburg, Paris and Bologna. $7\frac{1}{8}'' \times 4\frac{5}{16}''$.

1936. *The Little Wife and other Stories.* Published by Bernard Tauchnitz, Leipzig, Hamburg and Paris. $7\frac{1}{8}'' \times 4\frac{3}{8}''$. Cover design.

c. 1937. *Andalusia* by W. Somerset Maugham. A Borzoi Book published by Alfred A. Knopf, New York. Printed in the U.S.A. $7\frac{1}{8}'' \times 4\frac{1}{4}''$. Cover.

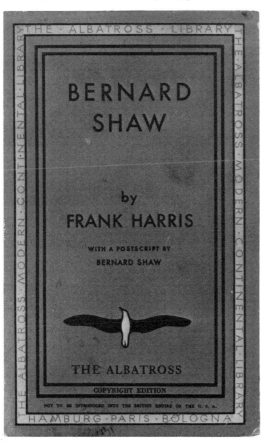

1958. *Tappan's Burro* by Zane Grey. Published by Penguin Books Ltd, Harmondsworth. Printed by Hunt, Barnard and Co. Ltd, Aylesbury. $7\frac{1}{8}'' \times 4\frac{5}{16}''$. Cover design by Dennis Bailey.

1964. *Tiermenschen* by Henry de Montherlant. Published by Deutscher Taschenbuch Verlag, Munich. $7\frac{1}{8}'' \times 4\frac{1}{4}''$. Cover design by Celestino Piatti.

1963. *Billard um halb zehn* by Heinrich Böll. Published by Knaur, Munich and Zürich. Printed by the Süddeutsche Verlagsanstalt und Druckerei GmbH, Ludwigsburg. $7\frac{1}{16}'' \times 4\frac{1}{2}''$. Cover design by Hermann Rastorfer.

1966. *Modern Physics for the Engineer.* Edited by Louis N. Ridenour. Published by McGraw Hill Paperbacks, New York. Printed in the U.S.A. $8'' \times 5\frac{1}{2}''$. Cover designed by Rudolph de Harak.

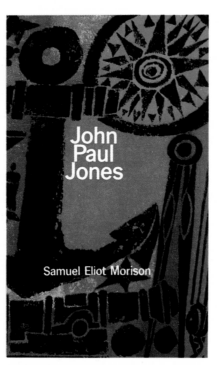

1966. *John Paul Jones* by Samuel Eliot Morison. Published by Time Inc. $8'' \times 5\frac{1}{2}''$. Cover design.

1960. *Münchhausen* by Erich Kästner. Published by Fischer Bücherei Frankfurt-am-Main and Hamburg. Printed in Germany. $7\frac{1}{8}'' \times 4\frac{1}{4}''$. Cover design.

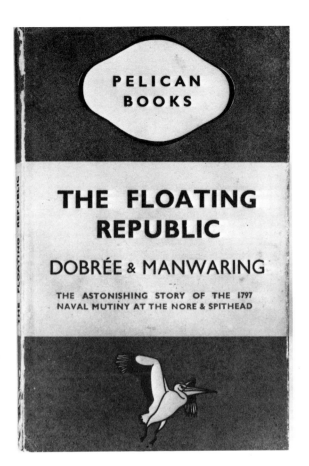

1937. *The Floating Republic* by Dobrée and Manwaring. A Pelican Book published by Penguin Books Ltd, Harmondsworth. Printed by Purnell and Sons Ltd. $7\frac{1}{8}'' \times 4\frac{1}{2}''$. Cover design.

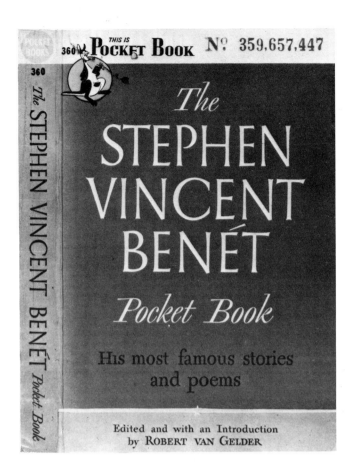

*c.* 1946. *The Stephen Vincent Benét Pocket Book* edited by Robert van Gelder. Published by Pocket Books Inc., New York. Printed in the U.S.A. $6\frac{3}{8}'' \times 4\frac{1}{16}''$. Cover design.

In England, the firm of Hutchinson had entered the paperback market a year or so later and sold a lot of books. They were followed by Heinemann's pleasant looking Evergreen Books, selling at one shilling, which were an attempt at publishing authors such as Aldous Huxley, John Steinbeck and David Garnett in paperback form. In spite of being printed on fugitive wood pulp paper, they had a slogan 'Evergreen books are books to keep' printed on the jacket flaps.

The jackets on these paperbacks added dignity and kept the covers clean. (Paperback of course is a misnomer, for all these books had drawn-on board covers of at least 2-sheet thickness.)

It was not until 1939 that a venture comparable to Penguins got under way in America. This was Pocket Books. Like Penguins they had sought and found new bookselling outlets through the five-and-ten-cent stores, the news stands, and most important of all, that universal meeting place, the drug store. The format was a little smaller than Penguins, the books were rather more bulky, with glossy laminated covers. Considering the huge runs, they were quite well made and well printed. Within a couple of years a rival firm had sprung up, whose books had an almost identical appearance. These were Avon Books, started by Joseph Myers, who were promptly and unsuccessfully sued by Pocket Books for plagiarism.

After the 1939–45 war, paperback firms sprang up all over the place and many hardback publishers moved into the field once more. Original publications began to supersede reprints and a new move was made into informative, educational publishing. Once again Sir Allen Lane had blazed the trail, with his Pelican series, begun in 1937 with such titles as Shaw's *Intelligent Woman's Guide* and *The Floating Republic* by Dobrée and Manwaring. By this time they had almost grown into a complete home library. The Pelicans were followed by other series, including in 1946 the Penguin Classics. In this series nearly a million copies have been sold of just one title, E. V. Rieu's translation of the *Odyssey*.

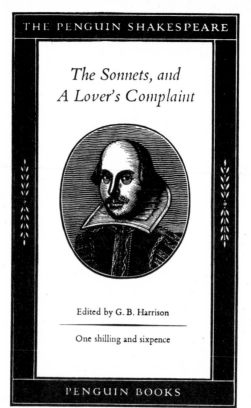

1949. *The Sonnets, and A Lover's Complaint* by William Shakespeare. Designed by Jan Tschichold. A volume from the Penguin Shakespeare published by Penguin Books Ltd, Harmondsworth. Printed by Wyman and Sons, London. 7⅛″ × 4⅜″. Cover design, printed in black on white board with a wood engraving by Reynolds Stone and text spread.

7

Lo in the Orient when the gracious light,
Lifts up his burning head, each under eye
Doth homage to his new appearing sight,
Serving with looks his sacred majesty,
And having climb'd the steep up heavenly hill,
Resembling strong youth in his middle age,
Yet mortal looks adore his beauty still,
Attending on his golden pilgrimage:
But when from high-most pitch with weary car,
Like feeble age he reeleth from the day,
The eyes ('fore duteous) now converted are
From his low tract and look another way:
   So thou, thyself out-going in thy noon,
   Unlook'd on diest unless thou get a son.

8

Music to hear, why hear'st thou music sadly?
Sweets with sweets war not, joy delights in joy:
Why lov'st thou that which thou receiv'st not gladly,
Or else receiv'st with pleasure thine annoy?
If the true concord of well tuned sounds,
By unions married do offend thine ear,
They do but sweetly chide thee, who confounds
In singleness the parts that thou should'st bear:
Mark how one string sweet husband to another,
Strikes each in each by mutual ordering;
Resembling sire, and child, and happy mother,
Who all in one, one pleasing note do sing:
   Whose speechless song being many, seeming one,
   Sings this to thee thou single wilt prove none.

9

Is it for fear to wet a widow's eye,
That thou consum'st thyself in single life?
Ah; if thou issueless shalt hap to die,
The world will wail thee like a makeless wife,
The world will be thy widow and still weep,
That thou no form of thee hast left behind,
When every private widow well may keep,
By children's eyes, her husband's shape in mind:
Look what an unthrift in the world doth spend
Shifts but his place, for still the world enjoys it:
But beauty's waste hath in the world an end,
And kept unus'd the user so destroys it:
   No love toward others in that bosom sits
   That on himself such murd'rous shame commits.

10

For shame deny that thou bear'st love to any
Who for thyself art so unprovident:
Grant if thou wilt, thou art belov'd of many,
But that thou none lov'st is most evident:
For thou art so possess'd with murd'rous hate,
That 'gainst thyself thou stick'st not to conspire,
Seeking that beauteous roof to ruinate
Which to repair should be thy chief desire:
O change thy thought, that I may change my mind,
Shall hate be fairer lodg'd than gentle love?
Be as thy presence is gracious and kind,
Or to thyself at least kind-hearted prove,
   Make thee another self for love of me,
   That beauty still may live in thine or thee.

The Siege
of Leningrad
Leon Goure
Foreword by Merle Fainsod

McGraw-Hill Paperbacks

Stanford University Press

$2.95

Rudolph deHarak

1965. *The Siege of Leningrad* by Leon Goure.
Published by McGraw-Hill Paperbacks and the
Stanford University Press. Printed in the U.S.A.
8″ × 5⅜″. Cover designed by Rudolph de Harak.

**Paperbacks for serious reading**

Sir Allen intended that the design and typography of his new series should
match the quality of the texts, and in 1947 he invited the famous Swiss
typographer, Jan Tschichold, to come to England to overhaul the typography
of all Penguin productions. Tschichold had already designed a handsome,
inexpensive series of books, the Birkhäuser Classics, which were proportioned
5:8 (7$\frac{9}{16}$ in. by 4$\frac{3}{4}$ in.). He gave his ideal proportions for trimmed page sizes
3:5 and 5:8.[2]

The Penguin Shakespeares, which he redesigned, were immaculate books,
set in Monotype Bembo and (like the Heinemann Evergreen Books) in paper
jackets. The series had an effective cover design with a portrait of the bard
engraved by Reynolds Stone, set within a wide black border.

Tschichold, with typical thoroughness, applied himself to instilling some
Germanic precision into the wayward methods of English printing. And he
achieved it. His typography (by then based on Renaissance classicism) was
distinguished by its neatness; his title-pages showed impeccable spacing, his
colophons on the verso of titles were set in minute (6 point) letter-spaced
small capitals. There were few hard-cover books of the late 1940's that
typographically could match the looks of these Penguin books.

The design of paperbacks is mainly a matter of packaging. In hard cover
books, much money and care is spent on the jackets, but the matter does not
end there. The binding case has to be designed and care taken with the
layout of text pages, illustrations, cover and end papers. For most paperback
publishers, providing they have what they consider to be a good selling cover,
the devil can take care of the rest. This, of course, was not the policy of
Albatross, Borzoi or Penguin, who remained faithful to their series designs.
But even Penguin wavered in the late fifties and started using coloured
illustrations on some of their covers. A new format was designed for these
books by Abram Games and one or two exciting covers appeared, including
Dennis Bailey's vivid drawing for Zane Grey's *Tappan's Burro*. Back in 1938,
the Penguin Illustrated Classics under the editorship of Robert Gibbings had
made use of wood engraved illustrations on their covers.

Dr Desmond Flower, in the paper that he read to the Double Crown Club in
April 1959, said: 'The realization in the early fifties that there did exist a wide
market for books concerning themselves with matters above the navel
encouraged a number of hard-cover publishers to start soft-cover lines on
better paper and at higher prices.' This educational market has come to stay.
With large international markets there is also more money available, so that
texts can be more easily commissioned, and more can be spent on layout and
presentation. An art director is now an obvious necessity, for design becomes
an integral part of the concept of the book. Graphic techniques for charts and
maps, photography and illustration all play a part, taking a step on from the
Tschichold conception of immaculate typography. American publishers such
as Prentice-Hall, with their Foundations of Modern Political Science series,
McGraw-Hill with their Paperbacks, Harper with their Torchbooks, Time Inc.
with their Time and Life Reading Programme, and the various University
presses are all producing books that are not only essential student reading but
are also exciting to look at.

The narrow format Washington Square Press paperbacks from Pocket Books
Inc. show much care in the design of their covers. Two of their titles, which
were exhibited in the American Institute of Graphic Arts 1966 Exhibition,
show an interesting return to art nouveau letter forms. Both Zane Grey's
*The Trail Driver* designed and illustrated by Jerry McDaniel, and Doris M.
Stone's *Projects: Botany* designed by Richard Adelson use typefaces that are
very like Otto Eckmann's Eckmann-Schmuck.[3]

[2] 'On Mass-producing the Classics' by Jan
Tschichold. Translated by Ruari McLean. *Signature No. 3* (New Series) March 1947.
[3] See pages 15 and 250.

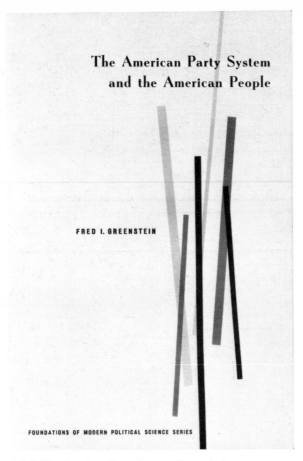

1964. *The American Party System*. Cover design.

1962. *Geometry* by H. G. Forder. A Harper Torch book. Published in their Science Library by Harper and Brothers, New York. 8″ × 5¼″. Cover design.

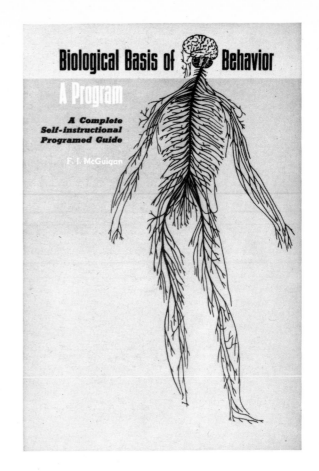

1963. *A Biological Basis of Behavior*. Cover design.

1962. *American Poetry and Poetics* edited by Daniel G. Hoffman. An Anchor Book. Published by Doubleday and Co. Inc, New York. 7⅞″ × 4¼″. Cover design by Ben Shahn.

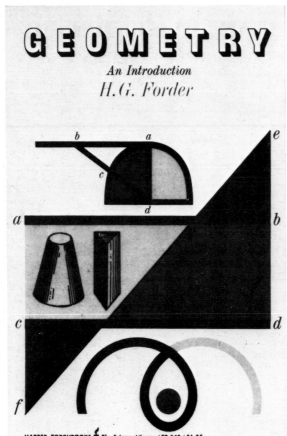

# Citizen Politics: The Behavior of the Electorate

CHAPTER THREE

In the United States, as elsewhere, all citizens are not equally active in politics. Some Americans have little political potency. They fail to act on their beliefs even to the degree of voting. Others, as we saw in Table 3 of Chapter 2, not only vote but also employ a variety of the more demanding avenues of expression available to the citizen, such as membership in pressure groups and letter-writing to public officials. Still others are far more politically active and potent than virtually anyone caught up in the broad net

18

of the normal public-opinion survey. These are the thousands of individuals in actual leadership positions—for example, elected and appointed officials at various levels of government, directors of interest groups and other associations, key figures in the communications industry, and elder statesmen such as Bernard Baruch and former Presidents Eisenhower, Truman, and Hoover.

It follows from the uneven distribution of activity that the views of some citizens have more political impact than the views of others. We therefore cannot be content with studying the behavior of the undifferentiated "general" public in our assessment of the citizen base of the political system. We must go on, as we do in the present chapter, to consider the behavior of the *effective* public. After our analysis of groups in the electorate and their effectiveness, we shall look at the dynamics of electoral choice.

## Groups in the Electorate and Their Behavior

### WHO PARTICIPATES IN POLITICS?

Figure 2 provides us with an indication of who the politically active members of the electorate are. Even in the simple act of voting, the range of participation from group to group is striking. Looking at the extreme cases, in 1960 nine out of ten of the college-educated voters interviewed by the University of Michigan Survey Research Center reported that they had voted. On the other hand, only slightly more than half of the Negro population seems to have exercised the franchise.

Of course, it is immediately evident that the "groups" shown in Fig. 2 are not discrete entities. Voters are not *either* college-educated *or*

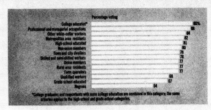

FIGURE 2 *Electoral Turnout of Key American Categoric Groups, 1960 Presidential Election.* Source: National survey conducted in 1960 by Survey Research Center, University of Michigan. Philip Converse of the Survey Research Center has kindly made these findings available.

19

*Citizen Politics: The Behavior of the Electorate*

---

1964. *The American Party System* by Fred I. Greenstein. In the Foundations of Modern Political Science Series, editor Robert Dahl, published by Prentice-Hall Inc, N.J. Designed by Walter Behnke. 9″ × 6″. Text spread.

1963. *A Biological Basis of Behavior* by F. J. McGuigan. Published by Prentice-Hall Inc, N.J. 9″ × 5$\frac{7}{8}$″. Illustration and text spread.

---

28    Receptors

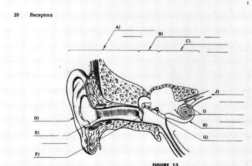

FIGURE 13

*227.* In Figure 13, write in the parts of the ear, in the blanks provided.

A. External Ear
B. Middle Ear
C. Inner Ear
D. Pinna
E. Auditory Canal
F. Eardrum
G. Ossicles
H. Cochlea
I. Hair Cells
J. Auditory Nerve

*228.* Without looking at the preceding discussion, draw a diagram of the parts of the external, the middle, and the inner ear, concluding with the auditory nerve that runs to the brain. State each step that occurs, from the point at which a vibrating object sends off a sound wave, to the point where a nerve impulse is transmitted to the brain. Be sure to label each part of the ear. Then check your diagram and steps for accuracy against the preceding discussion. (Standard size notebook paper may be used for all drawings that appear in this book.)

## RECEPTORS

Section III:  The Eye

*229.* We have just seen how the type of energy that
auditory     we call an _____ stimulus leaves a
             vibrating stimulus object, impinges on the ear, and sets
brain        off a nerve impulse that runs to the _____ .

*230.* In like manner, we shall now trace the process by which the type of environmental energy, that we call a visual stimulus, leaves a stimulus object and sets off a nerve impulse that runs from the receptor,
eye          called the _____, to the brain.

*231.* Some stimulus objects emit what we call RADIANT (rā′di ənt) ENERGY. A light bulb is an example of a
stimulus     _____ object that emits radiant energy.

*232.* Consider the various stimulus objects, in a person's environment, that emit RADIANT ENERGY. A stimulus object, such as a light bulb, itself produces
energy       the radiant _____ that it emits.

*233.* Other stimulus objects, however, do not produce
radiant      radiant energy, but rather they reflect _____
             energy coming from other sources.

*234.* For example, a light bulb in a room produces radiant energy that strikes the wall. That radiant energy is then reflected from the wall and is trans-
receptor     mitted to the organism's visual _____
             that we call the eye.

29

1965. *The Feminine Mystique* by Betty Friedan.
Published by Penguin Books Ltd, Harmondsworth.
Cover designed by Alan Aldridge. 7⅛″ × 4⅜″.

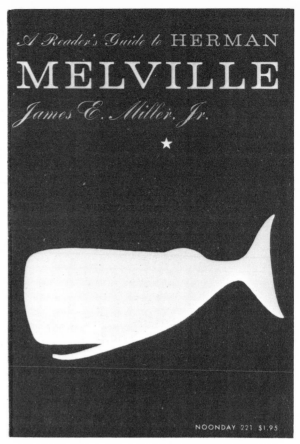

1962. *A Reader's Guide to Herman Melville* by James E.
Miller, Jnr. Published by the Noonday Press, New York.
8″ × 5⅜″. Cover designed by Robin Fox.

1965. *The Trail Driver* by
Zane Grey. Published by the
Washington Square Press,
Pocket Books Inc, New York.
7″ × 4″. Cover design by
Jerry McDaniel.

1965. *Projects: Botany* by
Doris M. Stone. Published by
the Washington Square
Press, Pocket Books Inc,
New York. 7″ × 4″. Cover
designed by Richard Adelson.

# Die russische Revolution 1917

### Von der Abdankung des Zaren bis zum Staatsstreich der Bolschewiki
### Herausgegeben von Manfred Hellmann

# dtv
# dokumente

1964. *Die russische Revolution 1917* edited by Manfred Hellmann. Published by dtv, Munich. $7\frac{1}{8}'' \times 4\frac{1}{4}''$. Cover designed by Celestino Piatti.

1965. *Berlin Alexanderplatz* by Alfred Döblin. Published by dtv, Munich. $7\frac{1}{8}'' \times 4\frac{1}{4}''$. Cover design by Celestino Piatti, and title-page.

1962. *Revolution from 1789 to 1906* edited by R. W. Postgate. A Harper Torchbook. Published by Harper and Brothers, New York. $8'' \times 5\frac{1}{4}''$. Cover design.

Alfred Döblin:
Berlin Alexanderplatz
Die Geschichte vom Franz Biberkopf

Nachwort von Walter Muschg

Deutscher
Taschenbuch
Verlag

And so the Army of the Potomac got a new commander—General Ambrose Burnside (left)—and the army which had not been lucky in its leaders now had the worst. It was Burnside's notion that he could run quickly down the Rappahannock River, jump across before Lee knew he was there, and charge towards Richmond. Not surprisingly, when Burnside got on the river in December, Lee was opposite him and busily entrenching on Marye's Heights behind the town of Fredericksburg. There was no bridge over the river, but Burnside expected to build one—while Lee presumably just sat quietly.

91

1961. *The Civil War as They Knew It* by Abraham Lincoln and Mathew Brady. A Bantam Gallery Edition volume. Published by Bantam Books Inc. Printed in the U.S.A. $6\frac{7}{8}'' \times 4\frac{1}{4}''$. Cover design and text spread.

1964. *L'Église et la République* by Anatole France. No. 5 in the Libertés series published by J. J. Pauvert, Paris. Printed in the Netherlands. $7'' \times 3\frac{1}{2}''$. Cover.

## Illustration in paperbacks

In Germany, the gayest looking of all paperbacks are from Deutscher Taschenbuch Verlag, who are known by their initials d t v. These are designed by Celestino Piatti, who uses a simple formula of a white laminated board, with the title set in Aksidenz Grotesk and printed in black, with a boldly drawn illustration vignetted in colour. The insides are immaculately laid out, with title-pages that look as if they belonged to the same world as the covers. Drömersche Verlagsanstalt from Munich publish the Knaur paperbacks with some colourful covers, designed by Hermann Rastorfer.

Paperback publishers were slow off the mark with fully illustrated books. The wide use of offset and gravure has done away with the need to use expensive coated stock for half-tone illustrations. Bantam Gallery Editions with such titles as *The Civil War as they Knew it*, with Mathew Brady's famous contemporary photographs, are a praiseworthy example of intelligent presentation and layout.

The designer of this book makes a lively use of negative prints both for his title-page spread and for section titles, which consist solely of the date of the year, set in an extended Victorian typeface. Dutton Vista Picturebacks edited by David Herbert is the first trans-Atlantic series of comprehensive pictorial surveys to appear in paperback form. These are fully illustrated, well designed books. *New Cinema in Europe* by Roger Manvell, shown here, is one of this series

In spite of indications both in the United States and in Europe of a considerable increase in well made, well laid-out paperbacks, the bulk of the books are still for the *roman policier* and the blood and sex markets. Once again we revert to packaging and find some very lively, good looking covers,

Jour de Fête France 1949. Director Jacques Tati

Pierrot le Fou France 1965. Director Jean-Luc Godard
Anna Karina

1966. *New Cinema in Europe* by Roger Manvell.
Published by Studio Vista Ltd, London and
E. P. Dutton and Co. Inc, New York. A
Dutton Vista Pictureback. Printed by Richard
Clay, Bungay. $7\frac{1}{4}'' \times 4\frac{7}{8}''$. Cover design by
Gillian Greenwood.

1964. *Napoléon le Petit* by Victor Hugo. No. 4
in the Libertés Series published by J. J. Pauvert,
Paris. Printed in the Netherlands. $7'' \times 3\frac{1}{2}''$.
Cover design.

standing out like flowers amongst all the corn. The use of display letters with no illustrations is still a rarity. The French series 'Libertés', published by Jean Jacques Pauvert, has a tall, narrow format, with cover design printed from large black sans serif capitals on brown paper. The texts are carefully set and well printed in Holland. These are thoroughly readable books and though printed on cheap paper, have an elegance about them, which comes from the care and thought that have gone into their production.

Since this book was first published, the great change in the appearance of railway and airport bookstalls has been the flood of Science Fiction titles. Another has been the presence of large-format illustrated paperbacks, increasingly popular especially in the United States. Brian Aldiss, one of the great SF authors, writing in *The Saturday Book* in 1964 drew attention to the cover artists of the old SF magazines such as *Galaxy* and *Fantasy*. He also described the swing towards paperbacks. He concludes prophetically: 'Nowadays the old covers and their mighty white cities, impossible architecture, man-devouring forests and other delectable props are steam engines among the diesel traffic of paperbacks. Their days are numbered. But science fiction, which today reaches a wider and more critical audience than it ever did, goes on; and in another twenty years . . . someone else may be nostalgically recalling the glories and idiocies of paperback SF covers.'

The two covers shown on page 255 are of a recent selection of Aldiss stories called *New Arrivals, Old Encounters,* and *Foundation,* the first volume of Isaac Asimov's classic trilogy. The artists are Tim Wright and Chris Foss, who more than live up to the traditions of the old SF magazine covers.

Scholem-Alejchem:           Knaur
Menachem Mendel,
der Spekulant

The IPCRESS File/LEN DEIGHTON

Secret File No. 1    3'6   Panther

'It's authenticity will make M.I.5 wonder where
he gets his material from'    DAILY SKETCH

1965. *Menachem Mendel, der Spekulant* by Scholem-
Alejchem. Published by Knaur at Munich and Zürich.
Cover design by Cristoph Albrecht. $7\frac{1}{16}'' \times 4\frac{1}{2}''$.

1961. *Borstal Boy* by Brendan Behan. A Corgi Book
published by Transworld Publishers, London.
$7\frac{1}{8}'' \times 4\frac{5}{16}''$. Cover design.

1964. *The Ipcress File* by Len Deighton. A Panther Book,
published by Hamilton and Co. (Stafford) Ltd. $7'' \times 4\frac{1}{4}''$.
Cover design by Raymond Hawkey.

1965. *Le Fils* by Georges Simenon. Published by
Presses de la Cité, Paris. Printed by Bussière at
St Amand. $6\frac{1}{2}'' \times 4\frac{1}{2}''$. Series cover design.

FG1464 A CORGI BOOK 5/-

BORSTAL BOY
BRENDAN BEHAN

THE BAWDY SWAGGERING OUTRAGEOUS BESTSELLER

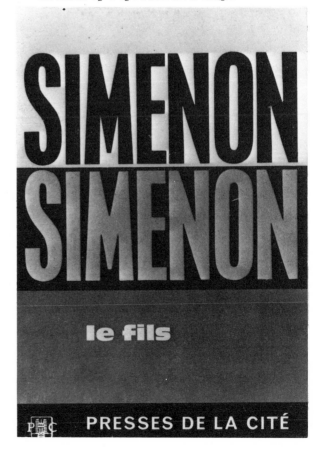

SIMENON
SIMENON

le fils

PRESSES DE LA CITÉ

1980 *Zorba the Greek* by Nikos Kazantzakis. A Touchstone Book published by Simon and Schuster. 8″ × 5¼″. Cover by Seymour Chwaste

1983 *New Arrivals, Old Encounters* by Brian Aldiss. Published by Triad Granada, London. 7″ × 4⅜″. Cover design by Tim White.

1973 *The Case of the Midwife Toad* by Arthur Koestler published by Vintage Books, Random House, New York. 7¼″ × 4⅜″. Cover by Trubshur.

1982 *Foundation* by Isaac Asimov. Published by Granada, London. 7″ × 4⅜″. Cover illustration by Chris Foss.

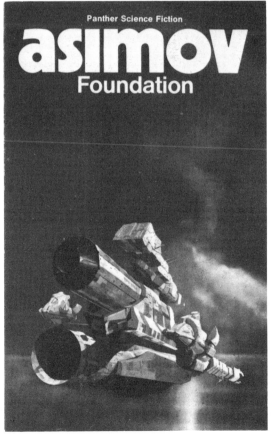

# 3
## Student Days

It was (I think) in our second session that EB and I, and Sam Heiman, a most cheerful and charming Design student, each had a bed-sitting room in the lodging-house of Miss Helen Groom at 58 Redcliffe Road, South Kensington. We often paid visits to each other's rooms and had great fun with dear Sam who was a Theosophist, a Jew, a Vegetarian, a Pacifist, a Liberal Catholic and much else of the same harmless character. We had breakfast together in the basement. Or rather we were supposed to breakfast together. But Sam preferred to consume mysterious compounds and beverages in the sanctity of his own room. Bawden was always down before me and would be sitting stiffly at table, reading as he ate. He did not look up as I entered. His social temperature was near freezing-point in the morning. When I bustled in announcing that it was a good morning or otherwise, he would go on chewing slowly, his eyes on a book, and would only murmur: 'Is it?' I hated this. I was always ready for conversation in the morning. So I took notice of what EB was reading. I remember that he went steadily through *Anna Karenina*, Fergusson on *Architecture* and Jackson's *History of Wood-Engraving*. He read to learn, unlike Ravilious who read for fun and whose favourite book was *Huckleberry Finn*. Once or twice I found EB deep in a trade periodical on ironmongery and hardware – his father was in that line at Braintree – which he would recommend to me, smiling faintly, 'as good sensible stuff' and 'literature'.

Bawden had a habit of wearing his hat indoors and his hats were dignified, mitre-like ornaments. He used to sit back on his chair at very dangerous angles. Sometimes he tipped the chair too far back until there was a crash. He would get up from the floor, resume his seat, still mitred and expressionless, and join again in the conversation. His hands, like those of William Morris, were always itching to do something (Morris as a school-boy made nets at Marlborough). We had to watch Bawden and catch him before he damaged the landlady's property. He might, bit by bit, during a conversation, with

– 24 –

1931 HOMAGE TO DICKY DOYLE specially drawn to show the use of colour applied by stencilling for the Curwen Press. Reproduced in Curwen Press Miscellany, 1931

– 25 –

---

1979 *Edward Bawden* by Douglas Percy Bliss, published by the Pendomer Press in England and Canada. 11¼″ × 8″. Illustration spread and jacket printed in black and brown and reproduced from a wallpaper design and typographic borders, both by Edward Bawden. Designed by John and Griselda Lewis.

## Art books

Art books still proliferate — more of them appearing in large-format paperback — though it looks as if the day of the coffee-table book is over, which is no bad thing. In no way a coffee-table book was Iain Bain's *The Watercolours and Drawings of Thomas Bewick* which the Gordon Fraser Gallery published in two volumes in 1981. This is an exquisite production, beautifully printed by the Westerham Press. The often minute watercolours (drawn the same size as the final wood engraving) sit on the page like little jewels.

Quite a number of monographs on contemporary artists have appeared, often from presses where the publishing aims have not been solely concerned with profit. The Lion and Unicorn Press at the Royal College of Art produced a handsome book on Stanley Spencer's drawings in 1964. In 1978 a new imprint appeared, the Pendomer Press, a trans-Atlantic venture operating from Godalming in England and Toronto in Canada. The moving spirit behind this was Simon Heneage. His first publication was *John Nash: the painter as illustrator* by John Lewis. This was followed by *Edward Bawden,* a study of the artist by Douglas Percy Bliss. This book was a revelation of Bawden's staying power as an illustrator and designer for books. His work over fifty years has a remarkable consistency.

As an example of the detailed planning of a series, the following account may be of some interest. Studio Paperbacks was a series of introductory handbooks on art and design that was launched in 1963. These books were aimed at the student market and intended to cover the basic principles of different subjects. They had to be relatively inexpensive, to be very fully illustrated, usually with colour, and to be designed in a manner acceptable to students and professional designers. To meet all these requirements meant long runs and economic machining. This was achieved by printing an American and an English edition at the same time, by offset on large machines, giving ninety-six pages printed on two sheets (twenty-four pages to view). These sheets were cut in

256

# Signs in action
## James Sutton

1965. *Signs in Action* by James Sutton. A
Studio Vista/Reinhold Art Paperback. Published
in London by Studio Vista Ltd and in New York
by Reinhold Publishing Corporation. Printed in
the Netherlands by Koch and Knuttel, Gouda.
$7\frac{3}{4}'' \times 6\frac{1}{2}''$. Cover photograph by Herbert
Spencer and text and illustration spread.

# Trademarks
## a handbook of international designs
## by Peter Wildbur

1966. *Trademarks* by Peter Wildbur. A Studio
Vista/Reinhold Art Paperback. Published in
London by Studio Vista Ltd and in New York by
Reinhold Publishing Corporation. Printed in the
Netherlands by Koch and Knuttel, Gouda.
$7\frac{3}{4}'' \times 6\frac{1}{2}''$. Cover design by Peter Wildbur.

Marble Arch, London
Photo Herbert Spencer

German street sign
Photo David Lock and Terry Smith

Safety for 50,000,000 motor vehicles is not materially
helped by this confused 'Christmas Tree' of signs –
downtown Washington DC
Photo United States Information Service

These monstrous Christmas Trees are confusing,
difficult to read and hideous. An ill co-ordinated
mass of verbiage.
Is every sign on p. 16 necessary? If the author-
ities tidied up the mess, the driver could see,
clearly, one sign. Even two or three co-ordinated
signs supporting rather than fighting each other
– or repeating the message – can be effective,
but completely different signs saying the same
thing can never be.

How it can be done.

Painted wood sign, Cortina, Italy ▶
Photo Publifoto Milan

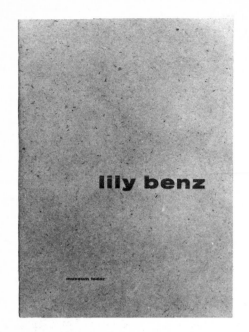

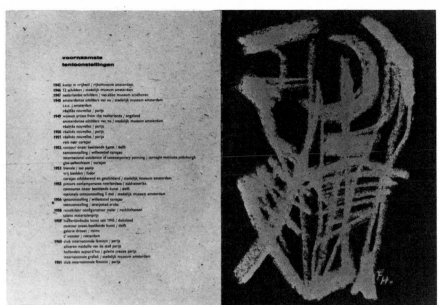

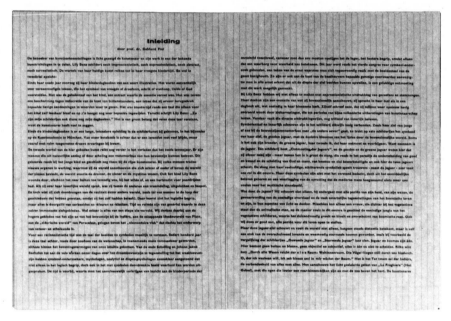

1950–60. Catalogue Covers from the Stedelijk Museum, Amsterdam. Printed on various papers and produced under the direction of Dr Willem Sandberg. Average size 10¼″ × 7½″.

**The Stedelijk Museum catalogues**

three, making three sections of sixteen pages. On one side only of one of the sheets, colour would be printed, though in collating for binding this could be scattered fairly widely through the book. The format, a squarish one (7¾ in. by 6½ in.), was perhaps not ideal for a jacket pocket, but most students do not wear jackets nowadays, and this size is far better for displaying illustrations, than, for instance, the upright Albatross-Penguin format. For most of the titles the type was set in a narrow measure, in one or two columns, which gave considerable scope for marginal illustrations, by the simple expedient of dropping one of the columns of type. The covers were printed in full colour, with some conformity of design. The formula proved a success.

New trends in book design have rarely come from the ordinary publishing houses. Such trends appear from other sources such as art galleries or in commercially promoted books, where expense would appear to be of little concern. These books, at their best, can be models of clarity in arrangement and design. They may range from prestige publications to service handbooks and even to catalogues. Where copy has to be made explicit, even appetising,

The Art of the Engineer

**The Art of the Engineer**
Two hundred years in the development
of drawings for the design of transport
on land, sea and air.

1978 *The Art of the Engineer* by Ken Baynes and
Francis Pugh. Produced by Design Systems.
Portfolio cover.

the clever hands of a hundred clever graphic designers have given it order
and clarity.

Exhibition catalogues were first given a new meaning by Dr Willem Sandberg,
the former Director of the Stedelijk Museum in Amsterdam. A brilliantly
exciting series of catalogues was produced under his care. That some of them
are typographically eccentric, with many more words to the line than makes
for comfortable reading, is almost by the way. Here was fresh thinking on the
presentation of type and pictures, and the use of unusual and often inexpensive papers. The Stedelijk Museum catalogues were packed with ideas that
the publishers of picture books might well have followed.

Another and different approach to catalogue design can be seen in the Welsh
Arts Council publication of *The Art of the Engineer*, written by Ken Baynes
and Francis Pugh and produced by Design Systems. This took the form of a
portfolio of twelve folded sheets tracing the development, through two hundred years, of drawings for the design of transport on land, sea or air. The
most effective portfolio cover is taken from a hand-coloured lithograph which
Scott Russell, I. K. Brunel's contractor, had drawn of a section of the *Great
Eastern* after the great ship had been fitted out in 1859.

A particularly notable catalogue was produced in 1972 for the Armand
Hammer Collection, which was exhibited at the Los Angeles County Museum
of Art, the Royal Academy of Arts in London and the National Gallery of
Ireland in Dublin. The catalogue was designed in Los Angeles by James L.
Wood and printed by the Anderson Lithograph Company in Los Angeles, with
a prodigal use of colour, particularly for the reproduction of drawings, some
of which had the merest hint of colour in them. No commercial publisher would
have contemplated such an extravagance, yet if colour reproduction, which
is so costly, in spite of (or maybe because of) great advances in electronic
scanning techniques, could be used for reproducing monochromatic drawings
or even the printed pages of books, it would lift the illustrations right off the
page, in a way that no monochrome reproduction could do.[4]

[4] I have noticed, when using 35mm slides, that
colour slides will bring the black and white pages
of books etc. to life in a way that monochromatic
film cannot do. The same lesson applies in the
printing of illustrated books.

1982 *David Gentleman's Britain* written and illustrated by David Gentleman RDI, published by Weidenfeld and Nicolson, London. Cover and illustration page.

1983 *Drain Pig and the Glow Boys in 'Critical Mess'* by Dan Pearce, published by Junction Books, London. 5¾″ × 8¼″. Cover design.

**In conclusion**

Some twenty years ago in a leading article in *The Times Literary Supplement* the anonymous writer said: 'For new types of books a new kind of author is emerging, a man who is able to handle words with skill and economy but whose books, in fact, evolve out of a balanced knowledge of both words and techniques of visual communication'.[5] This new kind of author-designer (like the 'directing intelligence' that Léon Pichon talked about) may play a bigger and bigger part in the book of the future, not as one who provides a 'prettifying' element, but as one who can act as an elucidating factor in the graphic presentation of a text, as well as assisting in the economics of production. David Gentleman is such an author. He is a painter, an engraver and a designer who can also handle words. His lavishly illustrated book *David Gentleman's Britain,* published by Weidenfeld and Nicolson in 1982, is an example of this kind of book that combines all the author-artist's skills. Such an approach of course does not apply to books to be read in the train or even in bed. For this, the Renaissance book, as for example those printed by Aldus in Venice in the early years of the sixteenth century and sometimes set in space-saving italic types, is a very satisfactory and utilitarian solution to the arrangement of type on a small page, but it provides no possible guide for the disposition of half-tone illustrations or other pictorial matter in the modern book. The Russian, Hungarian and German typographers of the 1920s made the first real contribution to solving this problem. A quarter of a century later typographers such as Willem Sandberg in Holland, Paul Rand in the United States and Max Bill in Switzerland applied further new thinking to the design of books and catalogues. Little has come from the modern book publisher that can compare in typographic skill with these productions.

As to the future of book design, in spite of radio, television and electronic aids for storing information, it would seem that there may still be a place for books. The question is, what kind of books? One answer would seem to lie in the paperback bookstalls, where the only sign of the designer's hand is in the covers, where, with the rare exceptions of SF titles, colour photographs of naked girls and heavy-handed typography are the main components. In the years since this book first came out there has been a marked decline in the design of such covers. The insides vary from the impeccable typography of Penguins or of the American and English University Presses to the abysmal standards of the pulp printer. As for covers, at the bookstall level I was hard pressed to find even four tolerable new paperback cover designs to include in this edition.

Apart from informative and educational books, the ever expanding market is for children's books. As children are conditioned by television, any stories that appear on the small screen tend to become immediate best sellers in book form. The comic strip either on the TV screen or in the Comics is a form of drawing a child can understand. The success of the adventures of Tintin or of Asterix the Gaul is an indication of where children's tastes lie. The reason for the enormous success of these books is not just in the drawings. Georges Remi (who drew under the pseudonym of Hergé) put much research into his drawings for Tintin, as does Albert Uderzo for Asterix. Both these series of books are compulsive reading (and viewing). There is a lesson here for any publisher or illustrator of children's books. All the design in the world will not compensate for the lack of a good story line and this does not only apply to children's books. Dan Pearce's *Drain Pig and the Glow Boys in 'Critical Mess'* published in 1983 is a strip cartoon book for adults, a brilliant piece of anti-nuclear propaganda that rivets one's attention from the very first page. The reader becomes utterly absorbed in the subterranean adventures of the uncomely little pig. This is the first book by this young cartoonist.

[5] *The Times Literary Supplement* 26 April 1963.